The SEO Standard

How to skyrocket your website's ranking
and grow your business online,
with the fundamental principles of
Search Engine Optimization

To Noah and Monia

CONTENTS

Introduction

If you are creating a website or already have one, there will come a time when you need the first, yet simple, essential thing a website requires: visitors.

Whether you have built a website for yourself or for a client, whether it was created with passion by you or by an experienced professional, the moment of publication is always exhilarating.

Finally, your project or business has an online presence, visible and accessible to anyone in the world. But that's not enough. For your website to be successful, it needs visitors who see that you exist, who read and appreciate the content you've published, and perhaps even purchase your products.

A website without visitors is like a library filled with books without readers—a place full of valuable knowledge that no one can discover. If you don't have users engaging with your content, the time and effort invested in creating your website may be wasted.

If no one sees your products or services, the money invested in building your brand has been wasted. It's a true loss of information and resources that could have been useful. Moreover, it's an economic failure, as neither you nor any potential visitors benefit from what your website offers.

Publishing a website is just the beginning; it's like planting a seed. The real work begins when you need to attract visitors and grow your website. These visitors, the lifeblood of your website, will be referred to as 'traffic' or 'users' throughout this book.

Just like water flowing from a mountain nourishes the land and the seeds within it, traffic feeds your website, bringing life and vitality to your content and pages.

A website without traffic is like a barren desert — a desolate, lifeless landscape. In contrast, a steady stream of quality traffic nurtures your digital ecosystem, allowing it to thrive and increasing your conversions. The flow of continuous traffic is essential for all online assets, and no one—whether managing a single website or many—can afford to go without it.

> The word *"asset"* refers to *"a property that holds value"* and is any resource you own that can be monetized. A website is an online asset. The ideal online asset is something that you no longer have to edit, for example, a pillar post or video on YouTube.

However, not all traffic is the same. There are different levels of quality, as you will see later on. But for now, let's focus on this fundamental point:

Traffic is the oxygen that sustains your website, just as oxygen sustains our bodies. Without it, the website suffocates and slowly dies. Just as we cannot survive without oxygen, a website cannot thrive without traffic.

This book will guide you through all the standard concepts in the world of Search Engine Optimization (SEO) and will teach you the effective SEO strategies you will need to generate a steady stream of free and qualified traffic to your website. You will learn how to attract visitors that will potentially be interested in your content, ready to engage with your brand, click your banners, and become loyal customers, all in an organic, free, and sustainable way.

We will also be discussing other types of traffic, separate from *free traffic*, such as *paid traffic* and many others.

Don't worry! Don't be discouraged by first impressions, terminology, or a few challenging concepts. With some studying and practice, you will master the fundamental concepts you need and find that everything becomes much simpler and more intuitive, almost automatically..

We will explore and address various topics, sometimes in general terms and sometimes in more specific detail. I will cover practically all the subjects you need to know if you truly want to build websites that stand the test of time, achieve significant numbers, and generate excellent financial returns.

This entire book aims to be a resource containing the immutable principles of SEO. However, let me be clear: I am fully aware that the digital world we live in today is constantly evolving and changing; in a few years, it will likely be very different.

Some may tell you that it is impossible to associate the word "standard" with search engine optimization because algorithms, technologies, and the web are always changing. They are not entirely wrong; changes are always occurring.

However, there are aspects, concepts, practices, and techniques that can be considered standard, even in the world of SEO. I have attempted to assemble them all in this book. Thus, it has the potential to be a lasting resource in the field of search engine optimization and organic traffic generation for any website.

What this book is for

In the following pages, I will guide you through a learning journey designed specifically to help you acquire the key concepts, proven techniques, and concrete solutions that I have developed and successfully applied to address the main challenge that all websites face after their publication: GENERATING ORGANIC TRAFFIC. Specifically, we will focus on SEO strategies, which will enable you to optimize your website for search engines and attract qualified visitors who are interested in your content.

Always keep this inevitable equation in mind:

zero traffic = dead website

In today's digital world, creating a website is just the beginning of the journey. The real challenge lies in attracting visitors and generating traffic, which is the lifeblood of online success. This challenge will sooner or later knock on the door of any website, regardless of its industry or nature.

Addressing the traffic issue is not only necessary but also requires an effective solution. If you do not have a budget for paid advertising campaigns, you will need to be patient and undertake a strategic and consistent work process, which could take weeks or even months.

Creating a steady and lasting flow of organic traffic is not an immediate process but a medium- to long-term commitment. It requires dedication, method, and the application of well-defined strategies, always keeping a long-term vision in mind.

Ignoring or underestimating the traffic problem can have fatal consequences for a web project. Following the wrong paths or relying on ineffective solutions can lead to a waste of time and resources, potentially resulting in the failure of the site.

You might spend a lot of time and/or money focusing on a factor that isn't crucial for generating traffic, leaving you with insufficient resources for the truly important aspects.

Devoting excessive energy to aspects that are not crucial for generating traffic, such as aesthetic design, technical complexity, or overly complicated user experiences, can divert resources from essential focus areas.

I speak from personal experience; there are mistakes that can easily undermine any project, often due to inaccurate beliefs or simply ignorance.

Not implementing an effective SEO strategy means giving up on one of the most powerful channels for attracting organic and qualified visitors.

Those who do not know do not understand. Knowledge is the first step towards understanding and solving a problem. In fact, if you know how to search for, generate, manage, and maintain traffic on your website, then the chances of your web project taking off will increase.

On the other hand, if you continue to ignore the dynamics and processes behind building a successful and profitable web project based on organic traffic—partially due to your lack of effort and partly due to personal beliefs that have been deeply ingrained in your mind and that hold you back—then you are more than likely headed for failure..

That being said, it's time to get to work. But first, have a look below, where I give an overview of what you will and will not find in this book.

I've made a list to help you evaluate whether or not this book is relevant to you. If you have no experience in SEO but want to gain insight into how it works, this book is for you.

This book will be of great use to you if...

... you have no background in SEO at all. It's a nice place to start, and it provides you with lots of tips and resources that you might need in the future. ... you're someone who wants to create your own website but lacks the necessary technical skills. It will be useful to understand what you need to do, what challenges you may encounter, and how to approach them—not in technical detail but from a conceptual and practical perspective. This is not a guide on how to write code to create a website but rather provides guidance on what you need to know before building it, offering you the tools to make the right decisions and learn how to generate traffic without paying for it.

... you want to learn how to optimize a website for search engines in order to generate visitors organically and without cost using search engine optimization techniques. It will also be useful if you need help grasping the requirements of search engines, standard optimization techniques, and the best practices for getting your content to reach top search results.

... you already have one or more websites but are not receiving visitors. You've read somewhere that SEO is important, and you're looking for practical solutions to increase traffic. This book will help you identify the root causes of the issues that are limiting you from producing qualified organic traffic and will equip you with the tools you need to turn things around and attract more visitors.

... you have a website with visitors but want more. You have a limited understanding of SEO but are aware of its importance in increasing traffic. You will learn the most effective ways for increasing traffic, ranging from the simplest to the most sophisticated. You will be able to determine whether there are any hidden barriers limiting the growth of your website. In this book, you'll learn how to identify and resolve these obstacles, guaranteeing that more people discover your online business.

... you want a solid foundation of knowledge on specific terminology, common business models, and industry dynamics to understand how to best leverage the potential of the web.

This book could be helpful to you if...

... you don't have a clear idea of what business you want to pursue yet but want to understand how to find one and apply it to the web, an idea that aligns with your skills and expectations. It will certainly be helpful to learn about the techniques, tools, requirements, and skills you will need to apply to your online business once you've chosen your topic, especially concerning traffic from search engines.

... you have no idea how to create a website but would like to start an online business in the future. It might be better for you to first take a course on website creation and then think about generating visitor traffic. However, having prior knowledge of what to expect can be extremely beneficial and may give you an advantage when learning how to technically construct the website.

... you already work in the SEO field, whether as a freelancer or as an employee in an agency. You will find validation for the techniques you already use and discover new strategies that can further enhance your results. You never stop learning.

... you're curious about how popular websites generate a large number of visitors and experience significant growth. It also provides valuable insights for those interested in the opportunities that online businesses offer for expanding their activities onto the web.

... you really want to explore the potential of a website beyond its surface.

What this book is not for

In the interest of transparency and fairness, I must also point out the reasons why you might *not want* to purchase this book. The information I have presented on these pages might not be for everyone.

Don't buy this book if...

... you already have an online asset (website, blog, eCommerce, etc.) and are fully satisfied with the amount of traffic you receive. If you are happy with the current level of visitors, contacts, or sales, especially from search engines, you are all set and do not need this book.

... you create websites for clients but are not genuinely concerned with whether the websites attract visitors because the client hasn't requested it and you have already been paid just to *"build the website"*.

... you want to learn how to create a website, a "step-by-step" guide from purchasing a domain to publishing, including coding and server management. This is not the right book for that.

... you want a technical and specific guide on generating visitors who do not come from search engines (e.g., paid traffic).

... you want to understand in detail how to make money online and the various methods for monetizing websites. I have only addressed this in a general way because it is not the focus of this book. First, you study how to obtain visitor traffic, and then you address the issue of how to monetize it. *What can you monetize without traffic?*

... you expect to find links to external resources or think that I will ask you to sign up for newsletters where I send spam emails every day urging you to buy something, or if you want to learn black-hat SEO techniques. There is no such content here.

... you want me to guarantee that the services, tools, and resources I mention will always be available. I cannot do that. What's important is to understand the underlying principles of each tool so that you can find similar ones in the future if the ones available today are no longer around.

... you believe I've covered all the various previous updates of search engines in depth. I do not focus on penalties because, given the techniques described and good practices, there is no need to worry about them.

What is SEO?

SEO is considered a secret weapon that gives your website a competitive edge over rivals who lack it, misuse it, or rely solely on advertising.

It allows your content to stand out from the crowd and rank at the top of search results, leaving behind competitors who neglect this fundamental strategy. Imagine your website as a high jumper in a competition: SEO provides the jumper with a longer pole, enabling it to clear the hurdle more easily.

SEO stands for Search Engine Optimization and is a varied and dynamic process, but it has one main goal: to bring someone who is browsing the web organically to your website so they can take the action you want.

You should know that search engine optimization encompasses many activities, which can be divided into the following categories:

- **Strategic Activities:** These activities are aimed at identifying your goal, finding your audience, determining your target demographic, researching keywords and search volumes, planning an editorial calendar, organizing a link-building strategy, and more.

- **Technical Activities:** These activities focus on designing the site's architecture, page layout, user experience, server and code optimization, mobile user optimizations, and speed enhancements, among others.

- **Creative Activities:** These involve writing content and structuring it on the pages, choosing the language, presenting resources in different formats, multimedia integration, content relevance, related topics, internal linking, and more.

Here's how SEO distinguishes you from competitors who either do not know about it or neglect it:

- Websites that do not implement SEO practices risk remaining invisible to a segment of potential customers, losing significant market share.

- Websites that use SEO techniques incorrectly or superficially generate disappointing results and risk harming their search engine ranking.

- Relying solely on paid advertising is expensive and ineffective in the long run. SEO offers a sustainable and lasting alternative.

And finally, a brief overview of the concrete benefits of SEO:

- SEO attracts high-quality visitors who are interested in your content and your industry, as they have used specific search queries to find your content.

- SEO results, when supported by solid foundations, are stable over time, ensuring consistent and long-term visibility.

- SEO offers a high return on investment compared to other marketing strategies, such as paid advertising, because once the website and content are implemented, no additional major actions are required, aside from maintenance.

- Good positioning of your content in search engines increases your trust, authority, and brand awareness, establishing you as an expert in your field.

Now that these concepts are clear, we can move on to the next topic.

The Internet is always changing

People who use the internet today and conduct searches on any search engine receive very different results compared to what they did in the past.

The job of an SEO professional is to know and understand the current types of searches, as it is essential to understand what the user really wants to find. SEO must take into account all the possible searches people might make and consider that not only users and their search habits change, but search algorithms are also continuously evolving.

Once you understand what a user wants, it will be your responsibility to ensure they find it, fulfilling their needs. You must provide them with optimized content based on the ecosystem they use.

Do you realize how quickly the internet changes? New technologies, new solutions, new platforms—everything moves fast. This presents a challenge for those who want to build an online business: given the rapid pace of change, *how can we keep up?*

Let's briefly and chronologically analyze what has happened since the internet became accessible to everyone. From a "search" perspective, the internet has gone through various "eras," which I believe are well-defined.

In the beginning, when we had just gained access to the World Wide Web, we needed directories to organize websites. I remember having to manually submit a website to each directory for it to be visible in the chosen category. You would include a link to the website, a brief description, select the category, and then wait for approval.

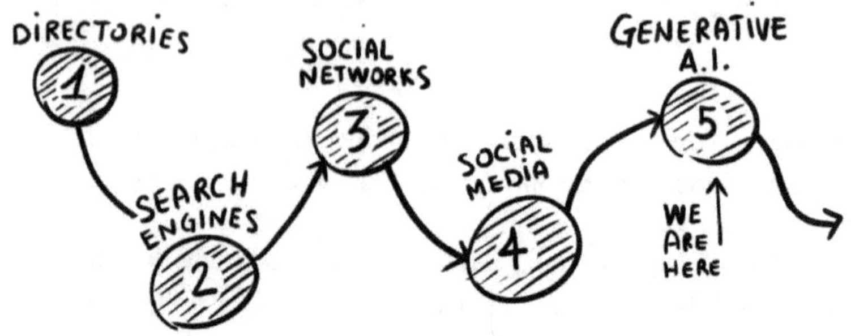

Then websites multiplied exponentially, and directories became too chaotic. It was difficult to find anything, and there was no merit-based order. Enter the era of search engines, with Google and its peers emerging.

The web continued this way for a few years, and everyone was content with it. People outside the web still interacted with friends and continued to meet new people just as they had in the previous 5,000 years of history, while occasionally sending emails on the web.

Suddenly, we found all our friends on the internet. We needed to connect with them through online messaging apps and later through social networks like Facebook.

Then, people on social networks (including our friends) began creating content, some interesting and some less so, posting photos, articles, and videos. This is when social media was born (YouTube, TikTok, Instagram, etc.).

Today, we are in a new evolution of the internet. There is too much information and too many tools; hence, we need assistants to help us navigate this digital jungle. Our phones are filled with apps, and the browser's bookmark bar is crowded with websites and platforms. Now, with just one app, an assistant equipped with artificial intelligence, we can save a lot of time.

But what's the point of this regression? It's to convince you that you can no longer generate traffic with SEO using content the way you did years ago.

Even though there are standard concepts that remain unchanged, you cannot use outdated techniques and pretend that everything is the same as before.

Both the internet and the people using it have changed. Consequently, SEO has changed and will continue to change. We can only adapt to people and their needs, along with all the requirements set by the traffic sources we choose, which, in the case of SEO, are search engines.

Let me give you a simple example. Richard is your ideal visitor: a young person who watches videos on his phone. So, thinking from an SEO perspective, what would you do between:

1. Creating a 2,000-word article on a desktop website with an explanatory infographic?
2. Creating a video and uploading it to YouTube, optimizing the content and description with a link to a detailed page on your site?

Which of the two solutions is "optimized" for search engines? It's the one that is optimized for Richard, the audience you are targeting. This is how an SEO professional should think.

You can no longer capture traffic the way you did before. You also cannot expect a single resource to capture all search traffic or all types of searches. It's no longer simple because everything has gotten more difficult and complicated. You need to create multimedia content and think cross-platform.

It's fine to choose to focus on just one type of search. But it's also fine to create different content for different types of searches, perhaps designing multimedia content even before writing it. This way, it can adapt to various platforms and thus reach different types of audiences.

In the scenario of Richard, I would have prepared a very interesting video for him and published it to YouTube, his preferred platform, methodically optimizing both the video and the channel.

I would then direct viewers from both the video and the description to a page on a website where I would provide additional resources and value. I would feature the video (with the precautions we'll discuss later), perhaps along with its transcription. I might also include a longer or different version of the video.

Additionally, I would find a way to engage the visitor by offering them the option to subscribe to my newsletter (in addition to subscribing to the YouTube channel).

After setting everything up, I would use YouTube's advertising tools to promote the video on the platform, giving an initial boost to the content. This would drive traffic from YouTube to the website , then to the newsletter list.

This is just an example of what it means to do SEO today and think cross-platform. Once, it was enough to fill a page's `<meta name="keywords">` tag with a list of keywords to do SEO. Today, times have changed; the internet is always evolving.

With SEO, you have to be adaptable, always keeping in mind the core standards.

UNDERSTANDING TRAFFIC

Now, to clearly establish the fundamental concept that will be repeated throughout the following pages, let's start with a question:

What is traffic?

Of course, as I mentioned in the introduction, we're not talking about the traffic of cars you encounter on your way to work in the morning. However, it is something quite similar.

> Traffic refers to the visitors to your website. Traffic is defined as those who browse the internet and seek information. Traffic includes users of websites, social networks, and online services. Traffic is made up of people; in fact, *traffic is people.*

Understanding what traffic is and how it behaves is important both conceptually and practically. But it's not complicated; in fact, it's quite simple.

We can understand traffic since it is made up of people. To easily grasp the concept of web traffic, we can compare it to road traffic. Imagine roads congested with cars heading to work or school in the morning; this is similar to the flow of users visiting websites in search of information, products, or services.

Just like road traffic, web traffic experiences moments of congestion and periods of smooth flow. Peak web traffic times generally occur during working hours, when people are active online at the office on PCs or at home on their smartphones. During these times, web traffic increases, similar to how roads become congested during rush hours.

However, several factors influence web traffic, just as they do road traffic. We will delve into the factors that influence visitor volume later. Additionally, special events or holiday periods can cause spikes in web traffic for some websites or sudden drops for others, much like how events or holidays can increase road traffic or how summer vacations boost traffic in tourist cities while emptying streets in major cities.

For example, during the COVID pandemic, web traffic surged significantly because people were confined at home and had little else to do but watch TV, use smartphones, or work on PCs. Perhaps some even read books.

By using the analogy of road traffic, we can better understand the concept of web traffic and the factors that influence it.

We can also envision the visitors to your website as people walking on a sidewalk rather than as cars. Think of those enormous sidewalks overflowing with people in major cities. In Tokyo, Japan, there's what seems to be the busiest pedestrian crossing in the world. It's called Shibuya, where thousands of people cross the street simultaneously in various directions when the light turns green, but they maintain an orderly *flow*. I imagine the internet just like that—a metropolis filled with people.

Flow is a term that describes something moving continuously from point A to point B along a path. It's exactly how users behave on the web, and that's why we refer to the flow as the pathway we want to guide traffic (users) through, directing them from where they start (A) to where we want them to end up (B).

In other words, just as you would design a route for pedestrians in a busy city to ensure they reach their destination efficiently, you design the user experience on your website to guide visitors seamlessly from their initial entry point to the desired outcome, whether it's making a purchase, signing up for a newsletter, or simply finding the information they need.

Imagine the Internet as a vibrant and bustling metropolis. Each neighborhood in this metropolis represents a niche, a specific market with its own interests and needs.

Within each neighborhood, we find a multitude of "houses" and "stores," that is, websites offering products, services, or information relevant to that niche.

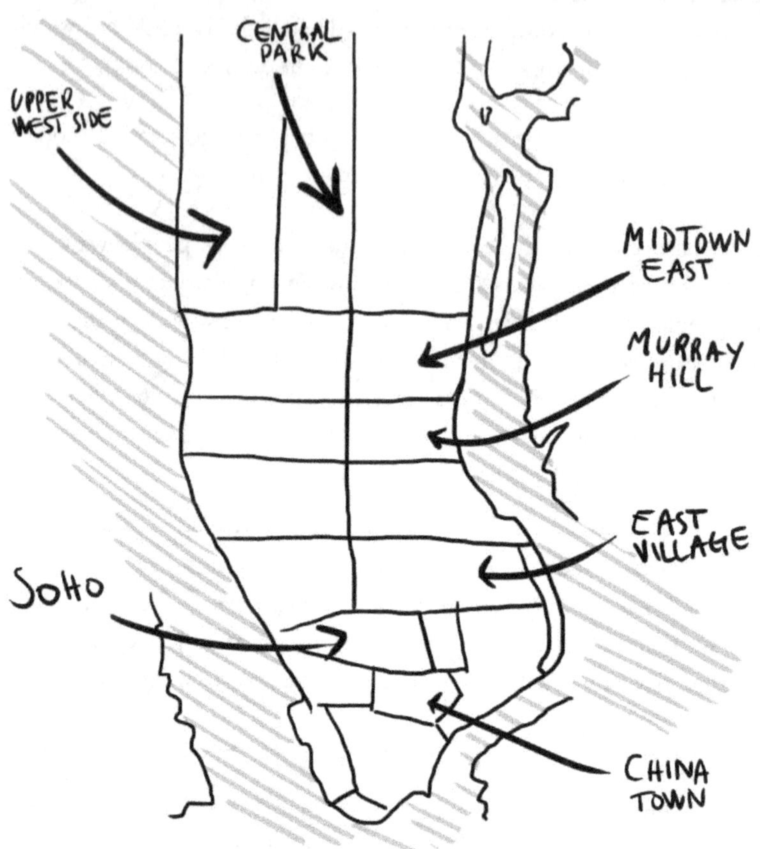

Let's consider the sports district: here you'll find sports equipment stores, virtual gyms, sports news websites, and blogs dedicated to various sports disciplines. Similarly, the beauty district will host websites for cosmetics, makeup tutorials, wellness tips, and everything related to self-care.

Just like in a real metropolis, the variety of niches and websites on the Internet is endless. There are districts dedicated to fashion, cooking, technology, music, travel, and any other imaginable topic. Each user can explore this virtual metropolis and discover the districts that interest them most, finding information, products, and services that meet their specific needs.

Every sidewalk, street, or corner of the city is filled with people constantly moving in all directions.

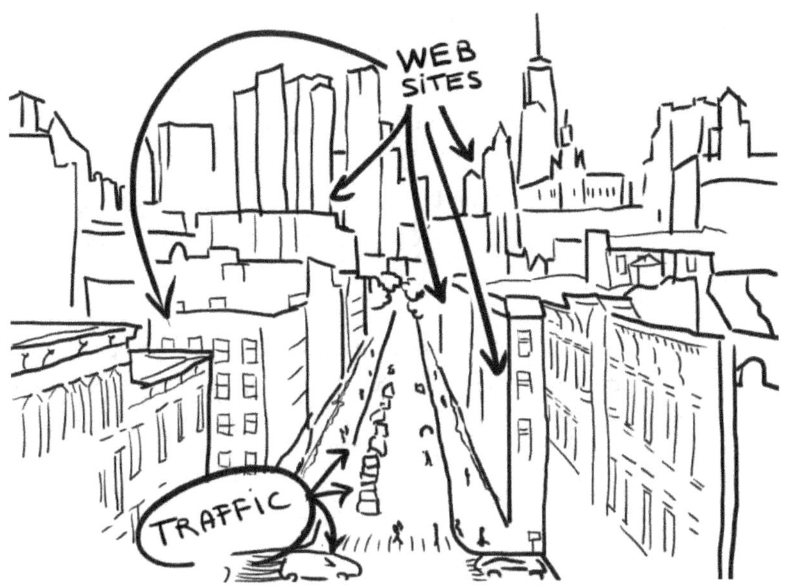

Just like the citizens of a bustling metropolis, internet users move dynamically and curiously between different niches and websites. Imagine citizens strolling on digital sidewalks, crossing virtual intersections, and boarding intangible means of transport such as taxis, trams, or subways. Each click represents a step in this ongoing exploration, discovering new topics and interests.

Just as a city dweller might decide to change neighborhoods to reach a specific store or gathering place, an internet user can switch from one niche to another with a single click and at the speed of light. From sports to fashion, from cooking to technology, the online world offers endless possibilities for discovery and exploration.

Just like in the streets of a real metropolis, the web also allows users to encounter people with similar interests, exchange ideas, and participate in discussions within forums, online groups, and social networks. The network thus becomes a space for meeting and exchanging, where different passions and knowledge intersect and enrich each other.

Internet users fall into two main categories: those with a specific destination and those who enjoy a leisurely, exploratory stroll without a fixed goal. The former seek specific information, products, or solutions to concrete problems, while the latter wander virtually, intrigued by what they encounter along their path.

In both cases, websites play a role similar to that of shops lining the streets: they contain everything users are looking for, from useful information and desired products to solutions to their problems. And just as a shopkeeper attracts customers into a physical store, the goal of a website owner is to attract virtual users.

This is the first mission to address after creating a website: to position yourself in the virtual showcase so you can be noticed by users searching for what you offer. Only then can you turn them from mere passersby into interested customers.

So, even you will have your shop in the metropolis. Perhaps you'll start from a simple basement or garage (after all, Apple, Amazon, and Google all started in a garage, *right?*).

Over time, your website will grow into a beautiful house or a 10-story building, and there will be space to welcome thousands of people each day, who will come and go, enjoying your content and buying your products.

What is traffic?

Web traffic is people. It's me searching for information on Google, and it's you visiting a news website to read some headlines.

When you open a website, you become traffic for that site. When you unlock your phone, tap the Google microphone icon, and speak, you become web traffic. *Open any app that provides an online service?* You become web traffic.

Every person on the internet is traffic and is a part of the total traffic on the network. A unit of traffic, so to speak, defined as a single person browsing and thus accessing content on the web, is 1 UV (*Unique Visitor*).

If we consider web traffic from a "data" perspective, then web traffic is the total amount of data sent and received by a visitor on a website, based on the number of pages they have visited.

However, we are interested in the definition of web traffic as "people," the individuals who send and receive data. So far, this seems straightforward. Let's dive a bit deeper in the next section, where we'll explore the main sources of traffic, analyzing how each can contribute to the growth of your site.

It's now essential to delve into the various sources from which this traffic can originate.

Section 1: Introduction to traffic sources

Where Will Your Website Visitors Come From?

Traffic is not always of the same type and is categorized according to its origin.

There are only 7 categories, each with a specific name. The category most relevant to SEO professionals is primarily the first one. The difference between the various types of traffic is fundamental, and it is also quite intuitive from the names you'll read.

Let's analyze all the categories of traffic types together.

- Organic Traffic
- Paid Traffic
- Direct Traffic
- Email Traffic
- Social Traffic
- Referral Traffic
- Bot Traffic

Organic Traffic

Organic traffic refers to all the visitors who arrive at your website organically.

What does "organically" mean? It means "naturally," i.e., without having clicked on a paid banner or coming from other websites.

In practice, these are users who come from search engines. Imagine a user searching for something on Google. The search engine generally provides a *link* to click, and the user lands on your site.

The same applies if a user searches on YouTube. The platform provides various links, including preview images, which, when clicked, lead to different videos. It's the same concept.

> A *link* is a connection between one page and another. It usually appears as blue-colored or underlined text, but it can also be an image. When you click on it, you are taken to another web page. In the world of the web, links and their structure are important; we will discuss this further later.

In our internet metropolis metaphor, a person is strolling, takes their phone out of their jacket pocket, and searches for something on the search engine.

> The *search engine* is nothing more than a website or service like Google, Bing, or similar that is used to search the web. In this book, when I talk about search engines, I am mainly referring to Google, which is the most dominant today. However, the best practice when performing SEO optimizations is to consider and check which search engine is most used in the country or market of interest.

The *search engine* displays a page with results, and the user clicks on one. A taxi arrives, picks up the user from where they are (on the search engine), and transports them to the neighborhood where the requested website is located.

Organic traffic is a type of traffic that comes to your website and doesn't cost you anything. It's free traffic, as you're not paying the search engine to display links to your content.

Moreover, it's often considered "valuable traffic." *Why is that?*

Because you can understand the search intent of the person who landed on your site. If you provide what they're looking for on your website, the user who arrives for free is also highly "*targeted*" in terms of their request. "*Targeted*" users are statistically more likely to engage with your product/service or information because they have found exactly what they were looking for.

Precisely because it's free and often "in target," this type of traffic is highly sought after, but few know how to obtain it (we'll figure it out together).

Organic visitors look for something on a search engine. The engine then proposes a link to a website (perhaps your own) and displays it graphically on a page (the SERP) within a *snippet*.

Once the user clicks on the link, they land on your website, having arrived organically.

> The "*snippet*" is the search result you see on search engine pages. It usually consists of a title and a description that help you determine if the proposed website contains what you're looking for. However, it can be much more complex, containing videos or images, structured data, or even becoming an informational card.

The question you should have in mind at this point is: *How do I get this organic traffic?* We will explore this in depth.

Since this traffic, as mentioned, comes entirely from search engines, your mission will be to ensure that search engines appreciate and recommend your website to their users.

The techniques needed to make your website appealing to search engines are part of SEO practices.

SEO, short for "Search Engine Optimization," literally means "optimizing pages for search engines." It refers to all the techniques used to optimize websites, pages, or web resources to make them easy for search engines to find and index.

Do you know how much of the web traffic is organic? About 50%.

Paid traffic

The traffic you obtain by paying a platform to generate it is called "paid traffic." When a user browsing the web clicks on an advertisement and lands on your website, that UV (Unique Visitor) is considered part of the paid traffic.

By now, you've heard the term "land" numerous times. It's commonly said that a user "lands" on a web page when they open it. Landing pages are specific pages designed for users to arrive at.

The reason it's considered paid traffic is simple: to attract this traffic, you use advertisements, and you, as the advertiser, pay for the advertisement.

The *advertiser* is the person or company that purchases ad space to publish their ad.

There are many types of advertisements, but this book won't delve into all the details. Ultimately, they all have one goal: to capture users' attention and get them to click, leading them to land on a website as part of paid traffic.

For example, paid advertisements include *"sponsored"* results in search engine SERPs, as well as banners and sponsored posts on platforms like Facebook, Instagram, or any other social network.

Out of all human-generated web traffic, paid traffic accounts for an average of about 10%.

The "SERP" (Search Engine Result Page) is the list of websites that a search engine displays for a specific search query. Most web traffic comes from the top 8-10 results on the SERP (around 91%). You will encounter the term SERP hundreds of times in this book.

The tools used to generate paid traffic can vary greatly, and we can visualize them in the metaphor of a metropolis.

Web banners are like the billboards, posters, and neon signs in a city. Other more "intrusive" tools could be compared to the "doormen" standing outside restaurants or clubs, trying to catch your attention and lure you inside for lunch or dinner.

Direct Traffic

Direct traffic is a type of traffic that holds high potential value because these are users who access your website directly.

A user who types your website's address directly into the browser's address bar is accessing the website directly and is part of direct traffic.

If someone is entering your address directly without going through a search engine, it likely means they already know you.

Perhaps someone told them your website's address verbally, so they found you through classic word of mouth. Or, more likely, the user already knows you because they've visited your website so many times that they remember the address by heart. Alternatively, they may have read the address on your business card, on a specific sticker, on your product packaging, or on a billboard advertisement.

All of these scenarios are great news, as each one indicates that you've done a good job with *brand awareness*.

> The term *"brand awareness"* is used to measure how well the public knows us, how familiar they are with our brand, and therefore our company or business. If a user, when thinking of a product, immediately thinks of your brand (which produces that product), you will have excellent *brand awareness* as well as perfect *positioning* in your market.

If your web project is new, if the website has just been launched and no one knows you yet, direct traffic will be virtually zero. In fact, no one is aware of your existence, either online or offline. Don't panic; this is normal.

EMail Traffic

This type of traffic consists of people landing on your website after clicking a link within an email.

It primarily comes from the email marketing campaigns you run. *Not doing them?* That could be a mistake; you should be doing them. We'll later discuss why these types of campaigns are very useful.

Since this traffic comes from emails, it follows that if you haven't set up any email campaigns—meaning you don't have a mailing list to which you send emails regularly—your email traffic will be zero.

This type of traffic is generated through all types of emails. This includes both the ones you send manually to individual addresses and those from a newsletter or a more complex system that manages lists, subscription forms, and automated *follow-up* sequences (which we'll talk about later).

Social Traffic

You're scrolling through your Facebook *feed*; you see the title of an article that catches your interest, and you click the link. You land on a website featuring the list of the 10 cutest kittens in the world. Congratulations! You've just become social traffic for the kitten website.

> The word "feed", which you'll read multiple times in the following pages, refers to the social network pages where information is listed in a column. The Facebook feed is the page where, as you scroll, you see posts from the people and groups you follow.

Social traffic, as you might have guessed, is the flow of users arriving from social networks. *How much of web traffic comes from social sources?* About 5%.

The situation is slightly different for traffic from Skype, WhatsApp, Facebook chat, or Messenger, which is still challenging to attribute, even though they do belong to social network platforms.

Referral Traffic

Referral traffic, derived from the English term meaning "referred" or "recommended," consists of people landing on your website through links from other websites.

If your statistics show a high percentage of referral traffic, it means you have many links on a single website directing people to yours. Alternatively, it could be that you have just one link, but it's on a very well-known and visited website, thus sending you significant traffic.

It can also happen if you've created some interesting content (a blog post, an infographic, a video, etc.) that gets shared and linked to. Since there is a link to your website in the content, you'll receive a substantial amount of referral traffic because these websites are recommending your content.

In all cases, referral traffic arrives at your website from other websites that have redirected part of their traffic to you. It's a great way to increase your *brand awareness* and enhance your *link building*.

Bot Traffic

We started by saying that traffic consists of people. In reality, a percentage of internet traffic is not composed of people.

This traffic consists of bots, programs that automatically scan the web for information. The term "bot" is derived from "robot."

Bots are usually programmed to perform repetitive tasks of information collection. One example is the classic Google bot, known as *Googlebot*.

Also called a *spider* or *crawler*, Googlebot scours the web using links as entry points, searching for new and relevant web pages. It then enters these pages looking for information to index and rank your website in search results. The term "spider" aptly describes something that works simultaneously across many websites with all its "legs."

> *"Spider"* is another term for the crawler, the robot, or the automated software used by search engines to analyze pages.

We will delve into the topic of crawlers and how to communicate with them later in the book. For now, it's enough to know that, on average, bot traffic accounts for 20% to 40% of internet traffic. So, don't be surprised if you find a portion of your site's traffic attributed to these automated programs.

You might imagine, in a way, that among the people strolling on the sidewalks of the "internet" metropolis, there are also some robots walking alongside humans, performing their assigned tasks. When I thought of this image, I was reminded of the cartoon "Futurama" with its futuristic cities shared between humans, robots, and aliens (this metaphor might be useful for you as well).

Conclusions on Traffic Sources

As you have seen in the chapters of the first part of this book, web traffic can originate from various sources, each of which is well defined.

Just like people walking through the streets of the imaginary city that is the web, visitors to your website can come from different places. These places, the origins of the visitors, are called "traffic sources."

Traffic sources are the origin, source, or place from which each individual user navigating the web comes. A user who follows the path *"Search Engine >> Your website"* will have the search engine as their traffic source and will therefore be categorized under organic traffic.

A user who follows the path *"Search Engine >> Another website >> Your website"* will have "Another site" as their traffic source and will thus fall into the referral traffic group.

Traffic sources correspond simply to the types of traffic you read about in the first chapter. Here again are the different types of traffic, excluding bots, as it is useful to always keep these in mind:

- Organic Traffic
- Paid Traffic
- Direct Traffic
- Social Traffic
- Email Traffic
- Referral Traffic

Visitors arriving at your website via organic traffic will be called "organic visitors." Following this logic, visitors arriving through direct traffic will be "direct visitors," those coming from Facebook or Instagram will be "social traffic," and so on.

The question you're likely asking yourself now is: *How can I attract visitors from these traffic sources? How can I ensure that organic traffic, paid traffic, direct traffic, or any other type of traffic ultimately ends up at my site?*

We will delve into this in detail, particularly focusing on organic traffic, which results solely from SEO optimization of your site. Your goal is to bring as many visitors as possible to your website, and to achieve this, we will utilize one or more of the available traffic sources.

A secondary, equally valid goal could be to attract high-quality visitors, thus focusing on quality rather than quantity. Often, the quality of a visitor is more valuable than the sheer number of visitors.

If we were to rank the existing traffic sources by quality, the scale would be approximately as follows:

1. Organic Traffic
2. Paid Traffic
3. Email Traffic
4. Direct Traffic
5. Referral Traffic
6. Social Traffic

It's precisely organic traffic, which you see at the top of the list, that I prefer because it's free.

Organic traffic comes from specific searches through a search engine. Organic visitors are also potentially very interested in the content they find. The downside is that sometimes it's difficult to capture this traffic, and it almost always requires a medium to long time to fully establish.

Paid traffic is also a type of traffic with potentially great value. Indeed, with the various targeting tools available on platforms that provide this type of traffic, you can capture the attention of precisely the people you're interested in. Essentially, you show your ads only to those who you believe will be interested, your ideal customers. However, paid traffic has a major drawback: it is, indeed, paid. If you don't invest your money wisely, you could end up burning through your entire budget without making any profit. The greatest advantage of paid traffic is its enormous scalability.

It's up to you to be skilled in investing money in paid traffic and to do it correctly and in the best possible way by creating profitable campaigns, optimizing the successful ones, and stopping those that do not produce results. But to do this, you need to be a master of online advertising, which is beyond the scope of this book.

Email traffic is very valuable because people who have given you their email likely already know you and trust your products or information. These users, having subscribed to your list or newsletter, are undoubtedly interested in your content and probably trust you since they've provided their email address.

The same applies to referral traffic. These are users "recommended" by another website and therefore come with a (potential) level of trust and expectation.

Finally, we conclude the quality ranking with social traffic. Social traffic generally has less commercial potential. The reason lies in the motivation that drives people to social media.
On social networks, people are often there to seek a solution to a problem, a solution that is not always easily monetizable. The positive side here is the potential for certain types of content to go viral on social media.

It's also important to clarify that if I buy traffic from a social traffic source, such as Facebook, for example, I'm bringing *paid traffic* to my website, not organic *social traffic*. Social traffic refers to traffic generated organically on social media without any advertising spend.

Section 2: Understanding your Audience

Strategic approach to understanding your ideal customer

But if internet traffic consists of people, like you and me, *can we get an idea of what they are looking for? But who are these people exactly?*

It's you when you check Facebook in the morning (you're direct traffic for Facebook) and click on a friend's post that takes you to YouTube (you're social traffic for YouTube). It's me when I open Instagram and post a photo (I'm direct traffic for Instagram). It's you when you click on a banner ad while reading your favorite online newspaper and end up on another website (you're paid traffic for that site), or when you go to Amazon and, before buying a book, visit the author's official website (you're referral traffic for that site).

It's me when I check my email and click a link in a message that takes me to Amazon (I'm email traffic for Amazon). Or when I open Google (I'm direct traffic for Google) and perform a search that leads me to Wikipedia (I'm organic traffic for Wikipedia). All these interactions between links, websites and people form *the web of the internet.*

But why do people browse the internet? They could be riding a bike instead of straining their thumbs scrolling through Facebook for hours, watching videos, reading headlines, news, or articles, *right?*

Understanding people's behavior and truly grasping the reasons behind their actions is essential for fully comprehending the traffic on the internet. Each person may browse the web for many different reasons. However, all these diverse motivations, whether subjective or objective, can be easily categorized into two main groups of users:

1. User seeking solutions to needs
   a. Users seeking answers to questions

2. User seeking solutions to discomforts
   a. Habitual users
   b. Users in search of stimulation

Solutions to needs

The first thing people look for on the web is solutions to their needs. Often, this need is simply the desire to know something, which translates into the need for information. And if you need something, you search for it online.

This category includes people who, through one or more searches, want to find a solution to a specific question. And when you want to know something and you have a phone that gives you access to the internet, *who else would you ask if not Google?*

Approximately 8% of searches on Google are posed in the form of a question. People ask search engines something, making a direct inquiry, and the search engine returns the answer. Or rather, it returns a list of resources containing the answers, ranked in the search results page (SERP) based on relevance as calculated by the engine.

Every day, people search for solutions to their problems, and the web is the fastest and most efficient way to find them. After all, the answer is right around the corner—just grab your phone, type the question into the search bar, and see the results. If you're lucky, you'll have solved the problem in less than a minute, or at worst, you'll need to perform more searches. Often, the search engine provides the answer without needing to click any links or open additional pages.

The solution to a problem could very well be an answer within a blog article, or it could be a product or service on an eCommerce site.

If you want to stand out from the crowd and succeed in SEO, you need to become obsessed with people's needs—your ideal customers' needs. If you want these people to read your website, purchase your services, or even just have Google recognize your content as high-quality, you must center your work around their needs and find a way to fully satisfy them.

Solutions to discomforts

The second major category of traffic consists of those who are simply looking for a quick solution to a discomfort they are experiencing at the moment. After all, every void needs to be filled in some way.

These people are not searching for information, products, or services. They are looking to alleviate discomfort.

This category includes TBH, "Traffic by Habit," and TPS, "Traffic Seeking Stimulation."

Discomfort is indeed an emotion that, at a specific moment, triggers a mechanism inside you that can easily become a habit. An action is activated to seek a solution to the discomfort itself.

When a person is waiting at a bus stop and has a few seconds of "nothing," a sense of boredom can arise. The result is an automatic response: the hand slips into the pocket, grabs the phone, and perhaps the quickest solution to boredom is scrolling through the Facebook feed.

People do this to find stimulation - any form of stimulation that can eliminate their boredom or current discomfort. If at any time of the day you feel lonely, you might pick up your phone and check your email, Facebook chat, or WhatsApp. *How many times do we do this each day?* Too many.

If you're feeling stressed, you might take a scroll through Instagram. It's all these online services I mentioned (Facebook, Email, WhatsApp, Instagram) that address your discomfort when you use them.

Once these actions are repeated day after day, they become habits.

What traffic finds

Now that we have explored the stimuli and reasons that drive people to browse the internet and open websites and applications, we need to answer another question.

What does traffic find?

What do people find on the internet? What does traffic discover when it flows through online search engines to find solutions to their needs? Where do people end up when they pick up their phones to resolve a discomfort?

There are two possible solutions:

- Websites
- Social Networks

Websites

Those who search for questions or information will almost certainly use search engines, primarily Google. The search engine suggests to the user that the answers they are looking for are probably available in the list of websites it displays.

Alternatively, if the question is specific, it may provide the solution directly in the SERP, at the top of the page, so it is immediately visible and allows you to get what you want while saving time.

By clicking on the links in the SERP, the user lands on a website that likely contains the answer to their question, the solution to their problem, the product they were looking for, or the service that will save them time and money.

Traffic will therefore land on informational websites, news portals, blogs, eCommerce websites full of products, etc.

On the other hand, those who consciously or unconsciously seek solutions to their discomforts are likely to end up on social networks. Each social network is designed, or potentially suited, to attract a particular type of discomfort.

If you feel lonely, you might open Facebook to see what your friends are up to. You might open Messenger, WhatsApp, or Telegram to send a message to a friend. Perhaps you'll open Twitter to read or post something.

If you're bored, you'll likely open Instagram and start scrolling through the feed to find images you like. When you finally find an image that appeals to you, you'll experience temporary relief and satisfaction from your discomfort, essentially a reward that momentarily makes you feel good. This reward process is what creates a habit.

If you're stressed, you might open Pinterest. If you're depressed, you'll check your email for incoming messages. And so on.

Social networks are solutions for the needs of this type of traffic. It's traffic influenced by emotions, mood, and feelings, as well as automatic habitual behaviors. In all these seemingly innocuous actions—feeling bored, opening a social network, starting to browse, and liking posts—there's a potentially dangerous process that I will only briefly mention, as it is not the focus of this book, but I would certainly recommend you explore it further.

The fact is, the more relief and temporary rewards you find on social networks, the more often you'll seek them out. You'll spend a significant amount of time on these platforms without even realizing it, as you'll be caught in a reward process that creates a habit.

For curiosity's sake, I'll point out that the average time a person spends on social media each day is about 2 hours. In practice, considering we sleep 8 hours a day, we spend 12.5% of our "waking time" on social media. Wow.

Your audience

But studying people goes beyond just understanding general needs or desires. To determine who you really need to target, you must dive into specifics by analyzing user profiles, their online behaviors, and their specific interests.

Only by doing this can you gain a complete view of your audience and deeply understand their needs to potentially offer a tailored solution by developing a customized communication strategy. This will complement the market study we will conduct in the next section of the book.

Throughout your audience analysis, you need to go through several stages:

The first phase is **audience definition**, where you clearly define what you mean by "audience." *Who are the people you will be targeting? What are their goals?* Write all the notes in a document that you will gradually develop.

The second phase is called **audience segmentation**. If your audience is broad and diverse, segment it by dividing it into more specific groups or subgroups and describe in your notes the criteria you used for the division.

Now it's time to do an even more detailed job: defining the *buyer persona*. The buyer persona is a fictional representation, but based on real data, of your ideal customer.

So, imagine creating a detailed profile of this person. The aspects you will need to analyze are:

- **Demographic Data Analysis:** Age, gender, location, education level, profession, income, etc.
- **Online Behavior Analysis:** Purchasing habits, preferred online channels, devices used to seek information, and goals.
- **Needs and Desires Analysis:** What problems or challenges they face and what goals they have.

This research should be conducted at the start of every project and updated considering market changes or shifts in customer behavior. *But why is it useful to create a buyer persona?*

Firstly, it provides a better understanding of the specific group of people who are relevant to you and your online project. It helps you gain a clearer insight into your customers' needs and desires, allowing you to offer products or services that are better suited to their requirements.

Moreover, defining your audience and buyer personas is essential for any marketing strategy, as we will discuss further. It is logical to assume that if you create targeted and personalized content, it will have a higher chance of conversion because it focuses efforts on the channels and messages that resonate most with your target audience.

For example, imagine you want to sell running shoes. By creating a buyer persona for a professional marathon runner and another for a recreational runner, you can tailor your messages and communication channels for each of them. But there are many other examples: a clothing store might create buyer personas for a trendy teenager, a career professional, and a homemaker. A bank might create buyer personas for a young adult buying their first home, a family with young children, and a retiree. *Does that make sense?*

All of this will be useful later when we discuss content creation and user experience. With buyer personas, you can identify more relevant keywords for your audience, improving your content's ranking in search engines.

But that's not all. Defining buyer personas can also help you set targets for advertising campaigns on different platforms. You might choose to focus a campaign on a single profile or create customized campaigns for each group, adjusting the message and channels based on their specific needs and behaviors.

To make the concept of audience and buyer persona even clearer, I can provide you with the example of the buyer personas I created before writing this book. In theory, you should recognize yourself in one of these:

Buyer Persona 1: **John, the Web Newcomer**

Demographic Profile:

- Age: 25-35 years old
- Gender: Male
- Location: USA (major cities like New York, Los Angeles), UK (London, Manchester)
- Education Level: Bachelor's degree in non-technical fields
- Occupation: Employee or freelancer in traditional sectors (e.g., marketing, administration)

Online Behavior:

- Internet Usage: High, primarily for social media, email and research
- Devices Used: Smartphone (70%), laptop (30%)
- Interest in Website Creation: Has considered starting a web project but lacks technical skills
- Preferred Channels: Facebook, Instagram and Google for searches

Needs and Desires:

- Motivations: Wants to start a website for a personal project or a small online business but doesn't know where to start. Interested in learning SEO basics to generate organic traffic without high advertising costs.

- Goals: Create a website that attracts visitors without significant advertising spend, and understand how to improve website visibility.

- Challenges: Lacks practical experience in website creation or SEO optimization. Confused by technical terms and complex strategies found online.

Buyer Persona 2: **Sarah, the Marketing Professional**

Demographic Profile:

- Age: 30-45 years old
- Gender: Female
- Location: USA (New York, San Francisco), UK (London)
- Education Level: Master's degree in Marketing, Communication, or Business Administration
- Occupation: Marketing Manager, Digital Strategist or SEO Consultant in a small to medium-sized company

Online Behavior:

- Internet Usage: Very high, frequently uses advanced digital marketing tools and follows SEO trends and updates
- Devices Used: Laptop (60%), smartphone (40%)
- Interest in SEO: Has a basic to intermediate understanding of SEO but constantly seeks to update knowledge with new techniques and best practices
- Preferred Channels: LinkedIn, industry blogs, Google for research

Needs and Desires:

- Motivations: Aims to optimize the company website or a client's website to improve Google rankings and attract more qualified traffic. Interested in long-term, sustainable SEO strategies.

- Goals: Gain new SEO knowledge and techniques to improve website rankings and increase brand visibility.

- Challenges: Faces online competition and needs to justify the ROI of SEO strategies compared to paid alternatives.

Buyer Persona 3: **James, the Digital Entrepreneur**

Demographic Profile:

- Age: 35-50 years old
- Gender: Male
- Location: USA (Silicon Valley, Austin), UK (London, Edinburgh)
- Education Level: Bachelor's or Master's degree in Business or Engineering
- Occupation: Entrepreneur, founder of a startup or owner of a small online business (eCommerce, digital services)

Online Behavior:

- Internet Usage: Extremely high, uses web analytics tools, manages ad campaigns and follows digital market trends
- Devices Used: Laptop (70%), smartphone (30%)
- Interest in SEO: Understands the importance of SEO but seeks practical solutions to increase traffic and improve conversions.
- Preferred Channels: Business blogs, YouTube for tutorials and updates, Google for specific solution searches, Podcasts

Needs and Desires:

- Motivations: Wants to increase organic traffic to his website to boost sales and ROI. Looking for SEO strategies that can integrate with existing marketing campaigns.

- Goals: Generate qualified organic traffic, improve conversions, and gain a competitive edge in the online market.

- Challenges: Manages multiple aspects of his business and needs SEO strategies that are effective but not too time-consuming or resource-intensive.

Buyer Persona 4: **Emily, the Small Business Owner**

Demographic Profile:

- Age: 40-55 years old
- Gender: Female
- Location: USA (Midwest, Southern regions), UK (Manchester, Birmingham)
- Education Level: Bachelor's degree in Business or related fields
- Occupation: Owner of a small local business (retail, service industry) with an emerging online presence

Online Behavior:

- Internet Usage: Moderate to high, uses the internet for managing her website, social media, researching ways to improve her online presence
- Devices Used: Laptop (60%), tablet (20%), smartphone (20%)
- Interest in SEO: Limited understanding of SEO but recognizes its importance for growing her online presence.
- Preferred Channels: Facebook, local business forums, Google

Needs and Desires:

- Motivations: Wants to attract more local customers online and drive traffic to her website. Looking for simple and effective SEO techniques that can be applied without needing deep technical knowledge.
- Goals: Increase visibility of her business in local search results, attract more customers, and improve online sales.
- Challenges: Limited time and resources to dedicate to learning complex SEO strategies, needs easy-to-implement solutions.

Now you know that studying the audience and creating one or more "buyer personas" help focus your efforts and are fundamental tools for any marketing activity, including SEO. One last thing: *remember that by choosing to be for everyone, you are, in reality, declaring that you do not want to be for anyone*

SEEKING TRAFFIC

We have now reached the second part of the book, and it should already be very clear to you what web traffic is and where it comes from.

If you still have any doubts, I strongly recommend re-reading the first part of the book and making sure you fully understand the differences between the different types of web traffic.

We know that web traffic is always present online and that it is like the internet's lifeblood, always flowing from one source to another.

We also know that traffic is always searching for something. Every day, billions of people use the internet for an average of 6 hours and 40 minutes. This figure refers to the total hours spent online by an individual each day, across all devices (mobile, desktop, tablet, and others), and includes time spent on social media (around 2 hours and 20 minutes), as well as time spent streaming video or music content.

A significant portion of this traffic ends up on social media—about half of the people active online daily.

This vast crowd of users is like a river that branches out into many different streams, each taking its own direction. I'm talking about a flow of users, a flow that you need to be able to intercept.

If you want people to read what you write, buy what you sell, or request the services you offer on your website, you need to capture a portion of this web traffic. You can't intercept all the traffic, of course; that would be unrealistic. But you must at least manage to divert a small part of this stream of users toward your content.

It's this specific traffic that your website needs to generate readers, subscribers, sales, and ultimately, *revenue*.

The term *"revenue"* comes from the Latin "re-venire" (to return), and it is always used to indicate a return, specifically in the sense of an economic return.

If you're selling bags on your website, you need traffic that sees the bags you're selling. You need users who might go ahead and buy a few. One thing is certain: if no one sees the bags, no one will purchase them.

If you want to start a blog or already have one where you talk about DIY (do it yourself), you need users to read the articles and watch your tutorial videos. You need traffic that views your videos and perhaps clicks on the banner ads placed in the sidebar or among the content.

If you have a website with videos on martial arts techniques and you are a kung fu master, you need people to watch the videos and, most importantly, fill out the contact form to book a trial lesson with you.

Your website without traffic is like a store without any customers walking through the door. It's an empty, useless, desolate room where only dust accumulates. Essentially, it's something that serves no purpose and helps no one.

In reality, if you owned a physically empty store, you could still rent or sell it and make a profit. However, an empty website is worth nothing.

Like any business, a website must have a way to generate profits, or it holds no value. And before generating profits, it needs to have a way to generate visitors—a way to intercept traffic.

Did you know that showing how much traffic a website has, along with its revenue, is a common practice when selling a website? It's a bit like showing the financial situation of a company you want to sell.

Imagine the example we mentioned earlier. We're in the vast metropolis of the web: the streets are full of traffic, cars, and pedestrians, and your little shop, which is your website, is being ignored by everyone.

No one stops because no one notices it. No one sees your search engine snippets or advertisements. No one visits your website. Pedestrians aren't even looking at your shop window because, in reality, you're not yet present in one of the largest shop windows on the web—search engines. This is the place where SEO experts aim to position content.

But wait a second! If you find yourself in this desolate situation, just know that it's normal. In fact, at this stage, if you've started from scratch, you'll have an empty website with no traffic. If you don't yet have a website, it's as if you don't even have a shop on the sidewalk yet.

If you have a website with no traffic, you might still be trying to figure out what people are searching for and what they want, which means you're still in the early stages of designing your ecosystem. Or perhaps you already have a website that's been online for a few months, with content in it, but you aren't getting any traffic because you haven't been able to tap into this flow. The solution exists, and you'll find it in the upcoming chapters.

I like to call these kinds of projects "ecosystems" because every website built using the techniques and concepts you'll read about—designed to first reach high traffic and then monetization—is really just a combination of elements in balance, forming a functional, dynamic, and self-sustaining system. Essentially, it's something you create that then almost feeds itself.

Your mission, for now, is simple: you need to build a website and make sure people visit it. You need to create an online business. You need to design a digital marketing ecosystem to acquire visitors, turn them into leads, and convert them into customers.

Returning to the example of the Kung Fu master, think about how he might not actually need a complicated website. For him, a YouTube channel showcasing his techniques, organized into clear playlists, and then directing users to a simple contact form or a Google Business profile might be more meaningful. There's nothing wrong with that, but the SEO concepts you'll learn apply to any platform, including YouTube.

Remember, running an online business instead of a physical one has major benefits. For example, you don't have to pay rent, utilities, or other similar costs. If you have an idea right now, within 3 hours, you could already have a blog with 3 or 4 articles up and running. You can even generate a website from scratch using AI. You can leverage the speed of online businesses in this way.

However, designing an online business, especially in the case of a dedicated website, is not something you can afford to take lightly. Just like any real business venture, an online business also requires detailed planning.

If you lack experience and start building an online business without knowing what to expect or what you'll need to do, you're clearly at a disadvantage.

Take all the time you need, then act with a plan; otherwise, you're just throwing money down the drain. I'll try to explain how not to make this mistake—the mistake of starting unprepared. To design an ecosystem that works or at least has a good chance of working, you need to start with something legendary and mysterious, something I didn't even know about at first: market research.

Section 1: Market Research

You cannot understand what you do not know

The first and most crucial step you need to take if you want to build an online business—in your case, creating a website that attracts traffic—is market research.

If you already have a website, you should have done this by now. I want to assume you've already done it, or at least I hope so.

So, if you bought this book just to learn how to attract traffic, you can skip the chapter on market research. However, I still recommend reading it because it's an integral part of the entire process. You can't just take one part of what I've written and implement it independently. The system works because it's made up of all its parts, and the parts work because they depend on each other.

Additionally, I want to provide the most complete information possible, even for those who don't yet have a website and are just thinking about creating one in the future.

The truth is, if you don't know your market, you're shooting in the dark, so get ready to waste some money.

Let me explain further.

Your Niche

Let's assume you're passionate about table tennis and you decide to create a website on this topic. You do it because one day you think you might be able to turn it into a business and maybe even make a living from it.

Keep in mind that it's almost never a good idea to create a website with the goal of doing business by focusing solely on a personal passion. First, you should verify if the topic has any actual commercial value. But let's continue with this assumption.

You always need to choose a niche, a topic, or a category to start from.

> The term *"niche"* refers to a topic, category, or field in which you will try to carve out a space for your online business.

Many people feel quite hesitant when it comes to choosing their niche. Often, they are unsure or afraid of making a mistake. In fact, finding the right niche, especially at the beginning, is not easy at all—it's very challenging!

However, there's nothing you can really get wrong at this stage. Choose a niche and start studying it, as I will explain shortly. Later on, you can decide if the niche is the right one or not.

The niche you've chosen might turn out to be wrong, in which case all you'll need to do is discard it and find a new one. Of course, you'll make this decision after gathering enough data.

The key is to get started. The worst thing is to get stuck, expecting to find the perfect niche right away. This paralysis, which has a specific name and stems from uncertainty in data analysis, is something we'll also discuss at the end of the book.

It's rare for me to think of a niche, do a quick check, and immediately conclude that it's profitable and suitable for building a monetizable website via search engine optimization. Instead, it takes several attempts, and eventually, through research, something interesting will emerge. But one thing is certain: you do not have to focus on all people, but rather on a subset.

Studying and evaluating your niche's market (both online and offline) is both necessary and essential. For market research, I primarily rely on a thorough analysis of *competition* and *trend* in the initial phase.

Niche and Competition

A niche, therefore, is nothing more than a broad or narrow topic, composed of the set of keywords that users type into search engines. All of these keywords and related words must be taken into consideration.

Each keyword has a certain level of "competition." For example, if 1,000 websites discuss and have optimized content for a particular keyword "X," then the organic competition for that keyword will be very high. This type of competition is exactly what matters to you if you aim to capture organic traffic through SEO.

Organic competition (referred to as "SEO difficulty) is a metric that indicates how difficult it is to rank organically for a particular keyword. This is different from "*paid*" competition, which refers to the level of competition for paid advertisements targeting that same keyword "X." It could be that many websites are optimized organically for "X," but very few advertisers target that keyword in their paid advertising campaigns.

The sum of the organic competition of the keywords within a niche forms the overall competition of that niche. So, let's say the niche "rice recipes" has a competition score of 8 because there are many websites covering that topic. Additionally, let's assume the niche "onion recipes" also has a competition score of 8. The macro niche "recipes," which includes both sub-niches, would have a competition score of 8 or higher.

That's why it's important to carefully study keywords, their volumes, and competition to choose a niche where the chances of success are higher.

If you start a project in a specific niche and later discover that you need to invest your limited budget in a highly competitive area, it's like running a marathon against a team of champions and giving them a 15-kilometer head start.

Especially if you're creating your first website, it's better to choose a small, low-competition niche. The smaller the niche, the easier it is to dominate. The larger the niche, the more likely it is to be competitive.

If you manage to find a large niche with plenty of products and users willing to spend, but with little competition, then you've struck gold—but, of course, this is very rare.

It's much easier to find small niches or sub-niches. This concept of focusing on smaller topics is called "*niching down*," and we'll cover it in a dedicated chapter later. Further on, we'll also discuss how to study your competitors, but first, you need to learn how to analyze trends and keywords.

The Trend

The trend is the first thing I consider when I need to "test" the ground for a niche or when I need to analyze new ideas that come to mind.

> The *"trend"* is the general progression of a particular sector over a specific period of time.

Consider this: 9 out of 10 businesses fail within the first 5 years of operation. Of those that survive, 90% fail within 10 years.

It is critical for a project to have positive data at the beginning of its planning. If this is not the case and you lack facts or numbers to back up your notion, it will be tough to achieve success.

Having a solid and growing trend as a foundation will provide you with a solid "initial state," with proven statistical data that will help build a strong foundation for your project.

At this point, your project can merely be a hypothesis, an idea, or an intuition that you will test. You will analyze and examine this idea to determine whether it is good or should be discarded.

From trend analysis, you can easily and reasonably predict the future direction and performance of the sector or category of interest.

Let's see how to simply analyze the trend of the topic you are thinking about to cover or of the website you already own.

To analyze the trend of a topic, I use a free and truly useful tool from Google; it's called *"Google Trends."*

This tool will instantly and graphically provide the situation of the chosen topic. In addition to showing the market trend, it will give you other interesting information about the niche you're considering, such as search history and the most searched keywords.

Here's how I typically use this tool:

First, I'm assuming you've already chosen a niche at this point. Let's say, for example, you've chosen the topic "table tennis" we discussed earlier.

I go to Google Trends and enter the niche I've chosen into the search field. In this case, since table tennis is also known as "ping pong," I enter both terms. This doesn't change the result in terms of the graph, which can be represented as follows:

The useful Google service reveals the classic graph I'd rather not see. The interest in the topic is waning, albeit slowly. Essentially, fewer and fewer people are interested in table tennis.

I understand that table tennis might be your passion because you play it every summer afternoon at the beach. I understand; I did it too. I understand how much you enjoy it. Unfortunately, no one cares what you enjoy; instead, they care about what they like.

Ask yourself: do you really want to start building an online business in a niche that is disappearing or, as the graph shows, is experiencing a decline in interest?

I would say no. That's why the first thing to do is to study the market, to see right away, in 2 seconds, if there might be fertile ground or if you're stepping into a quagmire.

Just for the record, let's try overlaying the graph of a niche that is currently very active compared to the previous graph.

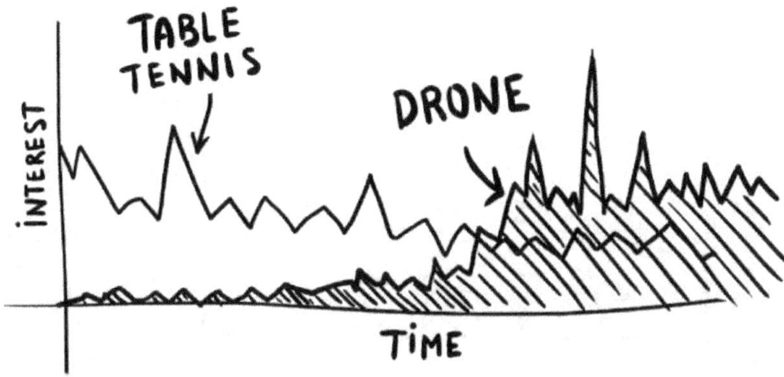

The curve with the most interest is the new niche I've added: the "drones" niche. Keep in mind that all the data I'm using for the graphs will be outdated by the time you read this book, so use them only for illustrative purposes.

It's immediately clear that interest in the topic of "drones" has been steadily increasing since 2009, reaching a certain level of stability. With just a bit of observation, you can see that shopping malls, which once had only 2 drones on their shelves, now have entire aisles dedicated to these remote-controlled gadgets. The overall volume of interest is still three times higher than that of your "table tennis" passion.

This indicates that, generally speaking, there is potentially more room in the drone niche. That space is where you should position your website.

I say "potentially" because, even though interest is high, you might later discover that the niche is dominated by 2 or 3 major, well-established websites that you'd prefer not to compete against, especially if you're inexperienced and have a limited budget.

But in general, *what should you look for when observing these trend graphs?*

When researching trends, there are two types of graphs you should look for and hope to encounter:

Graph type 1 shows slow but steady growth, indicating the gradual development of a stable niche over time.

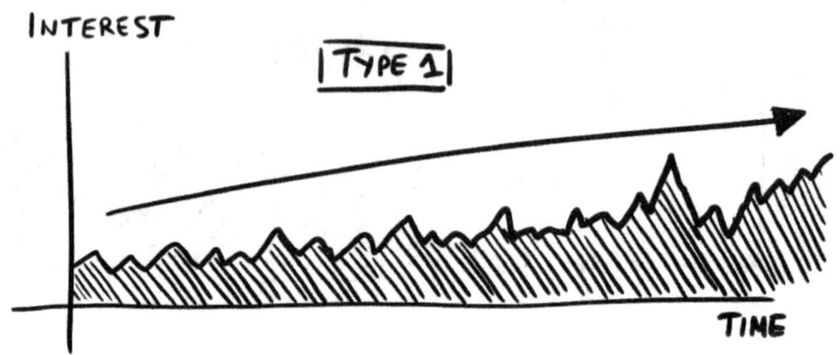

This type of graph is exactly what I would hope to find for long-term projects. The reason is that in these kinds of niches, you can rely on a volume of interest (and therefore web searches) that is not only solidified but also progressively increasing over time.

There is also a downside. This steady growth has usually been occurring for a long time, perhaps one or two years before you noticed it. Therefore, it has probably already been noticed by others or will be in the near future. So, you might not be discovering something new.

Whether you're working on your own SEO project or as an SEO expert for an external project, these are all factors to consider, and there are many more.

The second graph, which you'll always be happy to see when researching niche trends, is the one that shows a big spike. Let's call it a "type 2" graph. It is simply a graph that shows a sudden interest in a particular niche.

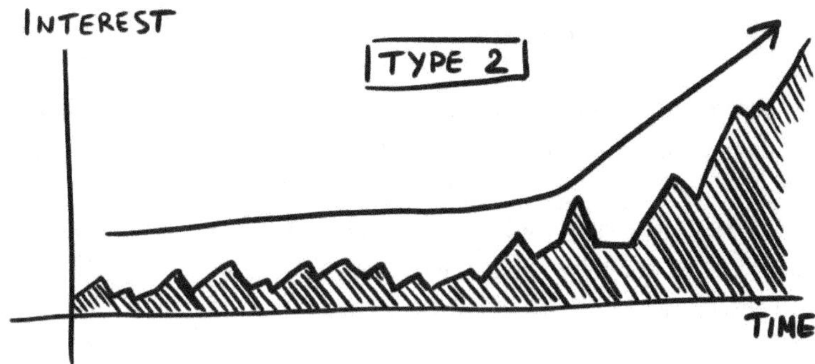

It's the case of topics or products that have experienced a sudden and recent "boost."

Often, this kind of situation is due to viral interest or perhaps a surge in searches caused by massive advertising campaigns in the media, such as in newspapers or even online.

It can also be due to news events reported by the media or perhaps sports results that draw significant attention to a particular topic. Or there could have been a launch of new technology or a specific geopolitical event.

The positive side of this situation is that, since the growth was truly rapid, you have a higher chance of discovering it first and, if you are well organized, taking advantage of it.

The negative side, in this case, is that you cannot be sure how long the interest in the topic experiencing the spike will last.

When you find this result, be cautious not to fall into the trap and carefully examine the time range. Ensure that the interest spike is not something seasonal or likely to be short-lived.

So, in simple terms, these are the two trends you would want to find: type 1 and type 2.

Having these two types of graphs in front of you, one showing consistent growth or one showing sudden growth, means you have found a niche with great interest and, hopefully, great potential commercial value. It's not yet time to celebrate, but at least you're starting off on the right foot with real data supporting your initial idea.

Another interesting tool for trend analysis that I want to point out, especially to understand which trends or topics are exploding, is "Exploding Topics."

It's an online tool with a nice interface that, thanks to excellent category division and good temporal filters, helps you understand what is growing the most and at what speed.

When conducting market research, the better the tools you use, the more time you save collecting data.

Google Trends doesn't just include the trend analysis tool but also all the analyses and infographics created from its data. It's a much more detailed and resourceful tool than one might expect.

The main tool we will use is called "Explore." With it, you can analyze the search terms you input, and it also offers a range of very useful filters. There are geo filters (even down to specific cities), time filters (including up to the last hour of searches or with customizable time intervals), and category filters (which allow you to search queries within specific categories).

Interesting, right? Additionally, you can choose the platform on which to conduct the search, including Google, Google Shopping, Google News, Google Images, and YouTube. This allows you to segment topics in great detail.

The set of terms that share the same concept defines "topics," which is a broader theme compared to the concept of "niche."

Related topics provide excellent information for SEO professionals. They help us understand what kind of website we might build and even what the structure of categories and the menu could be.

Topics are therefore fundamental to consider because Google pairs keyword searches (terms) with entity searches (topics). So Trends shows us two sets of data, both of which are very useful for implementing SEO strategies.

Moreover, these two data types (keywords and topics) are treated differently by Google. Just do an experiment by entering the same word into Trends, first as a query and then as a topic: the resulting graph will be different, and the associated queries will also vary.

A little trick I'll share with you: did you know that you can use operators in Google Trends? For example, the tool provides a list of queries limited to 25 results. So, if I want to remove certain words from the list of queries to make the result cleaner and more specific to the queries I'm interested in and free up space, I can do so using the operator "-": So, I'll write:

"query -a -b -c"

where a, b, and c are the words I want to exclude.

If I want to aggregate data, I can use the "+" operator. A classic example is wanting to aggregate a word in plural or terms in different languages. There are many other operators you'll need to explore on your own.

Another useful feature is year-over-year comparisons for each search term, which helps us graphically understand how the search for a particular query has changed from year to year. You can also compare data from country to country to see the differences.

In Google Trends, you can set up alerts and schedule them weekly. I can set alerts for specific topics, selecting the country of interest. This is very useful for automatic updates on a particular topic.

Another useful feature is the lists of the most searched topics year after year, with numerous fascinating categorizations. You can also explore the categorization and geolocation of each trend in the real-time trends panel. There are also courses, guides, and a newsletter.

The trends section is particularly useful for someone with a news blog, as it shows daily and real-time trends. The interesting part is that for each trend,

Google Trends also shows all related searches (along with the keywords) and all related news. This way, you can get a clear idea of the topic and the search keywords within a niche.

In short, this information provides several suggestions and demonstrates the themes and searches that are currently popular. Google Trends is a tool that will be very useful for any SEO expert during the market research phase.

Seasonality

The seasonality of some niches and topics is another factor you should certainly be aware of, simply because you'll need to pay close attention to it when conducting your market research.

> The term *"seasonality"* describes the general pattern of recurring interest in a specific sector over a given period.

A graph that might initially appear to be of type 2 could actually represent a seasonal topic. It could be that the chosen niche experiences peak at certain times of the year and have little or no interest during the rest of the year.

As a result, these are niches that can bring good results only during a specific time period. To identify these seasonal niches, simply extend the *time range* of the search, and the seasonal behavior of the market should become immediately apparent.

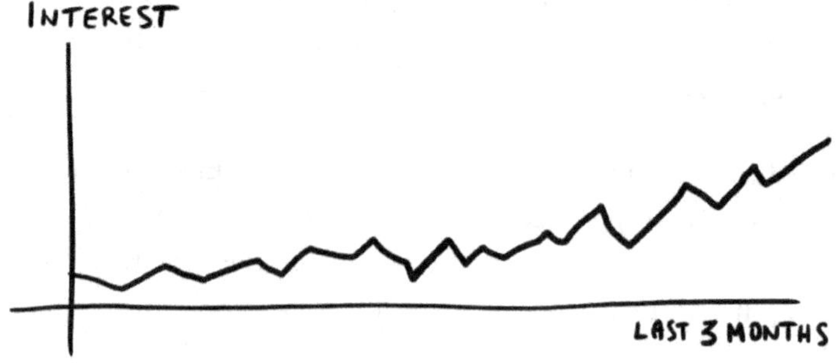

Let's take an example: the trend above is for the niche "Christmas trees." At

76

first glance, it might seem like a perfect example of a steadily growing trend with great prospects. However, simply extending the time range reveals that it is clearly a seasonal niche.

In the circle highlighted at the far right of the graph, you can see the range that the previous image covered. The wider image clearly reveals the seasonal nature of the niche, where each peak (triangle) represents the Christmas season.

Some niches may have long positive seasonal periods, such as the summer season, and equally long negative periods. In other cases, they may have brief peaks of high volume that occur only once a year, as seen with Christmas-related niches, like "Christmas trees."

So, is choosing the highly seasonal niche of "Christmas Trees" *a mistake*? Not necessarily. You can choose this niche, but you must clearly understand that it will only be at full throttle during a single extended period of the year. If that fits your strategy, then it's fine. If, however, you need something with a more stable and consistent volume, you should continue your search.

In conclusion, the trend analysis tool will be essential during the early stages of market research, allowing you to learn what people want, what intrigues them, in what quantity, and at what time.

Since you know that people are the traffic you need and will be looking for later, the insights extracted from this analysis tool are precious. It's common to find surprises or unexpected results during trend studies.

So, what are you waiting for? Take a break and start familiarizing yourself with this tool. Enter some topics and try to compare them with other similar or completely different topics.

Observe the trends, searches, most popular keywords, regions, and countries with the most interest. Think long-term, not just short-term. Think globally, not just locally. If a niche is well-developed, check its volumes in smaller countries as well. You might discover that it's a young market or not yet developed in some countries, which could present an opportunity.

Note down all the interesting trends you find and record them in a Google Sheet file named "Market Research."

Rename the first tab to "Niches" and organize it as follows:

Niche	Trend	Interesting?
Table tennis	Down	No
Drone	Up	Yes

Every time an idea comes to mind or you see something on Facebook that sparks an idea, write it in the "niche" column. Later, you can check the trend and update your file by filling in the other two columns at any time.

This is a systematic task that should become a habit starting now.

I write down all my ideas, including ideas for new niches, in a notebook that I always keep with me. I have dozens of these notebooks full of notes; when I want to consider one of the ideas I've jotted down on paper more seriously, I transcribe it digitally into a Google Drive file and start a more detailed analysis. I can access the file remotely from any location or device because it is stored in Google Drive's cloud. So, whenever a new idea comes to me, I can jot it down in an instant.

Later on, you will also take "interesting" ideas and study them in greater detail to determine whether they are valid or not.

It can also be useful, sometimes, to start with the assumption that the niche you found is not valid and try to find all the elements that might convince you to change your mind. This approach is especially useful if you are considering a niche that is also a passion, hobby, or personal interest. Pretend that the topic is incorrect from the start and try to find reasons to convince yourself otherwise.

During this initial trend research, you will come across the first *keywords* that describe the niche you are analyzing.

The concept of a *"keyword"* might be new to you, and we need to make sure it's clear because it will become central when we talk about SEO for content.

The concept is easy to understand. Every time you enter text into Google's search field, that is a query corresponding to a keyword. We will discuss this in more detail in a later chapter.

> In this field the term *"keyword"* or *"key"* refers to the set of words that a user has searched. One or more keywords make the "query" that a user asks the search engine. These are fundamental concepts.

Indeed, the tool you use for trend analysis also suggests some keywords, such as the most searched ones related to the topic you're considering or those that have recently seen a spike.

Here's a trick: if you type something into Google's search bar and then press the spacebar, a menu will pop up. This menu shows keywords related to what you've typed, ordered by the most searched ones in recent times.

Sometimes you might think finding information is difficult, but it's actually right in front of you.

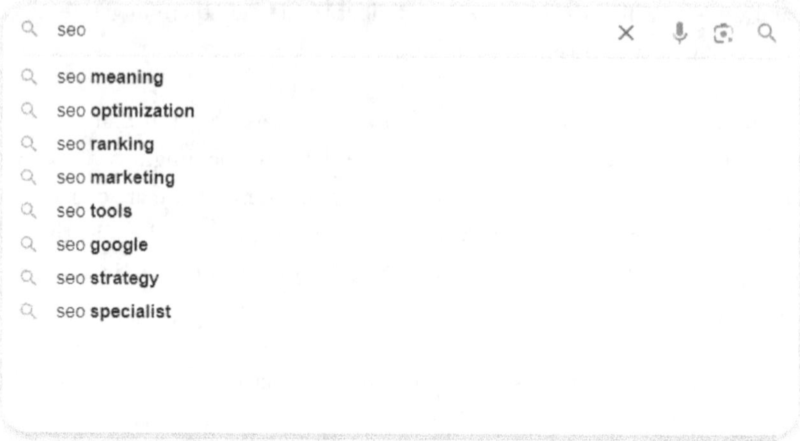

Later on, all these keywords will need to be analyzed in detail because together they form the set of searches that users (interested in that specific topic) perform over a period of time (usually monthly).

Keywords are thus the building blocks that make up the total search volume and traffic for the topic you are analyzing.

Section 2: Keywords Research

Now, let's look at another key component of your market research: how to position yourself in organic search, which is a critical step for the success of your online business when backed by SEO strategies.

The current situation should be that you have found a niche that seems promising in terms of trends and market. Great, so now you should start building your website, *right?*

No, wrong! You should not do anything else until you have thoroughly researched the search volumes for the niche in question.

You need to be as sure as possible that you are investing your time and money in a good niche. It has to be truly worth it.

Now we will talk a bit about search volumes. Volumes are the number of times that, typically over the course of an entire month, a particular keyword is searched for by search engine users.

> The *"volume"* refers to the number of searches for a single keyword during a specific period of time.

The concept is simple. Every keyword, meaning each search term that users type into the search engine, has a specific search volume. For example, let's look up the keyword from the niche we selected earlier, the drone niche. Let's check the monthly search volume for the keyword "drone" in the United States.

The resulting volume is 246,000 searches. Every month, the keyword "drone" is searched 246,000 times.

KEYWORD	TREND	VOLUME
DRONE	↑	246000

This means that almost 8,000 people in the United States search for that word in the search engine every day. This is very important.

Imagine you have a website about drones. Maybe you're passionate about the topic, and you've set up a small blog where you do unboxings or share videos of yourself flying your drone. You might give tips on how to pilot them, write articles, or post reviews on various models.

Let's assume you've done an excellent job with your content and SEO positioning, so when someone searches for "drone" on Google, your website always appears at the top of the SERP.

Let's exaggerate for a moment and pretend that the entire first page of Google for that specific search consists solely of pages from your blog.

At most, you would receive about 8,000 visits per day. *How come?* Because the keyword "drone" has that volume—8,000 daily searches.

If your goal is to reach 100,000 visits per day, a single keyword with that volume won't help you achieve it. This volume-related issue is something you'll always need to consider because you'll constantly be dealing with search volume numbers.

However, there's another thing to consider: the volume you extracted only refers to the exact keyword "drone." In reality, the drone niche consists of hundreds of different keywords, and the sum of all their volumes is much greater than 8,000 visits per day. In short, the topic "drone" encompasses thousands of keywords, not just one.

In fact, when you publish your pages on the website, they won't rank for just one single keyword but for many others as well. This happens because the content you write contains many different words and possibly various combinations of the main keyword.

The importance of the concept, however, does not change. If you write one article focused on a single keyword with a volume of 1,000, you'll get fewer than 1,000 visitors per month. This is because, as stated in the hypothetical example, it is extremely rare that you will occupy the entire first page of the search engine.

Also, during your research, you'll come across keywords with very low volumes, and you might be tempted to dismiss them immediately. However, it's possible that these keywords are highly relevant to your brand or strategy. In these specific cases, you can't afford to ignore them.

Keep in mind that for advanced volume research, you'll need to use online services different from Google Trends. I just want to explain the concepts; I'm not suggesting any particular service. Do your research—there are many available, and most offer a free plan that's useful for doing initial volume analyses and then deciding whether to subscribe to the service.

Organizing keywords

At this point, you should have a clear understanding that internet traffic is closely linked to keywords and their associated volumes.

However, people don't always search for the exact same word. When someone searches for drones, they don't always just type the keyword "drone."

As I mentioned earlier, they might use keywords from the same niche, related to the same topic, but with specific variations or additional details.

For example, they could add extra words, creating variations of the same keyword.

Keyword	Volume
drone	246000
drone with camera	74000
drone thermal camera	12100
drone show	12100
drone license	8100
can drone fly in air	320

In this case, each variant of the main keyword becomes a new keyword with its own volume, smaller than the volume of the main "mother" keyword (in this case, "drone").

Here comes the requirement for extensive organization and investigation. So, get comfortable and relax. If you skip this sometimes tedious task, you might end up getting lost in the details. You'll need to search for many keywords, including the variations of each word, and find a way to organize them properly. Later, this organization will be incredibly useful.

Especially in the content creation phase, if you decide to go forward with the niche you've analyzed, having clear and well-organized data will save you time and therefore money. Let's use the "cruises" niche as an example and investigate all the keywords connected to the "cruises" topic, starting with the easier paths, the most common and well-known keywords.

Keyword	Volume	Search Diff.
cruises	550000	66
norwegian cruises	246000	57
cruises lines	135000	63
cruises deals	110000	83
cruises virgin	110000	56
cheap cruises	74000	67
cruises from new york	33100	56
cruise last minute	33100	53
cruise seattle to alaska	33100	57
cruise from florida	27100	63
cruises all inclusive	27100	58
cruise hawaii islands	27100	61
cruises 3 days	18100	32
cruises out of new orle	18100	38
cruise xmas	6600	28

So, start with "cruises," which is the main keyword. You'll see a series of data arranged in a table, and you should sort it by volume.

This way, you'll immediately spot the keywords with the highest volume. Ideally, you want to find one with high volume and low competition. Export the file in ".csv" format and save it to your computer.

Now, look at the list, check the competition column, and pick the keyword with the lowest competition. Search for this keyword; let's assume it's "cruises 3 days."

Do the same: sort by volume, export the ".csv", and save it to your computer. Repeat this process in a loop for each interesting keyword you find. "Interesting" could mean a keyword made up of 2 to 4 words with a lot of volume, or one with high volume and low competition, or perhaps one that "surprised" you and you want to explore further.

You'll end up with a series of Excel files full of data, keywords, volumes, and competition (sorted by volume). For example, in the image below, I've extracted the data for the keyword "cruises 3 days."

Keyword	Volume	Search Diff.
cruise 3 days from miami	2900	21
cruise 3 days bahamas	2900	23
3 days cruises leaving from new	2900	31
3 day river cruises usa	1900	17
cruise 3 day mexico	1600	26
3 day cruises port canaveral	1600	14
cheap cruises 3 day	590	14
3 day cruise deals	480	21
3 to 5 day cruises	390	19
alaska cruise 3 days	390	6
3 day ohio river cruises	320	11

You can also expand the table by adding more data, extracted using a tool for studying keyword volumes and trends. For example, you can include information like CPC (cost per click), PD (paid difficulty), and trend data. Your table might look something like this:

Keyword	Vol	SD	CPC	PD	Trend
cruise 3 days from miami	2900	21	$1.25	53	⇧
cruise 3 days bahamas	2900	23	$2.30	48	⇧
3 days cruises leaving from new	2900	31	$1.21	44	⇩
3 day river cruises usa	1900	17	$1.42	42	⇧
cruise 3 day mexico	1600	26	$1.55	41	⇩
3 day cruises port canaveral	1600	14	$2.32	55	⇨
cheap cruises 3 day	590	14	$1.99	50	⇧
3 day cruise deals	480	21	$2.10	49	⇧
3 to 5 day cruises	390	19	$1.57	42	⇩
alaska cruise 3 days	390	6	$1.55	44	⇧
3 day ohio river cruises	320	11	$1.38	24	⇨

If the search difficulty (SD) is high, say above 35, it means that ranking a website or page for that keyword organically using SEO techniques will be difficult.

If the paid difficulty (PD) is high, it means that if you were to launch a paid campaign, you'd be competing with others targeting the same keywords and would need to bid higher for ad space.

If the CPC (cost per click) is high, it means that advertisers are paying a premium for each click, indicating significant commercial interest in that keyword.

You already know what a high volume means: many people are searching for that specific keyword. You also understand the implications of both positive and negative trends.

Now, you need to find a way to easily identify interesting data among all these columns and rows filled with numbers and figures.

To do this, I use conditional formatting in the data file. I set it up so that the cells in the table are colored green or red based on the parameters I set. For example, I want all cells with a "positive" trend to be colored green, while those that are not are colored red. I apply this rule to the entire trend column.

Next, I want the cell in the search difficulty column with a value below 35 to be colored in green. This way, I can quickly identify the keywords that are potentially more valuable—the easier keywords to work with. An AI tool can assist in this data organization phase and can quickly organize keywords and create pre-formatted Google Sheets files for you.

Clearly, if you're just starting out, you should stick to easier tasks and avoid overly competitive niches. I often also color cells with volumes greater than 1000 green to determine if there is sufficient user interest to justify the research.

Once you've identified some "easy" keywords with low competition, you start over. The data you've gathered should be more than enough to understand if a niche, or at least the more general keywords of a topic, can be fertile ground for your online business driven by organic traffic through SEO implementations.

If a niche has many "green" cells, then it's time to proceed with further research. To further investigate the potential, conduct an analysis using the same method.

It's not yet time to celebrate; it's possible that a more in-depth analysis may reveal that there's no opportunity for you. It's better to discover this now rather than later.

You don't have to do this additional research immediately. You can close the file and revisit it later when you're more relaxed. Taking some time off might clarify your thoughts. Certainly, after seeing so many numbers and words, a break is a good idea.

Search engines have many special ways of handling the *queries* they receive from users. *Are the keywords and queries all the same for them?* No, they aren't. Google takes the different "search intents" into great consideration when determining exactly what a user is searching for.

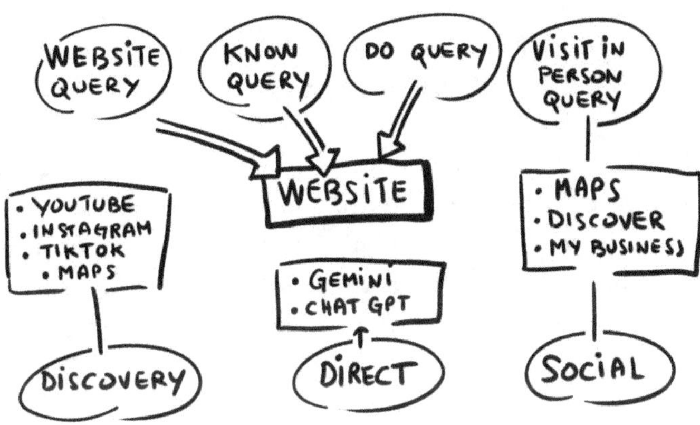

For example, this search engine divides keywords into 4 main categories.

- **"Visit in person"**: For example, "Grocery near me." These are keywords that likely indicate your intention to go somewhere, like "café, cinema." For this category, Google will likely show a map in the first position.

- **"Website Query"**: For example, "facebook login." These are keywords you type because you want to go to a website. For this category, Google will likely display a web resource in the first position.

- **"DO QUERY"**: For example, "book hotel." These are keywords you type because you want to do something or achieve a specific goal. For this category, Google will likely display a service or product in the first position.

- **"KNOW QUERY"**: For example, "Da Vinci paintings." These are keywords you type to learn something. For this category, if the question is simple ("know simple query"), Google will likely show a direct answer in the first position, citing the source. If the question is more complex, it will have a more detailed answer.

In all cases, the golden rule is that you must give the user what they are looking for. If you do this, the search engine will help the user reach your content.

What I've written will be useful not only from a cultural perspective and for understanding search dynamics, but also to help you filter out keywords you encounter in your research that are not suitable for your specific purpose.

But an SEO must keep an even more open mind and also consider searches that don't start from a search engine but instead begin on social media. Ideally, you should follow the user's search intent from the start of their journey. Perhaps your typical user begins on social media and then moves on to other platforms or tools before arriving at the search engine to conduct further research.

Clustering Keywords

Now you need to organize all this data. First of all, you should have filtered all the data you've gathered. This should give you a clear overview, allowing you to understand, on one hand, the potential volumes of the niche and, on the other, how difficult it might be to work in terms of competition.

Now, you'll need to work with the keyword lists you have and group the keywords. You'll need to find subtopics related to the main topic.

These groups will help you determine which categories or sections you'll need to create on the website once the production phase begins. The different groupings will also show you the total traffic volume you can aim for.

Take your usual data file on Google Drive and create a new tab. This allows you to work on a new tab while remaining within the same spreadsheet. You'll work without touching the previously collected and stored data in the first tab. A good idea is to make a backup of the source tab with the data.

Among all the keywords you've found and highlighted, identify all the easy (green) keywords that belong to the same niche and group them by topic.

Copy the keywords and their matching volumes from the "source" sheet. Create small groupings, and at the top of each group, place the keyword with the highest volume.

To make this work method clearer, let's revisit the research done earlier for the keyword "cruise":

Keyword	Volume	Search Diff.
cruises	550000	66
norwegian cruises	246000	57
cruises lines	135000	63
cruises deals	110000	83
cruises virgin	110000	56
cheap cruises	74000	67
cruises from new york	33100	56
cruise last minute	33100	53
cruise seattle to alaska	33100	57
cruise from florida	27100	63
cruises all inclusive	27100	58
cruise hawaii islands	27100	61
cruises 3 days	18100	32
cruises out of new orlea	18100	38
cruise xmas	6600	28

The keywords are organized with the highest volume words at the top. We take the one with the lowest SD (search difficulty).

So it would be "cruise xmas" which has an SD of 28. If you use conditional formatting, as I explained earlier, it would be the first cell to appear "green." Let's verify the keyword with a targeted and more in-depth search using the more general term (Christmas).

Keyword	SV	SD
cruise in Christmas	9900	45
Christmas cruise disney	1000	13
cruise to Christmas markets	880	52
Christmas cruise royal caribbean	720	19
cruise Christmas markets europe	590	10
Christmas cruise in europe	390	10
Christmas cruise norwegian	260	23
Christmas cruise Baltimore	140	19
Christmas cruise danube	140	6

On the right, the cells will almost all be green. *See how easy it is to find low-competition keywords now?* These are the famous long-tail keywords that I will discuss in the next chapter.

By doing this, you will create many small keyword groups. If a group is too large, you can probably divide it into two subgroups. This technique I use to divide and organize low-competition keywords is called "clustering" and is essential from various perspectives:

1. It allows you to organize your keywords semantically and give all the data a precise order.
2. It enables you to visualize and create an editorial plan, which will be necessary when you write or have content written.
3. It reveals what the categories of your website will be. In fact, the first keyword of each group, the one with the highest volume, will likely be used as a category.
4. It indicates which articles to write, their titles, and their corresponding categories.
5. It shows the hierarchy of categories and articles because keywords with lower volume than the first will be pages or articles under that category.
6. It indicates the structure of your website's internal links.

A useful tip at this phase, when you're determining the website structure, is to use the small trick I described before, where you use the spacebar to get Google to recommend related keywords, as well as the topics that Google Trends suggests as related, which I discussed in a previous chapter.

By the end of this process, not only will you have gained all the benefits essential for an SEO strategy, but you will also have found the traffic you were looking for. In fact, the people you need are those who search every day for the same keywords written and organized in your file. The traffic you need is right in front of you, even if it's not yet in the form of visitors.

For now, all you see are numbers, but these numbers, once your content is published, will become real people.

Long tail keywords

The more you practice keyword research, the more skilled you'll become at analyzing and organizing data on search volumes and competition. You'll soon realize that most user searches consist of multiple keywords, not just a single word.

Let me explain: users often enter specific questions or queries into search engines. *Remember the* "DO query" and "KNOW query"?

For example, look at this query: "best cheap drone with 4k camera."

> When a user types a word into the search engine's search field, they are "querying" its database for an answer. That is a "*query.*"

Some of the keywords you'll encounter in your research are much longer than 1 or 2 search terms. The example above even has 6. The reasoning is clear: the more detailed the question, the better (or should be) answer, since the search engine will be able to categorize it.

Many keywords entered into search engines are actual questions, for example:

"How to install a SIM card on a Google Pixel smartphone?"

Syntactically, these keywords consisting of multiple words are called "*long tail keywords*" and are very important for SEO.

> The term "*long tail*" refers to keywords that are in the "long tail" of the graph below, which means searches that consist of four, five, or even more words.

Long-tail keywords are graphically represented as the tail end of the curve that depicts the relationship between keyword length and search volume.

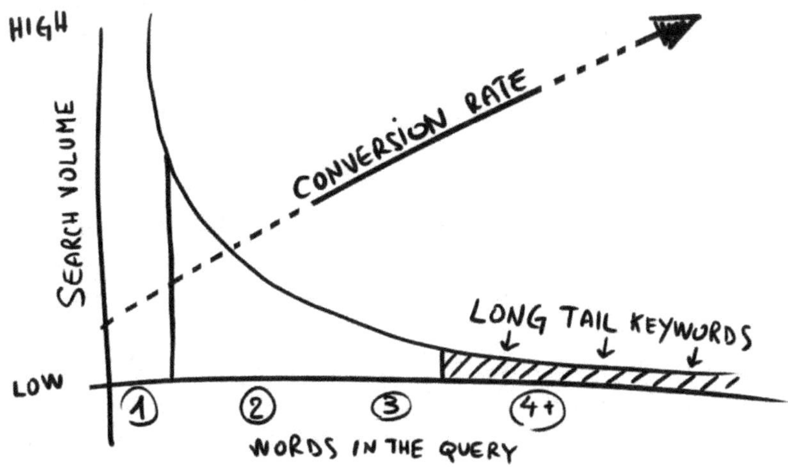

Long-tail keywords are important both from an SEO perspective and from a conversion rate (CR) perspective.

> *"Conversion Rate,"* or "CR," is one of those truly important indicators among all that you'll come across. For example, if you have 100 visitors on your site and 1 visitor purchases a product, you have a CR (conversion rate) of 1%.

The general rule is as follows: the more generic the keyword, the higher its search volume. The competition is usually greater in this case as well, meaning many websites will be ranked for that generic keyword. Additionally, if you need to drive paid traffic using that generic keyword, you will have to pay more for clicks, which means your PPC (*pay per click*) campaign costs will be higher.

The reason is that there are more people bidding on generic keywords. Essentially, advertisers bid money to have their ads appear in the SERPs for those generic keywords.

Conversely, the longer the keyword is composed of several words, the lower its competition will be. The reason is clear: there will be many fewer websites with pages optimized for such a long and specific keyword.

Additionally, the chances of converting the user will be higher, especially if the keyword is also a question with a commercial intent. This happens because a keyword in the form of a question is so specific that the search result is likely to be exactly what the user was looking for. Thus, the user's intent is fully satisfied.

At this point, with a perfect match between the query (keyword) and the offer (for example, a product on a website from the search result), it is more likely that the user will make a purchase or perform an action in the short term.

You will potentially find better CR (conversion rates) with this type of keyword. However, it is not limited to products for purchase. Even a user who enters their email address on a page with a contact form might be a high-value conversion for you.

Why? Because once you have a contact, you can market to them and persuade them to return and evaluate your products or services, as well as read your content.

	Short Tail Keys	**Long Tail Keys**
Volume	High	Low
Competition	High	Low
Intent	Low	High
Cost	High	Low
CR	Low	High

To help you understand what I'm talking about in more depth and to give you a sense of the volumes you can achieve with this system of keyword research and organization, let me share a brief reflection.

I live in a small town with about 7,000 inhabitants. I remember when I first truly realized the volume of traffic some of my websites were generating; It was over 15,000 people a day. There's always a strong emotion and great excitement when you pause to think that your site receives monthly visits equal to 65 times the number of people in your town.

Think about the busiest store in your town—*how many potential customers could it possibly attract each day?* Now think about how many users visit your site. When you take a moment to consider these numbers, you really understand the infinite possibilities that online businesses offer to people who are determined to succeed.

Keyword competition

As you have seen, each keyword corresponds to a specific Google SERP, which is a specific page listing the results that the search engine proposes to try to answer the user's query. However, SERPs are not always the same for every keyword or for every user.

They can change depending on the user's language or location. Your phone constantly locates you and shares your position with Google. Therefore, the search engine will show results closest to you for certain specific queries (such as visit-in-person queries).

For example, if you search for the keyword "pizzeria," the SERP will show the pizzerias nearest to your current location on a lovely interactive map. If you're in Rome and search for "pizzeria in Milan," the location won't be a determining factor.

As you've seen, keywords differ in terms of volume. Each keyword also varies in competition. Generally, it's much easier to rank first in SERPs with a long-tail keyword compared to a short, high-volume keyword.

It's not possible to find a profitable keyword with zero competition. It's very unlikely to find a high-volume keyword with zero competition. However, it is possible to find one with low competition.

Also, watch out for market saturation. If you notice that the search difficulty of every keyword you find is high or very high, it means that the market for that niche is saturated, and there might not be space for you to enter organically or it might not be worth the time/resources.

Now let's take a random keyword: "espresso coffee maker." If there are many web pages focusing on that keyword, Google will show them in its SERPs.

Remember that the number of positions on the first page of the SERP is finite; roughly ten positions are available, and 91% of traffic comes from the first page.

You, arriving after all these websites are already online, need to find a way to push at least one of those already on the first page out of their current position. *Do you agree?*

Otherwise, you will be unable to find a spot because the first ten positions on the page are already occupied. If you want to push websites already on the first page out of their positions, you will need to do even better SEO than they did! The better they did with SEO, the better you must be.

New, better websites will take the place of older, worse websites. New websites that are already worse than existing ones will quickly fail; old websites will stay where they are. You might even call it natural selection because it actually works more or less the same way. If your competitors have been online longer than you, they will have an advantage. If your competitors have a higher number of valuable links from other websites pointing to their pages compared to yours, they will have an advantage.

There are also many other factors affecting keyword competitiveness that you should consider. If you're working with dozens, or even hundreds, of keywords in a file, you may feel overwhelmed by the sheer number of keywords to consider. To identify the most important keywords or those that frequently appear within the keywords of the same topic, "cloud maps" are useful—graphic tools that help in organizing information.

Creating such a map is simple: just copy all the keywords from your file and insert them into a cloud map generator. Various free generators are available online, or you can use any AI.

The generator will produce a map highlighting the words that appear most frequently. This method can help you get a clear and quick overview. It can also help you see the entire collection of keywords from a different perspective you might not have considered.

Maybe you're underestimating a word that appears frequently, or perhaps you missed that term that users often use in their searches.

Keyword monitoring

When you have finished your keyword research, you will have hundreds of keywords to manage. For each of them, you will need to create a dedicated page on your website optimized for that specific keyword. You will also need to monitor all the keywords in the SERPs, or at least the most important ones, to keep track of their position changes.

You need to check the search result position for each keyword and verify whether the corresponding page on your website has moved up or down in the SERP.

There are several tools available to assist with this, some of which are free. For example, I use Semrush, but there are others as well. Within these online tools, you can add your domain and the various keywords you want to monitor. The tool displays their current and greatest positions, as well as a graphical representation of whether the keyword has moved up or down. Let's consider this example:

I have a website on "dog nutrition," and I wrote an article titled "Best Dog Food" based on the keyword. I enter my website's URL and the keyword "Best Dog Food" into the tool. The tool will query the search engine with that query, check which pages of the website appear in that SERP and their exact position, and then track future changes.

You can also use these tools to monitor websites that are not yours in the same way. This is a simple solution to keep an eye on the competitor pages you want to overtake. Additionally, the tool also provides the full SERP for each keyword you've entered, so you can immediately see who is performing better than you and take appropriate action.

When changes occur in search engine indexing or ranking algorithms, don't panic. Don't rush to read the manual and change a thousand things on your pages. Instead, evaluate whether your traffic experiences any negative impacts in the following hours or days, and only then take action.

Competitors Analysis

Another essential concept to understand before beginning any online or offline project is competition. This is the concept: if there are already 4 coffee shops near your home, opening another one doesn't seem like a good idea, at least in most cases.

But before you can beat your enemies, you need to know them, *right?* So, to find your competitors, if you don't already know them, is a very simple process. It involves gathering and studying data, just like you did for the keywords.

In fact, a simple Google search will reveal the websites that already dominate the SERPs for your keywords of interest. Even if you find a niche with simple keywords and low competition, you still need to study the low competition thoroughly.

This is because other websites will have joined the market or niche before you. As a result, you should become acquainted with all of them because they can be a valuable source of knowledge. Essentially, you should keep track of every competitor you encounter. Create a new sheet in your "Market Research" file on Google Sheets and name it after the niche you are analyzing.

Alternatively, if you've built a specific file to explore a niche in greater depth, simply create a new sheet called "Competitors". Organize the competitors' sheet for each niche as I do:

URL	Trend	Visitors	Top Keywords	How is monetised	Note
Competitor 1					
Competitor 2					

Then proceed as follows: look for an online tool that offers a free function to analyze competitors. I currently use Similarweb, but, as you know, any tool might no longer be available by the time you read these lines.

Enter one of your competitor's website addresses into the search bar provided by the service. Keep in mind that you will need to do the same with all the other competitor URLs.

The service will provide you with a range of useful information, some of which you should already know from your previous market and keyword research.

It will also show information about "similar websites" to the one you entered. Essentially, this way, you'll quickly discover websites similar to your competitor's and, therefore, likely find more competitors.

During these times, new competitors emerge that you were previously unaware of. Perhaps initially, you thought you only had to compete with two websites similar to yours, but then you find out there are ten. But don't worry, it's better to discover these things now than after investing thousands of euros and hundreds of hours in building a website.

Now gather the data you find and do this with each competitor you discover from the search.

In the "trend" column of the table, write "up" or "down" depending on whether the competitor's website traffic trend is increasing or decreasing.

In the "Visitors" column, write the number of monthly visits the website receives. You can average the last 3–6 months.

In the "Top Keywords" column, write the 2 or 3 keywords that bring the highest percentage of traffic.

In the "how is monetised" column, write the methods the competitor uses to monetize their niche. You usually see this immediately when you open the website, but sometimes you need to check more closely. This specific information will be useful when you need to monetize your website in the same niche because you might implement or at least test the same monetization methods as your competitors, saving a lot of effort.

Finally, in the "notes" column, write down any notes and observations you want to remember. Record things you find intriguing, good ideas you come across, and tools or automations you see on a competitor's website that capture your attention because they appear to be useful ideas.

Perhaps there is an original menu item that you could adapt, or the content has a distinct multimedia format that you could use for inspiration and improvement. Note everything that catches your eye and interests you. I often jot down the website's weaknesses, or at least the ones I can identify. By doing this, I can later improve my websites in areas where others haven't.

Analyze which keywords generate the majority of each competitor's traffic, as well as where their traffic is coming from. These are all data points that can be useful to you. Then, check which other similar websites the tool suggests and note these new potential competitors, for which you will need to conduct further keyword analysis.

As you can see, it's about conducting systematic and as detailed research as possible. One website leads to another, which in turn leads to others, and so on. You are essentially exploring a niche.

The data you gather will continuously increase, and you need to keep it well organized. Market research, in all its aspects, takes up most of the time during the initial phase of creating your SEO strategy or any online business. And it should be that way. The more precise and thorough the research, the better the foundation for the SEO techniques you will later implement.

By dedicating time to identifying keywords, competitors, and niches with a good trend, you are building the best foundation for your action plan. And remember, without a plan, you won't get far.

The SERP

Especially if you're primarily focusing on organic traffic, which is specifically what this book covers, you will always be dealing with the search engines' "SERP."

Understanding how the SERP works is also important if you rely on bought traffic, even if you buy traffic through Google and its search network.

I've already explained what a SERP is earlier, but I'll summarize briefly. When you enter a search (*query*) on Google, the search engine returns a page with results. In fact, it returns a list of pages, and at the bottom of the page, there's page numbering; This list is the SERP.

The SERP can take on a different appearance or layout depending on the device being used. Additionally, SERPs can contain various visual elements, such as carousels, video previews, products, maps, rich snippets, images, and many other things. Each SERP obviously hosts both organic results and "sponsored" results, which are essentially ads.

The first rule of the SERP is that the first page is the most important one. The second rule of the SERP is that the top positions on the first page are often the most important.

The first page is always where you want to position your website because it contains the results that appear first after the search. In practice, it's the most clicked area. Essentially, the first page has a higher CTR (click-through rate) than all the subsequent pages.

To make it clearer, let's give an example. If your search generates ten pages of results, practically everyone will click on the first page. So the first page has a higher CTR than the others. Specifically, Google's first page accounts for over 90% of the total clicks for any query.

CTR (*Click Through Rate*) is the ratio between the number of clicks and page views. If a page is viewed 10 times and receives 1 click, it has a CTR of 10%.

Now let's consider the individual positions within the first page of Google's SERP. On desktop, meaning on stationary or laptop PCs, the CTR of the first result represents 33.7% of the total for the page (on mobile, the figure is almost the same).

This means that out of 1,000 users who perform a search, 900 will find the results they're looking for on the first page, and the first result will, on average, receive about 300 clicks.

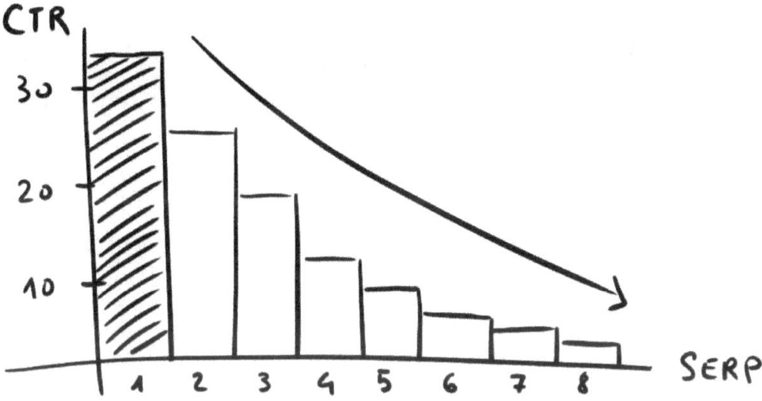

When I say that users will find the results they're looking for, it's not entirely accurate. In the sense that after reading the snippet, the user expects to discover the answer to their question on that page. However, they can't be sure of this until they actually read the destination page. Now, search engines take CTR statistics in the SERP very seriously.

Let's take an example. Suppose you own an ice cream shop in Pimlico, a neighborhood in London, and when searching "ice cream Pimlico" on Google, your website appears on the 3rd page, specifically in the 2nd position of the 3rd page.

If you've done a good job of copywriting in the description and title of the snippet that appears on Google (and this is done through "on-page SEO" optimization), you'll receive a higher number of clicks than the result that precedes you in the first position, still on the same 3rd page of the SERP.

Google, being intelligent, detects this and determines that, since your link is being clicked more than the previous one, it's probably more interesting for users searching for that term, so it moves you up in the rankings.

Now, let's say you move up 1 or 2 positions. The process of analysis and comparison repeats itself continuously, comparing you to the new results around you after your advancement in position.

This concept is valid throughout the entire SERP and is one factor to consider when trying to climb the search rankings.

Once you reach the top of the second page, depending solely on this strategy may make it difficult to reach the first page. You'll need to use a broader strategy, more or less diversified depending on the competition for the keyword.

Remember, there isn't just one SERP for a keyword. There's a SERP for every keyword, every user, every location, every device, and so on.

The snippet

As mentioned earlier, to improve the snippet that appears in Google's SERP, you need to work on on-page SEO optimization.

This will require directly optimizing the web page to ensure that the search engine collects and displays the data, rich snippets, and information that we want to communicate effectively. Specifically, speaking technically for a moment, you need to set "meta tags," such as a `<title>` and a `<description>`, within the HTML of the page, following certain rules.

To work on the "meta" tags you need, you can modify the page's code, or you can use plugins that simplify the task and save you from having to edit the HTML code of the pages. We'll cover this in more detail later.

However, simply knowing how to edit the snippets' titles and descriptions is insufficient; you need to do much more. You must stand out and entice users to click on your snippet rather than your competitors.

The right recipe to succeed is to use excellent *copywriting* along with on-page optimization of the meta tags.

"Copywriting" is the art of writing optimized texts that are both valuable for people searching for information, attractive to search engine algorithms, and, at the same time, through persuasive action, useful for converting people in your target audience. This means that first, you need to know who your target audience is; otherwise, you won't know whom to persuade or what to write.

The anatomy of a perfect snippet should consist of these elements:

The title, which must be of a length that prevents it from being "cut off" when the search engine displays it in the SERP. The title must always contain the main keyword. If you're writing an article focused on a long-tail keyword consisting of 5 words, you should include all 5 words in the title. Essentially, you will write the keyword exactly as it is. If you have space left, you can add other elements, such as a secondary keyword, incorporated into a phrase that piques the user's curiosity or grabs their attention.

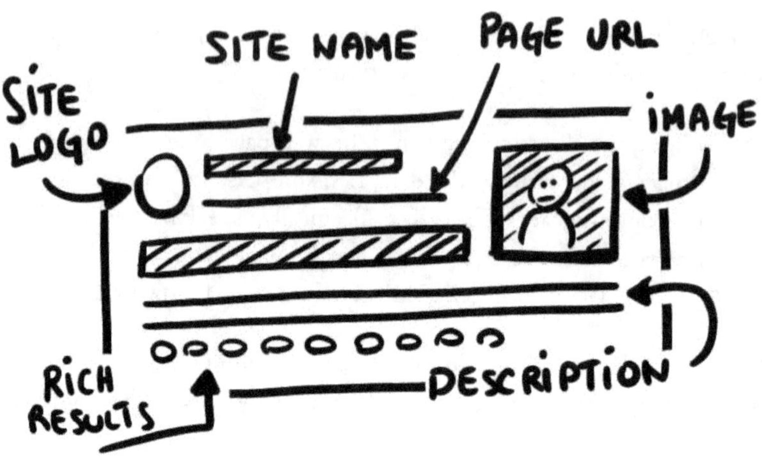

The URL, which is simply the address of the page, should be as short as possible but must always contain the keyword. So, the URL will partially or fully match the keyword.

Example: If the keyword is "Christmas decorations," the URL will be /Christmas-decorations/ or even /guide-to-christmas-decorations/.

The description, like the title, should be long enough so that it doesn't get cut off in the snippet. It must contain the main keyword. Additionally, it should include a copy that piques the user's curiosity and makes them understand that, by clicking on that page, they will find what they're looking for.

It's crucial that the user has the impression, or at least a vague certainty, that they will find what they're searching for there, and then you must provide it. The description should also contain a CTA (Call to Action), which invites the user to click without being overly *clickbait*.

By "*click baiting*," we mean something that tries to convince the user to click with too much insistence, aggression, or deception.

The snippet should also ideally be simple and intuitive. When you exit the King's Cross St. Pancras tube station in London, you have to orient yourself among many possible directions. Yet, you're able to do so in 1 second, even just stepping off the train, thanks to clear and intuitive signage that contains exactly what you need to know.

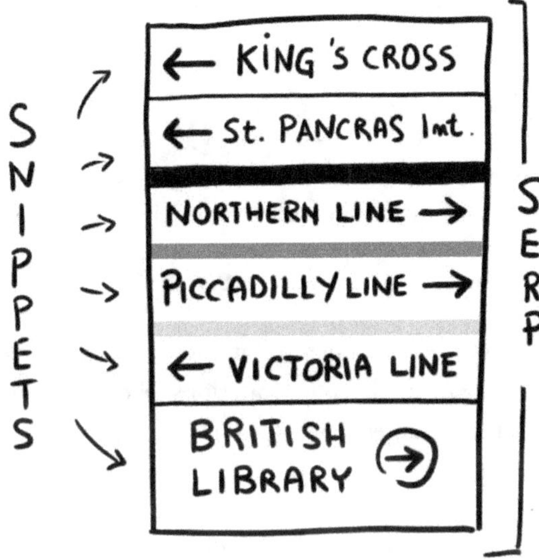

When you're filling in the data that will form the snippets for your pages, it's really helpful to see a preview before publishing the page. Some WordPress plugins, like Yoast SEO, provide a preview of the snippet before publication. It's a great help, although not always 100% accurate.

What you see below is the "snippet" that appears in the SERP when I search for the word "snippet" on Google.

If you don't know how to work with the HTML of your pages, that's definitely a plugin you'll want to install. I use it on almost every one of my websites because it makes it easier to optimize pages for keywords, which you should always do.

A few small notes:

The first is that WordPress, which I mentioned for the first time just now, is the CMS I use to create all of my websites, and it's the one I recommend you use as well.

> "CMS" stands for "Content Management System" and is an application created to manage web content, in our case pages, categories, and articles. Joomla, Drupal, in addition to WordPress, which is the most popular, are also CMSs.

Unless you need to create a complex eCommerce website or a website with specific features, funnels, or dynamic functions, WordPress is the simplest, most complete, and most accessible solution, ideal for working with organic traffic. The use of this CMS is implied throughout the book from now on.

The second note is that, like any plugin you install, Yoast SEO also has a weight and can affect your website's performance. Make sure it doesn't slow down the website too much, especially if it's hosted on a shared and low-performance hosting service.

The third note is that Yoast SEO, in some cases, should be taken with a grain of salt. Some of its features are useful, like the snippet preview. Others may not provide accurate feedback. There are aspects that visually indicate whether an article is "OK," but they frequently distract you from what should be your post's primary goal: to provide the reader with what they want.

In some cases, keywords, if written in small variations, may not be recognized correctly, and the plugin may "think" that they are not present. For example, a singular or plural form, in terms of keywords and from Google's perspective, is the same thing, but it might be detected differently if it's in plural form. I recommend not placing too much value on its keyword density and always performing a manual check.

What I write here about certain functions or features of plugins or CMSs might not be applicable in the future due to continuous software updates, so keep that in mind. We are interested in the standard concepts.

Returning to the snippet discussion, your mission will be to create highly optimized snippets for each page of your website. Each article will have its own snippet, and each snippet should have the 3 fundamental parts that I've listed, optimized as described. The ultimate goal is to create snippets that first capture the attention of traffic and then persuade users to click. If your snippet achieves better KPIs than those preceding it, it will have a better chance of gaining some positions in the SERP.

There's an interesting thing to know: all the work you do might be ignored by Google when it generates the snippet. Indeed, meta tags and meta descriptions can be altered and generated independently if the search engine deems them useful for the search intent.

> The term KPI (Key Performance Indicator) refers to those "key indicators" we consider to determine the success or failure of a performance. CTR, for example, is a KPI, but there can be many others.

We will go into more detail about meta tags in a later chapter because they are fundamental elements in on-page SEO optimization. Writing meta tags means "talking" to search engines and providing them with the information and instructions we want. It's as if Google were a teacher, and the page on your website is a student being tested. If the teacher comes to class and questions your website, the meta tags provide the answers. If there are no meta tags, the student is silent and will likely fail the exam.

GENERATE ORGANIC TRAFFIC

This is the third part of the book, a necessary phase to study in order to understand how to generate a consistent flow of visitors to your website through search engine optimization techniques.

The first phase was very conceptual; the second phase involved research and analysis, while the third will be more practical and technical. Once you've determined what web traffic is and how to locate it, the next step is to begin intercepting it. And that's exactly what we'll do in this third phase. I warn you that it is also the most boring part.

If everything has gone well so far, you should now be in a position where you've found a niche with a high volume and low competition, and you're ready to build your online asset.

You've already decided which neighborhood to set up shop in (which niche or topic), based on the city metaphor I provided you. It's a neighborhood with lots of foot traffic but few shops, and you're one of the first to open your business in this market.

Alternatively, you may not be one of the very first, but unlike others, you have something unique that sets you apart. Pedestrians are walking on the sidewalks (potential organic traffic), and there aren't many nearby competitors to cause you any trouble.

Another possibility is that it is a densely trafficked, well-served neighborhood with numerous other shops (competitors). There are cars with passengers (referral traffic) who, once they reach their destination, get out and enter the already established stores.

But there are also pedestrians (organic traffic) who are looking for something new, something better, and they're glancing around. You know where to find them and what they want, and you will soon be able to provide them with what they need.

The problem now is: *How do I get these pedestrians to enter my shop?*

To answer this question, you must first choose a specific source of traffic and focus on its unique requirements.

In this book, the source of traffic we'll be using to bring visitors to your website is organic traffic, coming from search engines.

Before we begin, it is best to make a few preliminary remarks and present some basic internet concepts for the benefit of knowledge, preparation, and a thorough understanding of what we will be covering. These need to be understood to fully grasp all the work behind SEO.

Section 1: Introduction to the Internet

From origins to the modern age of WWW

The internet originated as a military project called ARPANET, with the network's construction and the first connection taking place in 1969 in Los Angeles, USA.

The World Wide Web (WWW), however, was born in the 1990s thanks to researcher Tim Berners-Lee, who was working on a project aimed at allowing researchers to exchange information with each other.

Researchers faced an insurmountable obstacle: they couldn't share document links with one another because "links" didn't exist. Tim solved this problem by creating a common network that allowed researchers to create interconnected documents, thus introducing the concept of links.

He needed a protocol to transfer information in a standardized way. To achieve this, together with researcher Robert Cailliau he invented the HTTP protocol, thus beginning the development of the World Wide Web.

The web will be your working environment, so learn well how it works.

The HTTP Protocol

It's fascinating to understand how the HTTP protocol works. Let's say you open a browser (any browser) and enter a web address, a URL (Uniform Resource Locator), for a webpage.

When you click "enter" on the keyboard, the browser makes an HTTP REQUEST to the server that hosts the data. In response, the server sends back an HTTP RESPONSE containing the HTML code (which describes the content of the webpage) and other information (such as the "status code" and the "content type").

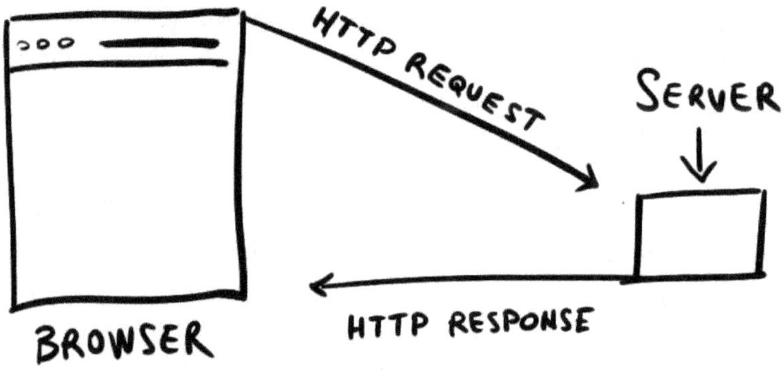

This, in simple terms, is the HTTP protocol that allowed the creation of the WWW. It is *not too difficult to grasp, right?*

But that was HTTP. At the time I'm writing this book, HTTP has been almost entirely replaced by HTTPS. The HTTPS protocol is an evolution of HTTP and has various additional security layers compared to the previous protocol, especially in terms of encryption and data integrity. You can look into these topics further if you wish.

The original HTTP 1.1 has evolved in terms of speed into HTTP/2, which allows for significantly fewer requests when we call the server from our browser. Fewer requests mean the response time is much faster.

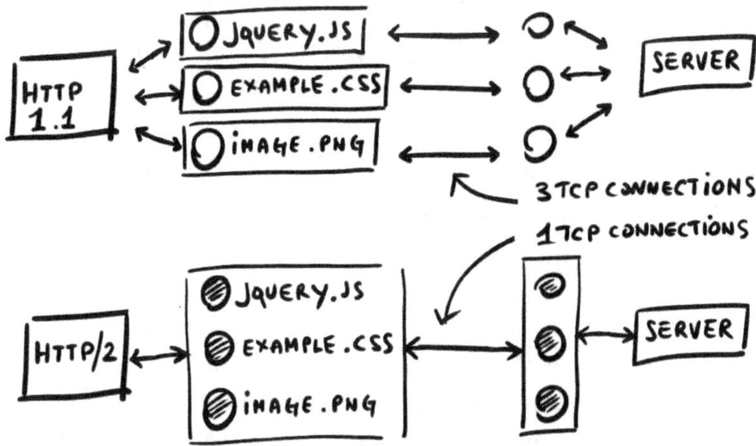

Imagine a traveler who has to carry his luggage. Instead of carrying multiple suitcases (HTTP requests), the traveler uses a single well-organized and compressed carry-on (a single connection), optimizing space and reducing weight (data traffic), thus saving effort and time. *Ok?*

Keep in mind that as of today, there is also HTTP/3, a further evolution in security and speed over HTTP/2. This new protocol will gradually be supported by various browsers and servers, further improving all aspects.

Security and speed are essential factors for today's web resources, particularly those that have to be SEO optimized. These two factors hold true today and will remain important in the future.

Status codes

"Status codes" are part of the information a server sends to the browser after an HTTP request. They are important from an SEO perspective because they help identify whether everything is working properly or if there are issues.

When managing a project from an SEO standpoint, it's crucial to understand the differences between various status codes. Without this knowledge, it's impossible to diagnose issues related to accessing resources on your site. The list of these codes is extensive, and I can't include it all here, but a quick online search will give you everything you need.

However, the most common and relevant ones for SEO, which you'll encounter most frequently while creating and managing a website, are the following:

- `HTTP Status Code 200 - OK`
  It's perfect; everything runs smoothly, and visitors and bots can easily navigate through the pages and follow the links within them.

- `HTTP Status Code 301 - Permanent Redirect`
  It indicates that all visitors on the page are redirected to another page because the previous page has been permanently moved.

- `HTTP Status Code 302 - Temporary Redirect`
  Similar to a 301, but the page has only been temporarily moved.

- `HTTP Status Code 404 Not found`
  The requested page was not found by the server. It could be that the page doesn't exist, or perhaps the link you used is incorrect.

- `HTTP Status Code 500 - Internal Server Error`
  Indicates a problem with the server and an issue accessing your resources.

- `HTTP Status Code 503 - Service Unavailable`
  The server is currently unavailable.

There are indeed many 3XX and 4XX status codes, and it's essential to be familiar with them if you want to work at a higher level.

You don't need to memorize them all, as you can always consult the list and look up the details for each code. However, it's important to be aware of the existence of these codes, understand why they occur, and know what they are telling you.

Section 2: HTML for SEO

So, what exactly is HTML, and what is it used for? HTML is a language used to describe the contents of a webpage. It helps the browser understand which content to display, how to format it, and where to place links.

It's a descriptive markup language (there are other types of markup languages) and it is essential to understand when thinking about optimizing content for any search engine because it's the most widespread standard language on the web. By establishing standard rules, HTML allows search engines to easily understand the page's code and compare it with other pages. In essence, it simplifies the task of comparing websites using any search engine.

Now imagine that HTML has two close friends, CSS and JavaScript, who always accompany it. These two inseparable companions "enhance" HTML, enabling the multimedia and dynamic features of modern websites.

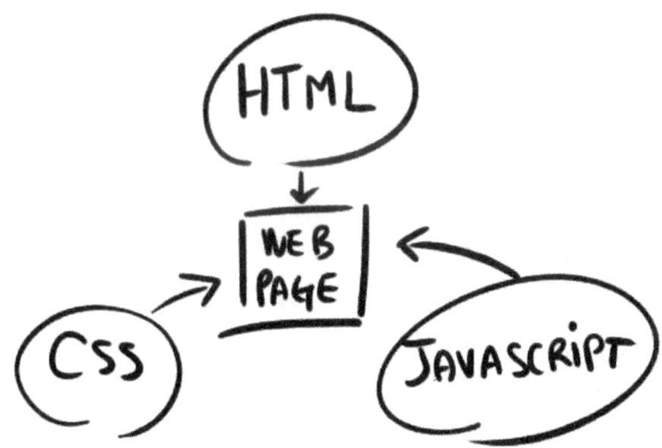

HTML provides the structure for the content of a webpage, CSS defines its visual appearance, and JavaScript adds dynamic behaviors. These three languages, working together in synergy, allow for the creation of rich and engaging user experiences.

HTML structure

HTML, and thus all pages built with it, are made up of TAGS. Here's a small example just to give you an idea if you've never seen one before.

```
<!doctype html>
<html lang="en">
      <head>
            <title>This is the page title</title>
      </head>
      <body>
            <h1>This is the primary topic of the
page</h1>
            <p>This is just a paragraph</p>
      </body>
</html>
```

Everything you see are TAGS. The `<html>` tag, the `<head>`, `<title>`, `<body>`, `<h1>`, `<p>`, and so on. Each tag has an opening part and a closing part. For example, `<head>` is the opening tag, and `</head>` is the closing tag of that tag.

Tags define and describe different areas of an HTML page, mainly the `<head>` and `<body>` sections; the `<head>` section contains metadata and links to external resources, and the `<body>` section contains the visible content of the page. We'll also see that many more tags have been defined with HTML5. The tags you insert into the page, the code you use, where you use it, and how you use it are all fundamental for creating an online asset that can be well perceived by search engines. We are about to enter into what is purely technical on-page SEO.

For example, the `<head>` section is crucial for Google and any other search engine. It must be crafted carefully because if it's not written properly, the crawler may encounter indexing errors.

Moreover, and it's significant to know, both HTML and HTTP are standards set by the W3C (World Wide Web Consortium). And fortunately so; *can you imagine the web without this standard? How would search engines evaluate the quality of pages if they were written in different languages? And how would browsers interpret codes across different protocols?*

The good news is that W3C also includes hundreds of members, including Google, Adobe, Microsoft, Intel, and many other major tech players on the web. Their involvement makes W3C an authoritative organization.

In this book, I will focus on the fundamental aspects of creating SEO-optimized web pages without delving too deeply into the technical details of the code. To further explore and apply your knowledge, I recommend consulting specific resources or using platforms like WordPress, which we will discuss later.

Keep in mind: the internet has always evolved and will continue to evolve towards the creation of more standardized code, ensuring better interpretation and accessibility of content by web browsers.

HTML5

The fifth version of HTML, currently recommended by the W3C, is HTML5. This recent version of the language adapts to the modern web. HTML5 represents a significant advancement in creating engaging web experiences. With its new features, such as native support for video, audio, vector graphics, and APIs for offline application development, HTML5 has paved the way for a richer, more interactive web, making it a more dynamic and versatile environment.

This new version has enabled the creation of engaging web experiences. Native support for multimedia elements like video and audio, combined with the ability to create games and animations directly in the browser, has transformed websites into genuine entertainment platforms. Additionally, thanks to APIs for geolocation and access to device sensors, it is possible to create highly customized and interactive web applications that adapt to the user's context and provide tailored information and services.

The code is increasingly precise, even by identifying areas of the website through some "semantic tags" (`header`, `footer`, `article`, `nav`, `section`, etc.), which facilitates search engines' work.

The introduction of semantic tags has marked a turning point in creating web content that is accessible and optimized for SEO. The areas of a page are no longer limited to the `<head>` and `<body>` tags but can include many other tags that describe different sections. For example, here are some of the main ones:

- `<article>`
- `<aside>`
- `<footer>`
- `<header>`
- `<main>`
- `<nav>`
- `<section>`

You will need to explore these tags in more detail on your own, as there are many more, and this is not a specific guide for HTML.

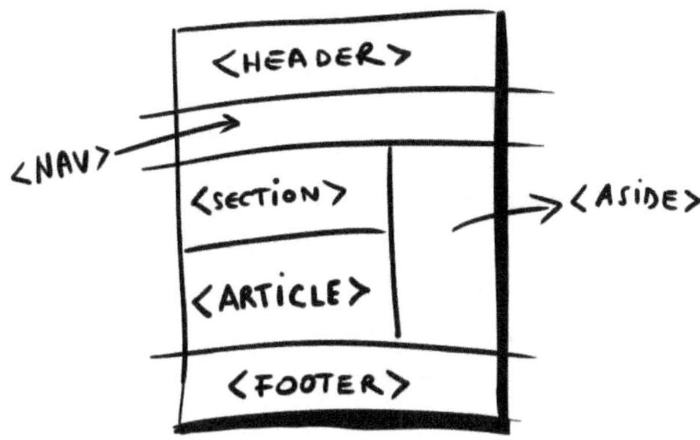

These tags, which provide semantic information about the structure and content of a page, allow search engines to more accurately interpret the meaning of different sections of a web page, thereby improving its visibility in search results. Additionally, semantic tags help users with visual impairments by making content more accessible through assistive technologies like screen readers.

From an SEO perspective, the better we can help crawlers understand how our pages are made, the better. Therefore, using the tags available in HTML5 is clearly an opportunity to be exploited. Of course, if a page has clear HTML but very poor content, the effort is pointless.

In short, HTML5 is a modern language for the modern web, and you will need to deal with it when optimizing the code of your web pages or those of your clients. Use it to its full potential and take advantage of every opportunity it presents, keeping in mind what we've discussed.

A quick tip: there is a fast and simple tool, completely free, that helps you check if the HTML of any page contains errors or if it is not entirely correct. It's validator.w3.org/, and you can use it during your experiments to check if you're doing things right.

Extensions and index.html

Here are the final notes to jot down to understand this first section on the relationship between HTML and SEO.

HTML pages can have various types of extensions, including .html, .htm, .shtml, and .shtm, but the most important page is always the `index.html`.

This page should always be placed in the root of the domain or, if the website has several subfolders, also in the root of each individual folder.

```
/index.html
```

When a user types a domain into the browser, the web server automatically looks for the `index.html` file within the site's main folder. This default configuration allows access to the homepage simply by entering the domain. Therefore, it is good practice to link the homepage directly to the main domain, avoiding the need to specify the complete file path. This approach not only simplifies the link structure but is also important for SEO, as it allows search engines to easily identify the main page of the site.

Consistency in link structure is a key factor for SEO. Linking the homepage to the main domain and using a consistent link structure for all other pages of the website helps search engines better understand the hierarchy of the pages and index the website more effectively.

Additionally, a clear and intuitive link structure enhances the user experience by making navigation within the website easier.

OpenGraph

Open Graph is a protocol developed by Facebook to enhance content sharing across social networks.

By adding specific meta tags in the `<head>` section of an HTML page, you can provide additional information about titles, descriptions, images, and other elements. These meta tags are used by social networks to generate customized and engaging previews.

The term "social graph," from which this protocol derives its name, represents the network of relationships and connections between people and content within a social platform like Facebook. Open Graph extends this concept to the entire web, creating a richer and more integrated sharing experience.

When you paste a link to your website into Facebook's feed, the social network automatically looks for Open Graph meta tags in the `<head>` section of the page. These meta tags contain structured information describing the content of the page, such as the title, description, and main image. Thanks to Open Graph, Facebook can generate a personalized and engaging preview of your content, increasing the likelihood that users will click the link and visit your website.

If social networks are part of your strategy, it's crucial to have control over this content, so for each piece of content, page, or video, you'll need to specify the information to be transmitted to social media through Open Graph.

It might seem complex, but there are tools to preview Open Graph data, and all meta tags can be managed easily without writing code manually if you use WordPress with plugins like Yoast.

Remember that whenever you change the information or update the Open Graph tags, you must notify Facebook to refresh the information. This is done using Facebook's own debug tool, but keep in mind that each social network has its own debug tool—there's not just Facebook, but also Twitter, LinkedIn, etc.

Schema.org

Another crucial piece of the SEO puzzle to understand is Schema.org. It's a kind of shared vocabulary, created by major market players like Google, Microsoft, and Yahoo and developed by an open community.

Schema.org is a standard supported by major search engines that allows you to provide additional semantic information about web pages beyond what meta tags offer. By using this markup, you can specify the type of content (e.g., article, product, event) and its properties (e.g., author, publication date, price).

Why should you use this? The goal is to enhance search engines' understanding of your content, increasing the likelihood of obtaining enriched search results. Schema.org includes hundreds of tags you can use to embed information. To implement these on your website, you'll need to study them in detail on the official Schema.org website.

What do you gain by adding these tags to your pages? You provide crawlers with more specific information, giving search engines a broader context to evaluate your page. Additionally, Schema.org markup enables the creation of "rich snippets," which make search results in SERPs more attractive. For example, when you see search results with star ratings, that's a rich snippet in action.

From a generic SEO perspective, the most interesting Schema.org markups are:

- <logo>: This helps search engines to display your brand image or official website logo in search results.
- <breadcrumb>: Generates a navigation path that helps search engines understand and define the website structure and page hierarchy.
- <FAQPage>: Allows search engines to display your "Frequently Asked Questions" directly in the search results, making them easily accessible and improving the user experience.

Schema tags are inserted using a special JavaScript called JSON-LD within the `<head>` of the page. There are other methods, but Google recommends this one. You can also add them through plugins without touching the code if you use WordPress. You need to determine whether you need consistent structured data across all pages or articles or if different content requires customized data.

If you need customized data, use a plugin that allows you to insert custom HTML code into the `<head>` section of individual articles or pages. Then, you can use AI to quickly generate the JSON-LD code and, before publishing, review it by consulting the documentation on the official Schema.org website. Do not rely solely on the generated code; once published, use the validation tool available on the official website to ensure the data is interpreted correctly.

I use the method described above or, alternatively, insert the Schema at the beginning of the HTML of the page by going to the HTML view in WordPress and pasting the code.

If, for any reason, you choose not to use Schema, at least make the information on your page easily interpretable for a crawler. For example, a small trick to simulate the presence of structured data on pages without using any tags or JavaScript is to include tables or bullet points.

Inserting information in this manner allows Google to interpret and view the data in the same way as structured data does, and it is taken into consideration.

In terms of SEO, Schema.org is much more important than OpenGraph and it should be taken seriously, so take your time to consult the resources on the official website to find the ideal code for the resource you are publishing online.

Section 3: Google and SEO

Rules to become the search engine favorite

Now, let's get a deeper understanding of something that will be critical to your SEO job. In fact, I need to explain to you what Google's index is and how the search engine works.

When we talk about a search engine, we have always referred to Google, which is the most efficient and widely used today. But seeing Google as merely a search engine is a huge mistake.

In reality, it is a massive ecosystem with billions of monthly users; an ecosystem today made up of various services such as YouTube, Maps, Gmail, Chrome, Android, Play Store, Discover, the Vocal Assistant, Gemini A.I., and the search engine itself. I am probably forgetting something. So, Google's search engine is simply one component of a vast ecosystem. *Does it make sense?*

In fact, take a moment to look at the search bar on Google's page. What you see is not just a search bar but a gateway to its ecosystem.

And when you think specifically about Google's search service, imagine it as an enormous library full of rooms. This vast library contains the index, which is a collection of all web pages.

Before adding a page to its library or index, the engine thoroughly analyzes it. It checks the content, the links, and a series of parameters to determine the "value" of the specific page in order to compare it with other similar pages with similar content.

Additionally, before a page is added to the search engine's index, it undergoes a security check. It is scanned to ensure that it is not malicious or does not contain malware or any other dangers for users.

Once the page is analyzed, the engine adds it to its index and places it on a shelf in a room of its library. However, each shelf also has drawers, and the drawers contain words. Each drawer corresponds to a specific word.

When a user types a keyword and your web page is related to their search, the engine "suggests" it to the user, along with other "suggestions," putting everything in a page with a hierarchy that tries to be as compatible as possible with the user's request.

Subsequently, the engine continues to periodically analyze the page, looking for changes, updates, new links, etc., to keep the library up to date.

But that's not all. Your page, whether it's an article, a product, or something else, is now information within Google's ecosystem and could be suggested on other Google services or platforms, even in different formats.

The *ranking* of your page, i.e., the position of the page in the SERPs for specific keywords, will now be influenced by various parameters (both on-page and off-page) that will be continuously updated.

> When I talk about "ranking," I'm referring to the classification of results in the search engine results pages (SERPs).

But what do you care about in this story? You need to get organic traffic, right? So all of this information is important because, if you want to receive organic traffic, you have to make the search engine like your site.

If the search engine doesn't like your content or other parameters we will cover from now on, you can forget about having a good ranking and, therefore, good organic positioning. In other words, you can say goodbye to the ninth wonder of the world—organic traffic. (The eighth wonder is *compound interest*).

Let's dive deeper into how a search engine works. We can break down its operation into two phases: the **crawling phase** and the **indexing phase**.

Crawling

Crawling is the first phase, during which the search engine identifies new URLs and determines their location. This is because, before a search engine can analyze data from the internet, it has to locate the websites and pages that contain it. *But how does it locate pages on the web?*

All search engines use web crawlers, which are programs (software). We've already touched on their functionality in previous chapters, but let's explore the concept further. Crawlers roam the web, looking for URLs they don't know about in order to add them to their index, or library, which, as previously mentioned, contains all URLs on the web.

Crawlers use the links on web pages as a gateway to other sites. They find a link and follow it until they reach the page that link leads to.

If they find a page they already know, they'll flag it for potential updates. If the page isn't present, they'll add it to the index.

But Google doesn't have the only crawler, of course; every search engine has its own crawlers. The software Google primarily uses is called "GoogleBot," but in reality, there are many different bots running everywhere on the web.

Each Google crawler has a specific role in indexing and analyzing web pages. Understanding the function of each crawler can help you better optimize your website for search engines through SEO and improve its visibility in Google's search results.

The list of bots can change over time, but if you read Google's guidelines, you can find the most common crawlers, which, as of today, include these:

- **Googlebot Smartphone:** This crawler focuses on indexing web pages viewed on mobile devices. It analyzes how pages are rendered on mobile devices and evaluates the user experience.

- **Googlebot Desktop:** This is the most common crawler and is responsible for indexing most web pages. It analyzes the text content, images, and other elements on the pages to build Google's search index.

- **Googlebot Image:** As the name suggests, this crawler specializes in indexing images. It analyzes images, their ALT attributes, and captions to understand their content and classify them correctly.

- **Googlebot News:** This crawler focuses on news and frequently updated content. It indexes news articles from news websites and blogs, making them available in Google's "News" section.

- **Googlebot Video:** Similar to Googlebot Image, this crawler focuses on videos. It analyzes videos, their metadata, and transcripts to understand their content, classify them correctly, and provide previews.

- **Googlebot StoreBot:** This crawler specializes in indexing online products and product feeds. It analyzes product data, prices, availability, and other relevant information for online shopping.

- **Google-extended:** This crawler is used to gather additional information about web pages, such as external links and relationships between pages.

- **Google-Inspection Tool:** This crawler is used by Google Search testing tools, such as the Rich Results Test and URL Inspection Tool in Search Console. It simulates the behavior of Googlebot to test a web page's compatibility with Google's requirements.

And these are just the most common crawlers, each specific to a particular type of resource or data. Additionally, there are special bots.

This information is significant because, when working at a high level with SEO, during the on-page optimization phase, you can give specific instructions to each individual bot.

Google is likely to integrate additional AI algorithms into its existing crawlers to improve the understanding and indexing of both traditional content and AI-generated content.

In the future, it will probably be possible to give specific instructions to bots on how to manage AI-generated content within a website's resources.

What's crucial to understand at this stage of crawling, especially from an SEO standpoint and to avoid technical issues, is that you must do everything necessary to allow the crawler easy and quick access to the resources where your content is located.

A crawler won't wait longer than 5 seconds to check a page before moving on to the next. You need to ensure that the crawler not only understands it at the code level but can also access it without any blocks and render the content quickly.

Indexing

What does the search engine know about each page in its index? Interesting question, *don't you think?* Google knows the content of the page, including the media material and all the text, every single word.

This is the second phase, the indexing phase. In this phase, the search engine examines all of the webpage's content and places it in all of the library's drawers based on the words it discovers on the page itself.

So, if your page contains 100 different words, the engine will place your page in 100 drawers. If a user types the word "bat" into the search bar, the engine will open the corresponding drawer for the word "bat" and consider only those pages.

The search engine can also open multiple drawers because it understands the meaning of synonyms related to the word you're searching for. So, there's no need to title an article "How to **see** and **observe** the lunar eclipse" since Google understands the meaning of both terms and recognizes synonyms in their specific context.

As we've already mentioned, to find pages, GoogleBot follows all the links it finds online. It also decides how many pages to crawl from each website and how frequently to crawl it.

And what are the specific HTML elements that the crawler analyzes to find more pages? They are as follows:

```
• HREF: < a href=""> text </>
• SRC: <img src="">
• SRC: <iframe src=""></iframe>
```

The crawler takes everything it finds within the `href` tag, which is simply the tag that indicates the presence of a link. It also analyzes everything inside the `src` tags: videos, images, and all embedded multimedia elements (such as YouTube videos and audio files).

When talking about the web, *"embed"* means inserting a multimedia element (such as a video, an interactive image, a social media post, a form, or an application) within a webpage. Instead of creating a link that redirects the user to an external page, the embedded element is displayed directly within the page itself.

What types of files can Googlebot read and index?

- HTML
- PDF (also recognizing links within these files)
- CSV
- PostScript (.ps)
- Microsoft Excel (.xls)
- Image formats like .jpg, .png, .webp
- Video or multimedia formats like .mpeg, .mov, .mp4
- and many others...

If you're studying search engine optimization, it's important to touch on the commands and operators you can use on Google.

Yes, because in the Google search bar, you're not limited to just typing a word or topic you're searching for. The search bar supports various operators. Here are some of the main ones you can type into the search bar:

1) `site:google.com`

    This operator returns the main pages (not all) of the website listed after the ":"

2) `site:google.com youtube`

    This operator returns the main pages (not all) of the website listed after the ":" that contain the word "Youtube".

3) `site:google.com filetype.pdf`

    This operator returns all the most important PDFs (not all) from the domain google.com.

And to check if the search engine has indexed one of your pages, simply go to Google and type the following string:

```
site:www.francescobaldi.com
```

If pages appear in the SERP, it means that the search engine has indexed the website and added some of its pages to its index. When you use the "site" operator, it shows you the most important indexed pages. This way, you can tell if the website is being indexed correctly. AS I said, if you add a word after the URL while still using the "site" operator, you can search for that word within that specific website, for example:

```
site:www.francescobaldi.com seo
```

Once a page is indexed, the search engine's bot will occasionally revisit it to check for updates or changes. *But what determines Google's crawl frequency?*

The crawl frequency depends on several factors. First and foremost, it depends on the quality of the page—so the page should always be free of errors. If the page is of low quality, Google bots may even ignore it. The authority of the links pointing to the page also plays a role, meaning that a popular website will have a higher crawl frequency.

For this reason, one of the simplest and most direct ways to quickly index a page is by placing a link to it on the homepage.

Search Console

Google Search Console (GSC) is the main tool for SEO professionals because it provides a wealth of valuable information directly from Google's search engine itself. All search engines have their own search consoles or webmaster tools. In fact, aside from GSC, there's also Microsoft Bing Webmaster Tool, which, as a search engine, has a significant share of search volume, especially in certain countries.

GSC also allows you to upload sitemaps to monitor the performance and efficiency of your pages. Keep in mind that you don't even need to use this tool until your website is ready for publication. Once the website is online, you will refer to this tool and its dashboard to evaluate the state of crawling, indexing, and overall performance of the site.

Observing the console, you'll see that in the crawl statistics, there are data points on crawl requests, download size, and the server's average response time. From here, you can also view any errors in detail, even for individual webpages.

In the security section, Google alerts you to any security issues or rule breaches, but in the "links" section, you receive a report of all backlinks received, along with the accompanying anchor text.

Through the "URL Inspection" tool, you can scan a page and obtain various details about it. For example, you can check for errors in the HTML code or SCHEMA before requesting a new indexing.

In the "indexing" section, you'll find other relevant information. Google displays all pages, indicating which are indexed and which are not, as well as highlighting any errors or issues. For each page, you can dive into the details of the problems, fix them, and then validate the correction to initiate proper indexing. Within this section, you'll also find the URL removal tool. As mentioned earlier, in the sitemap section, you can submit your site's sitemap or multiple sitemaps and check for any errors.

A specific section of the Search Console requires our particular attention: the "Experience" section, and more specifically, the "Core Web Vitals." These are a set of metrics that Google uses to assess user experience in terms of loading, interactivity, and visual stability of individual pages.

By dividing the data into mobile and desktop categories, the tool can determine how many pages provide a poor, good, or improved user experience and identify those pages.

Thanks to a timeline graph, it's easy to pinpoint the exact moment when an issue occurred with the "Core Web Vitals" parameters.

The tool will indicate the specific issues for each page that prevent it from achieving a satisfactory score in terms of user experience. To self-evaluate the "Core Web Vitals" metrics for each page on your website, you should ask yourself the following questions:

- Do the pages have good Core Web Vitals scores?
- Are the pages published securely?
- Are the pages' contents displayed correctly on mobile devices?
- How easy is it to find the main content of the page?
- Is reading hindered by an excessive number of ads?
- And many more...

As you continue reading, you'll realize how much Google values these metrics, but also how striving for a perfect score shouldn't become a source of unnecessary stress.

PageSpeed Insight

Is it possible to evaluate the performance of a page immediately after it has been published without having to wait for indexing on GSC? Absolutely. When you publish a page, you can use Google's PageSpeed Insight tool to test the URL of the newly published page.

This tool will analyze the page's performance and notify you within seconds whether it passes or fails the Core Web Vitals check. It will also give you a score divided into performance, accessibility, best practices, and SEO.

Your main but not mandatory goal here should be to reach a level sufficient to pass the Core Web Vitals check. You don't need to stress about achieving scores of 100/100. Instead, use the tool to identify any errors or unoptimized elements and fix the issues.

There are many metrics that the search engine considers to evaluate the user experience, and as an SEO expert, you should at least be familiar with the basics. This way, not only can you manage optimizations for personal or small projects on your own, but you can also have better oversight, leaving the technical work to a developer if necessary.

Perhaps the most crucial concept to understand is 'rendering' of pages, which is closely related to other concepts like 'DOM', 'CSSOM', and 'Render Tree.'

I will explain it in simple terms in a later chapter when we cover advanced concepts, as it's not a priority at the moment. It will be up to you to dive deeper and practice.

Section 4: Organic Traffic

Standard concepts to achieve the most valuable traffic source

We've arrived at the book's core: organic traffic. We will explore this in depth. This highly valuable type of traffic is captured by providing users with just one simple thing: what they are searching for.

But that's not enough. You also need to make the search engine (and therefore its crawlers) understand that your pages contain what the user is looking for. *It does make sense, right?*

So, the information users are seeking is the holy grail of organic traffic. However, it's not enough to create a one-page website with a single answer to one, high-volume question if you want to achieve consistent and tangible results in terms of traffic.

It would be too easy, *don't you think?* Since this traffic has to pass through a search engine before reaching you, your website will be positioned in the search engine's SERP based on the parameters and algorithms that the search engine uses to generate its results.

The amount of traffic you get will therefore be a direct consequence of the results produced by those same parameters and algorithms that operate within the search engine. And search engines don't care if you've repeated a keyword 100 times on the page; they don't care if you've bolded or underlined it because the crawler analyzes both the content and its relevance.

If the *search engine* likes your website, it will send you traffic and make you happy. If it doesn't like it, it will simply "do nothing," meaning it will exclude you from the top positions in the SERPs that it provides to its users.

But how can you make sure that the search engine likes your site? You need to build a website with specific characteristics, all focused on one fundamental goal:

"You must provide users with what they are looking for, in the form of clear, comprehensive, valuable and understandable information, both for the user and the search engine."

We'll go into more detail from now on as next chapters will be entirely dedicated to this type of traffic, which is the one that interests us the most as SEO professionals.

First, a clarification is necessary. Most likely, many of the concepts you'll read in this chapter are ones you've already come across elsewhere. You might have even found them online during your research on the topic if you've already tried to learn about it.

The reality is simple, and you need to understand it well: if you take 100 pieces of information you find online, you'll realize that about 10% are truly valuable, correct, and, if implemented, can deliver results. Another 50% are useless or outright wrong. Finally, a solid 40% are worse copies of the already incorrect 50%.

In short, a small percentage of the information you've already gathered is useful, while the rest is not. Here, however, you can be mathematically certain that I've only included what works. Not because some of these things are also found online, but because I've tested, implemented, and verified them through hundreds of experiments, investing both time and resources.

Everything I've written here is based on real data. The fact that you can find some of this information online is irrelevant. What truly matters is that this information works, and you won't have to waste time figuring out which 10% of the data is correct or waste money running into walls because of the 90% of useless or incorrect information found online.

I can teach you to accomplish in 3 months what took me two years. I can save you from unnecessary trial and error and the burden of having to filter the information you receive.

Ranking factors

How do you get your website to rank in the top positions of the first page of the SERP for a keyword that matters to you?

Google takes over 200 factors into account to determine a page's ranking in search results. However, analyzing each individual factor in depth would be a monumental task and, in many cases, not very productive. It's much more effective to focus on the key factors that significantly impact ranking and tailor them to the specific needs of your website.

In my experience, out of all the factors considered, about 20% truly make a difference in a site's ranking. And from that group, another 20% are responsible for the majority of results—a classic example of the famous Pareto principle.

It's on these specific points that you need to concentrate your efforts to achieve significant results. All of them deserve your full attention.

> "Pareto" was an Italian economist who formulated the well-known principle stating that "the majority of effects are caused by a small number of factors," later summarized as "20% of the causes result in 80% of the effects."

In this section of the book, we will cover both technical SEO principles and content SEO, but we will focus only on the truly important factors. These are the ones where you should concentrate the majority of your resources and energy to build an online asset capable of capturing organic traffic.

Don't get distracted by dozens of secondary parameters that would only drive you crazy with increasingly complex tasks or waste your time and money. Let's go through them one by one.

The content

The first factor that greatly impacts the organic ranking of a website is, without a doubt, the content of the website's pages.

It may seem obvious, but in reality, it's often overlooked. That's why it's important to clarify this right away: the content of your pages, its quality, the presence of keywords, and their relevance are all fundamental factors.

I remember when I first started reading online *marketing* resources. Among all the information, the concept of content being the primary focus emerged almost immediately, like a pillar you should never forget.

> *"Marketing"* is the strategy and process you use to satisfy and retain customers over time (branding). The marketing system consists of three phases: attraction (or profiling), education (nurturing), and sales. Without a market, there is no marketing.

"Content is king," Bill Gates said in 1996, referring to the internet as a platform of "content," and he was right. Various search engines have since positioned themselves as intermediaries between users and the information they seek, developing algorithms to filter that information.

If someone browsing online is searching for information "A," and you've written information "B" on your website, it's highly unlikely that you'll be ranked in the search engine's SERPs for the keyword "A." You're simply not in the drawer for that keyword—*remember Google's index?*

It seems logical to me, and this basic and rather obvious rule applies to all keywords.

I've said it before, and I'll say it again, as if it were an unbreakable law: you have to provide the user with what they want. If you're not doing that, then perhaps you've made a mistake in defining your audience or your buyer persona. In terms of content, you need to create material that can fully answer their question. To do so, you should write content in a page or a long article that provides the user with all the information they were searching for—and more.

But that's not all. The article must be well-written, readable, accessible, detailed, and provide information relevant to the main keyword and the user's search intent. *Do you remember the different types and categories of search we discussed in Phase 2 of the book?*

So, when you write content, you always need to keep two different aspects in mind: optimizing it for the reader and optimizing it for the search engine. However, when you write, you should always focus on providing value and creating resources that people actually want.

Let's talk about the basic standard concepts to keep in mind and always apply when writing content for a website.

When writing a page or an article—any type of content—you should have one major goal, which should also be the article's goal: to provide the user with what they are looking for and answer their questions. Sorry if I'm being a little repetitive but it's simply important.

Naturally, to achieve a goal, you need a plan. The plan you need is simple, structured, and easy to replicate. It is based on three decisive concepts: *inform, persuade, and entertain.*

To *inform* the user through an article, you can't just write content randomly, throwing together concepts or repeating phrases, words, or keywords without any sense. *Don't you agree?* Yet, I assure you, most people do exactly that. Hoping to rank for a keyword, some create a page packed with that one keyword repeated hundreds of times, perhaps even underlined or bolded. *Funny, right?* On the other hand, you also find pages with just three lines of content hoping to rank in top positions.

A person who knows how to write a good informational article first researches the topic. Then, they can elaborate and structure all the gathered information, or at least the most relevant bits, in a simple, original, and easily digestible way.

The preparation of an article is critical, while the actual writing is essentially a transcription process that becomes nearly automatic with practice. This is especially true when a website consists of articles that follow the same structure and type of content.

After the article is written, you'll need to review it both in terms of content and SEO optimization. You'll have to ensure that it follows the framework you'll see in a later chapter.

In fact, in addition to a content review, important articles or landing pages require a technical inspection. This is particularly useful to ensure that all links function properly, the page loads quickly, and there are no other technical or compatibility issues.

In each of your articles, you need to *engage* the reader. You must keep their attention high by making them feel that the page they're reading will provide what they're looking for. They might find it a bit further down in the text, in a paragraph or a later section. Perhaps they'll not only find what they're searching for but much more...

If the reader gets the impression or sense that they've landed in the wrong place, they'll leave immediately. I mean, if in the first sentence of ten words, three of them contain grammatical errors, that's already a more than valid reason for the reader to leave. The same goes for encountering six banners before reading a single line of text or having to close three pop-up ads. The user will simply leave.

Once you've established that the user understands they're in the right place and the reader has found what they were looking for, you can then try to guide them toward the next action.

You've already "given for free" the reader the answer they were seeking, so you've gained some trust and activated the principle of persuasion known as "reciprocity."

> The term *"reciprocity"* refers to the principle that makes someone feel "indebted" to you. The classic example is when you invite a friend over for dinner, and they say, "Next time it's on me." You treated them to dinner, so they feel a sense of obligation and want to return the favor in some way. Maybe they even brought a bottle of wine to the dinner as a result of this reciprocity.

Remember that your mission is to generate traffic to your website, and you need to think of various strategies to either attract or maintain it if you already have some. Thus, your writing style, language, and tone are all essential in delivering and helping the reader understand your message.

For example, when someone is reading an article and has found what they were looking for, you could suggest they explore another page. Ask them, using a link or a *call to action*, if they want to dive deeper into the topic.

If you need to sell something, you must *persuade* the reader to click on the "add to cart" button or direct them to a landing page. Perhaps afterward, you can convince them to add another product to their cart, maybe with a special offer, and do some up-selling or cross-selling. If you want to keep them on your website longer, you'll need to persuade them to stay and consume more of your content.

In this way, a user who is already part of your traffic but would have only been a single *pageview* can easily turn into two pageviews or more.

The visitor might stay on your website longer, browse through more pages, view more banners (which might pay you per *impression*), and gather more useful information.

The ideal process resembles a loop; it's beneficial for you because it increases reader loyalty, and it's beneficial for them because they consistently find valuable, useful information. This creates a kind of *"win-win situation,"* where both you and the reader benefit.

A reader who finds great content, well-written and full of valuable information, is more likely to trust your site. As a result, they might sign up for your newsletter, buy one of your products, or at the very least, remember you the next time they're looking for information. This means your traffic could return again, but this time as direct traffic instead of organic, which, as we've seen before, is very valuable.

If you think about it, this entire chapter on how to create content-rich articles is based on what you can offer to users. Always remember this:

"Write first for users, then for search engines."

Making an article "good" for search engines is relatively easy, and it's simply the result of a repeatable process that I will explain in the upcoming chapters. Making an article "good" for a reader, however, is much more difficult. But if you manage to do it, you'll reap the benefits for a long time.

Remember, if a reader enjoys your content, they'll spend more time on your website and might even share the article on social media. Furthermore, metrics like "time on page," "bounce rate," and "social engagement" are all KPIs that search engines take into account when ranking. Sure, they might not all be considered in the short term, but in the long run, a quality project will always beat a disorganized and poorly written one.

There are also several ways to define different types of content, which is useful to know in order to categorize the resources you'll need to create. Let's see them:

- **Hero Content:** This is the content that makes a "boom." It grabs attention, goes viral, and generates buzz. Think of a super creative video, a spectacular infographic, or a highly engaging contest.

  Its purpose is to create an immediate impact and get people talking about you. It can be a page that uses images, videos, or other elements to deliver the message directly, with the goal of converting users, increasing engagement, or boosting brand awareness.

- **Pillar Content:** This is the backbone of your content strategy. It's a highly detailed, long, and comprehensive article or webpage on a broad topic, supported by more specific content.

Its purpose is to position you as an expert in the field, generating authority as well as backlinks and organic traffic.

- **Hub Content:** This type of content aggregates and connects other pieces of content. It can be a category listing resources, a comprehensive guide, or a thematic hub. While it's less detailed than pillar content, it's often broader in scope.

  Its main purpose is to organize content and make navigation easier for the user, acting as a starting point for exploring other resources, including pillar content.

- **Help Content:** This is content that answers the most frequent and specific questions users have. It includes FAQs, quick guides, tutorials, and any content focused on single keywords aimed at addressing a user's need or problem.

  Its purpose is to build user loyalty while also improving search rankings for specific queries.

This table should help you to have a view of the different types of content I am talking about. Each one has its own characteristics, format, and goal.

	PILLAR	HERO	HUB	HELP
GOAL	Authority, Organic Traffic, link building	Conversion, engagement, brand awareness	Organization, internal linking	Problem solution, retention, Organic Traffic
WORDS	6000+	2000	3000	2000
FORMAT	Article, Tutorial	Landing Page, Video, Infographic	Category Page	Article, FAQ, Tutorial, Video
FOCUS	Broad and complex topic explained in detail.	Call to action, offer, news, key message.	Topic Overview	Answers and solutions to specific questions

The ideal structure of content for a project with excellent SEO foundations is as follows:

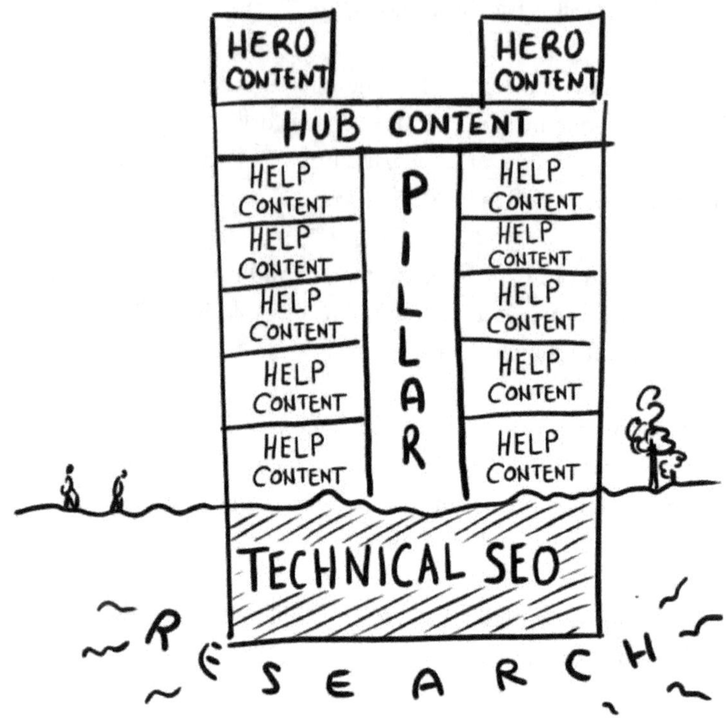

Note how the entire structure is supported by the solid foundations that only technical SEO can guarantee. If you build a content strategy on rotten or defective foundations, the first pass of the crawlers will cause the whole structure (and project) to collapse.

In terms of market research, if you build the structure on unsuitable ground, it will eventually sink like quicksand.

The right pattern

The best content not only answers the user's primary question or request but also allows for a deeper dive into the topic as well as an expansion of it through related resources.

All content should be written clearly and understandably for both human readers and search engine bots that need to *crawl* the pages and update their *index*.

Now, the first thing to consider is: 1 keyword = 1 dedicated page. Each page should be optimized for a single keyword. Therefore, if you're creating a blog with 20 identified keywords, you need at least 20 pages.

Second thing: The page should always include an HTML `<title>` tag with the exact keyword you want to rank for. If the keyword is on the left side of the title, it is given more importance and is seen first by users when they view the search results in the SERP.

Keep in mind that Google calculates the pixels occupied by the title. So, if you write a title that's too long, it will be truncated in the snippet. This behavior depends on the screen size and resolution, not the number of words. Thus, on smaller screens, the `<title>` might be truncated, whereas on desktop screens it will be displayed in full.

A `<meta name="description">` tag is also crucial, and it should contain the exact keyword along with a variant or a complementary keyword. If you have space, you can also include a call to action, but in general, it should be a continuation of a well-written `<title>`. What we have said for the `<title>` length is also true for the `<description>`.

These two elements, the `<title>` tag and the `<description>` tag, along with the page URL, will form the snippet of the page in the SERP and should always be included and optimized on every page. Additionally, they must always be unique, so there should never be pages with identical titles or descriptions.

I have already discussed how to best write and organize the snippet in a previous chapter.

Let's proceed to understanding how to organize the content of the page. After the chapter about HTML in the 2nd phase of the book, you should have already delved into the main tags; they will come handy now.

You're familiar with the <h1> tag, but since all of them are essential in SEO, let's start with a brief introduction:

The <h1>, <h2>, and <h3> tags are fundamental elements in HTML5 used to define the structure and importance of headings within a web page. They are mainly used to structure content, and we do know how much search engines like to find structured data, *right?* These tags create a visual and logical hierarchy of the content, making it easier for both users to understand and search engines to index.

> *Headings* are relevant both for the reader, as they make the text more readable, and for SEO, as they determine the topic or subtopic of the content, making crawling more efficient.

The <h1> tag represents the main title of the page, followed by <h2> for primary subtitles and <h3> for secondary subtitles. This hierarchy helps crawlers understand the importance of each section of the page, and it also makes the page more accessible to users who use screen readers to navigate the web.

Your page should always contain a single <h1> with the exact keyword. When I say it must have an <h1>, I mean exactly one, not two. There should be no two "heading 1" (<h1>) tags in the same section of the page.

As of today, Google can index pages with one <h1>, multiple <h1> tags, or even without any <h1> tags. Generally, since the <h1> represents the title of the main topic of a page, and since a page often has a single main topic, it strongly suggests including one. Until recently, the rule was to have only one <h1> per page. However, with HTML5 and its widespread adoption, this concept has evolved. The current standard allows each section of the page (`header`, `footer`, `article`, etc.) to have its own <h1>. Therefore, today <h1> is considered the main title of a section within a page rather than the main title of the entire page.

The title of your page (<title>) and the main heading within the page (<h1>) are not always the same. Although they sometimes coincide, it is generally better to keep them distinct. For example, in e-commerce and product contexts, <title> tags are often very specific, while <h1> tags are shorter. Conversely, in editorial contexts such as blogs or forums, the two titles tend to match.

Despite these variations, I believe that maintaining a distinction between <h1> and <title> is the best choice for optimizing both user experience and SEO. The <h1> title should be shorter and focused on the main content, while the <title> can be longer and contain more information. This distinction encourages visitors to your website, helps them to quickly grasp the page's content, and allows search engines to properly index it.

After the <h1>, include an introductory paragraph about the topic of the article. In this paragraph, which is enclosed by the <p> tag in HTML, include the direct keyword and possibly a variant. Keep it concise, ideally within 30-40 words, and avoid using poorly crafted variants of the keyword—make sure they are relevant.

The first few words of your text are your hook. In these brief lines, you need to grab the reader's attention like a fisherman with his bait. A well-crafted introduction not only piques interest but also creates an expectation that the rest of the text should fulfill. Spend time crafting these 40 words and an effective hook to keep the reader engaged.

After the first paragraph, include an image using the <img> tag. This should not be a random image; it must be relevant to what the user is searching for and the topic discussed. The image should be of excellent quality and, above all, original.

From a technical standpoint, the image should be lightweight. An optimized `.jpg` or `.webp` format will work well. I will explain image optimization for SEO in more detail later.

For now, it's important to fill in the image "title" and "alt" attributes, including the chosen keyword, along with a description of the image, or describe the image while incorporating the keyword into the description. If you want to add a caption to the image, that's great—include a variant of the main keyword. After the image, you can include another brief paragraph <p> if you wish, or you can skip it.

Now, insert the first heading <h2> on the page, which should be a title containing a word related to your keyword. It could also be a variant of the main keyword; the crucial thing is that it clearly indicates the topic you will discuss in the subsequent paragraphs.

After this <h2>, you will add additional explanatory paragraphs <p> that elaborate on the <h2> heading. These will be further paragraphs that discuss the topic indicated by the <h2>. If another subheading is necessary, include an <h3> within the <h2>.

Always follow and respect the heading hierarchy; as I repeat, it makes the content more readable for people and helps search engines understand the document structure. Google clearly understands the hierarchy of tags on pages.

The article will continue in this manner, following the structure outlined in the schema below, repeating until the end.

Example 1	Example 2
| ```
<h1>
   <p>
<img>
 <h2>
    <p>
    <img>
    <p>
. . . .
 <h2>
    <p>
    <p>
. . . .
``` | ```
<h1>
  <p>
<img>
 <h2>
    <p>
    <img>
    <p>
      <h3>
          <p>
          <p>
   <h2>
      <p>
      <p>
``` |

Within the central paragraphs `<p>` of the document, remember to include the exact keyword for which you want the page to rank, along with some variants.

Also, include the exact keyword in the last sentence of the final paragraph. In summary, the keyword you want to target should appear in the `<h1>` title, the first paragraph `<p>`, the central content (a few times and in the form of variants), and the last sentence of the final paragraph `<p>`.

Once the entire page is complete, add a table of contents (TOC) to the page. The TOC is a list of links that, when clicked, take the user directly to a specific section of the page using anchors. Place the TOC before the first `<h2>`. You can use simple WordPress plugins that automatically add it to all pages, but we'll discuss this in detail in a later chapter.

You can decide which types of headings will make up the TOC for your page. Guess what? tables of contents facilitate and improve navigation for users and signal to search engines that your content is easy to navigate. As a result, your article will be better in this aspect compared to articles on other sites that don't have a TOC.

Here are some additional concepts that should be obvious but are always worth emphasizing:

Write in grammatically and syntactically correct language, using simple and easily understandable terms. You can also write in Spanish, French, or English if your website targets keywords in different languages; the important thing is to always write correctly and use simple words. Only use complex words and sentences if the topic warrants them. Use the language that your reader expects, which aligns with your target audience.

Avoid using unusual colors or special fonts. Bold text should only be used for its intended purpose, which is to make important information easily accessible for those who are skimming through, not for highlighting keywords.

The content should be comprehensive. If a competitor's page that ranks for your target keyword contains 500 words, *how long do you think your article should be to try and surpass it in the SERPs?*

Definitely not just 505 words. Aim for 2000, 3000 words, or even more. Make it the best content available on the web about that particular topic. Don't assume that if an article is long, no one will read it.

Remember, you have a structure (headings, table of contents, etc.) that helps make information easily accessible. As a result, when the user visits the page, they may quickly navigate to the area they need by clicking the table of contents. Or, it's the search engine itself that directs them to the right part of the page after clicking the snippet link in SERP.

If the competitor has explained certain concepts, provide a better explanation. If they have included 5 images, include 15, and optimize them so that your 15 images together are more descriptive, original, and lighter than their 5.

The advantage of working this way is that, although it may seem more labor-intensive at first, it is more profitable in the long term.

A 3000-word content will not only include the main keyword but also dozens of long-tail keyword variants or related keywords that are pertinent to the topic. Each of these keywords will have its own search volume.

In the end, the page will rank for all keywords, not just the main one. Even if the additional keywords don't make it to the first page, they will still rank in the SERPs and generate traffic.

Typically, 80% of the traffic to the page will come from the main keyword, while 20% will come from related keywords. This proportion should be familiar to you, *right?*

Images optimization

Optimizing images is another important aspect, especially if you need to include many images in your content. If your web pages don't contain images, perhaps because you follow a purely descriptive style, then this optimization isn't necessary for you.

However, in general, you should always optimize your images, even if you only have one per article. I never recommend including just one image in an article, but if you must, at least make sure it's optimized according to the rules I'll explain in this chapter.

Search engines give importance to images, often displaying them before the text in search results. This means that if the image isn't optimized, the snippet will perform much worse because users simply won't click on it. The same applies to videos, which are also gaining prominence in the SERPs.

But what does optimizing images mean? It means making them small, both in terms of compression (reducing their file size in KB) and in terms of loading speed (server-side optimization).

Here's the method I use. First of all, I decide on a maximum image width, considering where the image will be used. Let's say, for example, 900 px.

I open Photoshop and create my 900 px image. Then, I use a function that was developed decades ago but still does its job well, called "Save for Web." I save the image for the web as a `.jpg` and set the compression between 50 and 65.

The image I create is highly compressed in terms of size and remains very lightweight, while retaining much of its quality.

It's also essential to ensure that images can adapt to different devices to enhance the user experience. You'll need to check if this feature is enabled in the WordPress theme you're using . I can assure you that applying this optimization to all the images across your website makes a huge difference. If you don't have Photoshop or prefer to accomplish the same thing in *batches*, you can install an image compression plugin for WordPress. The plugin will go through all the images in your WordPress folders and optimize them according to the parameters you set.

> *"Batch"* refers to a list or series of identical commands executed sequentially. For example, you decide on a command or action once and have it automatically repeated X number of times on Y different elements.

Additionally, I optimize images to speed up server-side requests and loading times. To do this, in specific cases, I use the `.webp` format, which reduces image size even further.

All these measures make the pages load faster. This means users will see the content sooner, and guess what? the user experience improves. Consequently, Google will notice this improvement in UX, and you'll usually rank higher in the SERPs.

Did you know that many websites still don't have optimized images? Yet, it would take little effort to achieve significant improvements and surpass competitors.

Listen to this story; once, I created a completely original article that was 5000 words long. It was intentionally long because I was conducting an experiment to see if Google had a word limit beyond which it would consider an article too long for users and, therefore, wouldn't rank it well.

I thought 5000 words was excessive, especially for content viewed on mobile devices. I followed all of the procedures outlined in this book when creating the page, and it ended up containing more than 25 images. There was a lot of text, but also plenty of images. After publishing it, I monitored the SERPs daily to see what would happen. Even though my articles usually get indexed within a day, this one still wasn't visible in the SERPs after a week.

After two weeks, nothing. I thought that maybe, since the article was so long, it would need more time. After three weeks, still nothing. I began running tests on the page to figure out where the issue might be.

To make a long story short, I realized I forgot to optimize images. Each one weighed 250 KB, and with 25 images, that's about 7 MB for a single page. Once I optimized them, reducing each to 60 KB, the page was already in 4th position on the first page of search results for the main keyword within 24 hours.

There are plenty of image compression tools available online or as plugins, so you'll need to choose the one that's most convenient for you.

Let's talk about other important elements regarding images when discussing SEO; those are elements that aren't related to size or speed optimization, but instead focus purely on information optimization for the images.

Every image will be a file with a name on a server. Let me explain further. Suppose you have a blog about garden plants and you've written an article on blackberry plants, focusing on the keyword "blackberry" and related keywords (blackberry bush, blackberry flowers, etc.). When adding images, the file names of these images should contain the keyword. For example, in the section on blackberry flowers, you should include an image named:

```
/blackberry-flowers.jpg
or
/flowers-blackberry.jpg
```

In the subchapter (Heading-2) where you talk about the fruits of the blackberry plant, you'll include an image named "blackberry-fruits.jpg," and so on. You should never upload images with names like "image1.jpg" or "dasdoh3nas.jpg" (I just hit random keys for that one), or images taken directly from a camera with names like "IMG_52.jpg."

The image file name and the `alt` attribute are also crucial, as we will see shortly. The search engine reads the file name and uses it to understand if the image you added is relevant to the topic you're discussing and to the keyword you're aiming to rank for. It also uses the name to index the image in the SERP. Besides the image file name, the tags you can associate with each image are also very important. Always fill in the `title` tag of the images, including the relevant keyword.

Images can also contain a link; thus, some of them are clickable. In this case, since Google uses the "alt" attribute of the "img" element as anchor text, you should always make sure to include descriptive text in the "alt" attribute of each image.

```
img src="image.jpg" alt="text that describes the image"
```

But that's not the only reason. This text in the "alt" attribute can also appear in other places, such as when the image is accessed by screen readers. For this reason, ensure that the text is functional for people who actually use it.

The caption and the text <p> surrounding the image provide better context, increasing the likelihood that it will appear higher in image search results.

Also, remember that Google does not index CSS images, so keep that in mind and be careful of code like this:

```
<div style="background-image:url(image.jpg)">My image</div>
```

I'm teaching you to be meticulous in search engine optimization. That's why I also recommend considering the originality of the photo you use. Think about it for a moment. I believe that using images downloaded from the web is inefficient. *Why?*

Because everyone has access to that photo; it has already been seen, indexed, copied, used, and reused. It would be much better to create your own image, generate or take a photo, so you can provide original, never-before-seen, new, and unique content. The search engine would certainly prioritize it and give more visibility to such content.

You can get an idea of how widespread an image is by using the Google Lens tool, and you'll see how any image is often repeated across multiple websites and, therefore, cannot be considered "original."

Video optimization

Nowadays, we know that most people prefer watching a video rather than reading an article or a page with an index, chapters, and text.

Even in the SERPs, it's noticeable that the top results are often videos. The search engine does not even direct the user to the video, but instead offers it immediately in the SERP, making it playable and beginning exactly where it believes the solution to the user's problem is.

So, let's follow this logic and think: *What could an SEO expert do to make their content more visible?*

The best technical SEO practices for optimizing videos are simply those that make them more visible, clear, and accessible to users. So, first of all, if you have a video, place it on the page as early as possible. If you have a page explaining a topic and a video, put the video at the top of the content, not at the bottom. Make the video important, and Google will do the same.

In fact, Google suggests creating a dedicated page for each video. However, be careful where you place it; the video should be placed in a context that is consistent with the video's content, the page title, and the text surrounding the video. Additionally, if the video is not part of the main content of the page, the preview could not be shown in the SERP. This means that if the video is not the primary content of the page, the search engine will not prioritize displaying its preview in the SERP.

Organize a specific video sitemap and include as much useful information as possible for the crawler. Consider implementing "schema" tags if you want to add even more information. Always check that the `robots.txt` file or the robots `noindex` tag doesn't block access to the page.

Ensure that the video is placed within a dedicated section of the page, using ideal HTML5 tags such as `<video>`, `<embed>`, `<iframe>`, or `<object>`.

To appear in Google's video search results, you must also provide a "thumbnail." If you're using the `<video>` HTML tag, you can do this by specifying the `poster` attribute. Alternatively, you can specify the thumbnail location in the video sitemap with the `<video:thumbnail_loc>` tag or through structured data.

I could talk about video optimization for many pages, but the truth is, you need to verify and study the details of each method on your own, even by directly using the documentation provided by Google, which you can find on Google Search Central.

And all of this only covers the technical optimization of videos on your website. You also need to think from a strategic perspective. If video content is a fundamental medium for your business, you'll definitely want to leverage the potential of other platforms within Google's ecosystem, where other specific SEO strategies must be implemented. I'm talking, for example, about YouTube but also external platforms like TikTok.

For instance, ask yourself this question: *What does the user want to see?* Come up with 2 or 3 possible answers. Then ask another question: *How do I produce this content?* Once you've answered these questions, all that's left is to experiment and test.

User Experience

What I've explained so far are some of the main factors and some of the most important variables. These are fundamental principles—things that, if not implemented, will make your project truly weak and short-lived.

However, there are other factors that should not be ignored, which you must implement if you want to create a competitive and SEO-optimized asset.

In this chapter, for example, I will talk about *user experience*, a crucial factor that heavily influences how relevant your website is to Google. We briefly touched on its importance in the chapter about "links," and we will also address it in the chapter on "website speed," because "speed" is always closely related to the concept of user experience.

It's one of those parameters you need to monitor because it's decisive for search engines, and thus becomes an essential factor for the success of a web project based on organica traffic. First, you want users to go beyond the first page of your website and explore other pages. Secondly, because Google will rank you higher in the SERP, bringing the benefits you're already aware of.

> *User experience* can often be found abbreviated as UX and indicates the overall quality of experience when using a website.

Search engines are becoming more skilled at identifying and penalizing websites that do not consider the most crucial factor: users and their experiences on the website to which the engine sends them."

For example, it is still common as well as unappealing to come across websites with cluttered menus that make navigating impossible. As a result, they are practically useless, as a menu should specifically assist navigation.

Other times, and you will have experienced this yourself, when you land on an article, you are met with an impenetrable wall of text with no spaces occupying the entire page. Text that, according to the author, we should hypothetically read but will never read from a desktop or a smartphone: a wall of text in practice! *Would you find it easy and enjoyable to read?* That would be a flat-out no.

Many websites present you with a variety of things as soon as you click on them, such as pop-up coupons, pop-ups asking you to subscribe to their newsletter, a notification asking you to subscribe to their pop notifications, and then three or four pop-up banner ads, including a video with audio. All of these cover the content and obstruct navigation, decreasing your enjoyment of it.

This happened to me a little while ago. I was looking for the guitar chords to a Nirvana song; I typed '*tabs nirvana frances*' into Google ("frances" is the first word of the song title). I opened four different sites from the search results, and each contained everything except the song's chords. There were huge menus, advertisements, self-starting videos, associated articles about other songs, pop-ups, popunders, and notifications, but no chords. *What kind of 'user experience' do you believe I had?* A bad one. But the user experience is not just that; it is much, much more.

It begins long before the user navigates a website, for example, via the SERPs. Consider this: If users look at your snippet but do not click on it, resulting in a low CTR, their experience will be poor. As a result, after a few days of rotation, your snippet will land on another page farther down the SERP.

Instead, let's say the user clicks on the snippet link in SERPs and assumes it lands on your website. *How long did it take him to land? How long did the page take to load?* This is also a factor in the user experience.

Clearly, fast pages correspond to a better experience. Another plus point for the UX! Pages that take 20 seconds to open, even with fast connections, clearly contribute to the desire to pick up the phone and throw it off the pier (there is a pier near where I live).

Imagine that two users are browsing your website. The first user finds a well-written and intriguing article and reads all of it, then opens another page, to which you have linked on your website, and reads that too, enjoying the content. Another user, on the other hand, enters your website and after 3 seconds leaves because he has not found anything interesting.

The first user has a very good experience and has produced an excellent *'time on page'* and *'session time'* score. The second user indicates to the engine that your website is uninteresting.

One website has a 'returning visitors' rate of 25 per cent, while another website has a 'returning visitors' rate of 1 percent. Obviously, if a user returns, it means that the experience he had was considered excellent; and that is why he returns. Another plus point for UX!

In short, user experience is something you should always optimize with users in mind, not search engines. Then, automatically, the engines will detect your excellent UX scores and reward you in SERPs.

If you're wondering how search engines collect so much information about the user experience, consider that when you browse, you may be doing it with the Chrome browser (which belongs to Google) and you may be doing it while logged into your Google account. *Can you see where they get their data from?*

The design of a website, its graphics, font style, paragraph style; and overall visual impact are also part of the parameters that contribute to the user experience.

Sites that are graphically unattractive result in a bad user experience. Often, if I see a website with an extremely unattractive logo, I close it without viewing anything else, because the logo represents your brand and is the first thing that appears at the top of the header. Maybe it's a bit of an exaggeration, but that's how it is: if someone hasn't put the effort and work into creating a professional logo, I don't expect to find professional content on the site.

So make a website that is also visually appealing! I have a very solid background in graphics, and that is perhaps why I am very fussy about it. I worked for years in computer graphics. I used to create children's 3D TV series for television companies. A great attention to detail and professional knowledge of many graphics programmes was always required. So the design and appearance of a website is always something I take very seriously (sometimes too seriously).

All these parameters taken individually may seem irrelevant, but taken as a whole they are clear and important signals to Google that the content on the page was relevant to the user.

Perhaps the following question is popping into your mind: *how to increase user experience?*

Enhancing the user experience is quite easy, in theory. These are the four most commonly used ways for improving it:

1) Intelligent and planned use of well-optimized internal website links and maximum clarity in menu links.
2) A focus on optimizing website speed, pages, and navigation within the website structure.
3) Create long, engaging, interesting, and well-structured content to keep users glued to reading pages.
4) Allow the user to flow without blocking them, letting them consume the information, and helping them with a minimalist and pleasant design.

Think how nice it would be to be able to know, directly from your users, what they are looking for on your website, what they like, and what they don't like. Well yes, that would be great. The good news is that you can actually do it.

Before we figure out how to implement this function, let's work on the concept behind it for a moment. *Why should you know what the user likes and dislikes?* It's obvious: to improve the *user experience.*

If you know what a user failed to find, and therefore why they are leaving your website, you can fix the problem and insert that missing content. By doing so, you will avoid the same behavior for future users, because not a single user will ever leave due to a lack of information.

This is based on the concept of the *feedback loop,* which is related to the concept of "cause and effect" and works like this: you receive feedback from a user and implement a test solution to see if the result is different or not. You do this to see if the user is now satisfied or not and will stay on the website instead of leaving. All you do is test whether the effect remains the same by changing the cause. By implementing this concept everywhere and infinitely (in loops) you will always find the solution to the problems you have to solve. The feedback loop protocol will also serve as the foundation for all of the future optimization processes.

In this case, if we want to collect feedback from users, it is simple to implement. To do this, you can use an external service through which, with just a few steps, you can install a WordPress plugin and create surveys that your visitors can answer with a simple click.

They are not invasive and are perfect for understanding what users don't like and would like instead. This is all information you can use to improve your website, and once you have collected enough data, you can always deactivate the plugin.

You can also use the same system to ask more general questions and then work out, after you have obtained a statistically valid number of answers, what articles to talk about and what topics to cover for the next content publication.

I suggest waiting for a statistically valid number of responses because if you only get one response in a week from a user saying, 'I couldn't find the contact page,' it isn't necessarily a problem that needs to be solved. Maybe the user is the one who failed for other reasons, not because the contact page is not in the menu. However, if 36 users per day inform you that they can't reach you because they can't find the contact page, it's time to investigate and resolve the problem.

Heatmaps are another useful tool for gathering information on user experience. A *'heatmap'* is a visual tool that shows you how users interact on a web page. With this tool, available through free or paid services on the web, you can see the areas of the page that are the 'hottest'. These are the areas where users click more or move the mouse over more frequently or simply focus their attention more. Heatmaps are another intuitive tool for understanding which elements work and which are ignored by users.

Domain Name, Age and Quality

Now, in case you want to create a website from scratch, you need to know a few things about the domain you choose.

If, on the other hand, you already have a website online or have already purchased a domain, these are also things you should know because you can always start new projects and then buy new domains.

Yes, the domain name selection is important in website indexation, particularly at the start of a new project.

Let's use an example so you can understand the concept easily. Let's say you are thinking of making a website about 'washing machines'. You then examined the trend in the washing machine market and established that it is expanding, or at least consistent, and you want to give it a go. I'm speaking hypothetically because I haven't investigated this particular topic.

You've reached the point when you need to choose a domain name for your website, and you've concluded that your primary keyword will be 'washing machines'. "Keep in mind that, especially in the short term, the website on the hypothetical domain 'washing-machines.com' has a better chance of being ranked for the keyword 'washing machines' than the possible domain 'washer.com'.

Usually, when I buy domain names, I choose the domain name with the key that has the most volume that I find in my niche. In the event that the selected keyword is a key that is too generic or has too much competition, I discard it and move on to the keyword with the next volume.

Remember that a keyword may not even be a single word. In fact, often the domain names I use have two or more words. I chose these 'long' names from the list of *'long tail keywords'* that I have studied in my keyword and volume research.

Let's talk about the age of a domain. Although it is disputed that a domain's seniority, and hence its age (domain age), has any influence on its ranking algorithms, my personal experience has shown that this is not the case. Perhaps the age of a domain has no direct effect on the ranking of your website, but it certainly has some indirect effects.

To understand this, let's assume you have two domains. The domain where website "A" is located has been online for 10 years, and the website has a lot of content. The domain of website "B" has been online for 2 months and also has a lot of content. Both are optimized on the same keyword.

It is assumed that "A," having been online for much longer, has built up much greater authority over time than "B," who in fact, in all likelihood, has not yet had time to do so.

Furthermore, "A" has had 10 years to build up excellent content, not to mention a large number of links, which will give it further authority in the eyes of the search engine. Website "B," which has been on the market for a short time, has no incoming links from other sites because it has not yet had time to generate them.

Thus, there is indeed a correlation between the age of a domain and ranking, and it is especially noticeable when looking at the indirect effects of being online for much longer.

A domain that has been online for as long as "A" has is much more likely to receive links, and thus authority, from other sites and consequently trust from search engines.

Anyway, it is not certain that "A" will always remain in a better position in SERPs than "B." This needs to be established.

Say that "B" becomes a surprisingly popular website only a few months after it's published. Google would be aware of all this traffic, which might be millions of monthly visitors. This, combined with the anticipated consequential backlinks it will receive, will result in it rising in the SERPs.
The search engine simply assumes that if you have been online longer, it means that people are reading your content, probably because you are

publishing good content. This, combined with the fact that older sites have a high number of backlinks, enhances the domain's quality and, as a result, its overall ranking.

Let us now focus on the quality aspect. I'd like to share some interesting information with you about the URLs you'll use for your site(s).

Let's say, for instance, that you want to make a website about 'trainers'. You do some research and see that, unfortunately, the domain with the .com extension that you are interested in is already occupied, but fortunately, it is for sale, or maybe a website that has already been online for a long time is for sale and you decide to make an offer to buy it.

In both cases, it would be a good idea to do a domain check. Similar to what one would do before purchasing a house, a thorough review of the land registry to ensure that everything is in order. Even with websites, these checks are made, because a 'quality' factor of the domain comes into play.

If the domain you are purchasing does not presently host any websites, it does not imply that it has not previously hosted any. And if the old website has a history of spammy content behind it, which has produced backlinks of poor quality, this could be a problem and certainly diminishes its value.

Even if a website is already complete and online but has been put up for sale 5 months after it was published, you should still evaluate the domain's quality. Perhaps the publication is too recent, and you will need more time to have it properly indexed by the engines. So if you wanted to get off to a flying start, maybe this is not the right website to buy.

You need to check if the domain has a story behind it and, more importantly, what that story is. You have to find out whether it has purchased links and to which pages, as changing these links will result in the loss of the link or the need for redirection. You have to check each link's relevance and authority to ensure that the search engine can trust your online asset without problems.
If, on the other hand, you are planning to compete against a domain that has already been online for a long time, you need to do a competitor study. This website, which you intend to overtake in SERPs, will have two separate aspects that you'll have to consider. The first is the competition factor of its

pages and therefore its content. The second element, which we will focus on in this chapter, is the domain's competition factor and thus its quality.

If your analysis reveals that both the domain's and the pages' competition parameters are extremely competitive, forget it; do not even attempt to target it. You would not be successful if you started a project from scratch with a small budget. If, on the other hand, the domain has a high level of competition but the page parameters are not particularly competitive, there may be an opportunity. You could exploit this weakness in its 'content', and attack the competitor by creating better content to overtake it in SERPs.

Social Media

Even if Google, from a certain perspective, ignores social media, having a large and active community sends positive signals to the engine and generates a lot of traffic.

But why does Google ignore social media? Google treats social media pages, and thus Facebook pages, in the same way that it treats regular website pages. It treats them in the same manner; therefore, it indexes them using the same parameters. Clearly, all the flood of parameters, which we have seen and need to manage as much as possible for better indexing cannot be controlled on social pages.

However, when it comes to using social page numbers as a ranking factor for socially related sites, search engines tread lightly the topic.

Many people place a high value on the number of followers a social media profile has, but not everything that shines is gold. If my website has a Facebook page with 20,000 likes and another website has one with 500,000, these numbers mean nothing to Google.

The reason is simple: it is far too easy to manipulate social numbers, such as by purchasing fake followers, 'likes,' or other similar services. As a result, all of those people who know how to buy followers and likes would have a significant impact on the engine's SERP. Yet, as in the case of domain seniority, indirect effects come into play with social media, which the engine algorithms take into account when indexing your site.

Social media is populated by users and users are people. All social media works because of these people. They are the ones who like, share, comment or read the Facebook, Twitter or Pinterest feeds. They watch YouTube or TikTok videos. Google is interested in people, their actions, and their behavior; this is what you should focus on.

Essentially, the more people who follow your page, and thus the more likes or followers it has, the more likely it is that the content you publish will be seen and shared.

Consequently, if they are shared, they are more likely to receive links. So in the end, it's all about links. It is about the links that come from social shares and those you cannot manipulate.

It doesn't matter which social platform you use. If the content is good and is read by the right people, i.e., your target demographic, it will most likely be shared and possibly get links, simply because it was the right content at the right time for the right person.

Of course, don't expect 1 share of your Facebook post to equal 1 link. The conversion rate (CR), in this case, will remain to be seen and will depend on many factors. And don't expect a link shared on a Facebook page or group to have the same value as a link from a PR8 website either.

Nonetheless, if you have a high number of shares, you will gain more visibility among those who use social media and, as a result, among those who are likely to share your content, increasing your visibility.

The process is very simple. You write a high-quality article on your website and share it on your page, which has 2000 followers. Facebook's algorithm only shows it to a small percentage of your 2000 followers. If you thought it showed up on everyone's Facebook page for free, I'm sorry to disappoint you. Assume that out of 2000 people, 20 see it and 5 share it.

At this point, not only does Facebook's algorithm detect that the article is interesting and therefore shows it to other people, increasing its organic reach, but another wonderful thing happens. With your added reach, the 5 shares also reach 1 'content creator'. A content creator is a person who has their own blog or website and chooses to include your articles in one of their articles. It is someone who not only consumes content, but also publishes new content.

Thus, a new link is born.

Then, social networks boost your website's SEO from a different perspective. They are tools created to connect people and create communities. So your Facebook page or group, or any platform, is a community, and you should treat it as such because it is valuable.

Your Facebook page's audience consists of users who are interested in your content. Learn how to establish, grow, and feed this audience with consistently captivating content.

These users, or at least a portion of them depending on the reach of your posts, will read your content with interest, contributing to an improved *user experience* score on your site. Furthermore, if users come across your results in SERPs while searching, they are more likely to click on a link to a website they are familiar with because they may already follow it on Facebook, rather than one they are unfamiliar with. When you enter a club, do you first greet people you know and hang out with or maybe strangers? Again, this all contributes to increasing the CTR parameters on snippet clicks in SERPs.

Building a community is a must if you want to create online assets, because communities are assets of their own.

Even from the point of view of promoting your content or products, these social assets will prove to be very useful tools because they already contain the audience interested in your niche. Therefore, when you create advertising campaigns for this audience, you will pay much less for traffic or clicks on your ads by 'targeting' people in your community.

So make use of the tools that social networks offer you, always keeping these dynamics in mind. *Remember the Open Graph protocol we talked about earlier? It is precisely one of these tools.*

To summarize again, social media does not influence positioning directly but rather indirectly through these mechanisms.

- Increasing the visibility of your website, bringing in more organic and social traffic.

- Shares, likes, and comments on social media can be interpreted by Google as positive social signals, indicating that your content is valuable and relevant.

- If your content is shared on social media and linked from other websites, this can lead to acquiring high-quality backlinks.

- High engagement on social media can indicate a dynamic and active website, enhancing the user experience.

Everything clear? Let's go and discover some interesting new concepts.

Local SEO

Imagine being a tourist on a warm August day, strolling under the pleasant shade of the trees in Kensington Gardens, London. Suddenly, you get hungry and start looking for an Italian restaurant. *What will be your first action?* Most likely, you'll grab your smartphone and search for "Italian restaurant near me." At that precise moment, local SEO comes into play.

Local SEO is a set of strategies aimed at making your business appear among the top search results when a user is looking for specific products or services in their area. Like a website, it's a virtual storefront that's always open, designed to capture the attention of those searching for what you offer. However, it's a different channel compared to the traditional website, and the difference lies in this channel being more related to a particular search intent: the so-called *"visit in person queries."*

Local SEO involves implementing all available optimizations to rank a local business in the SERP. These optimizations differ from those generally used to rank website pages in that they focus on using and optimizing one of the Google ecosystem's platforms: Google Business Profile.

In short, it's like a business card for your company within Google's ecosystem. By carefully completing your profile and providing various information such as the address, opening hours, photos, and reviews, you've already begun the local SEO optimization process for your business.

I won't go into detail about optimizations within Google Business. Once you've opened a business profile, take the necessary time to fill out every required field with information that is as thorough and helpful as possible for users. You'll be fully capable of doing this with the concepts you'll read in this book.

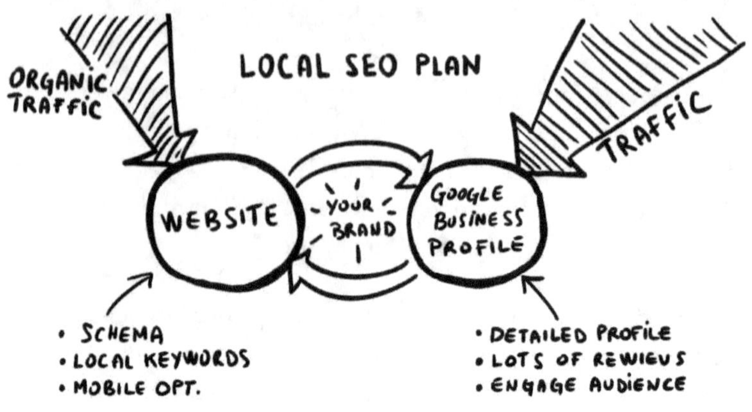

Aside from completing your profile (with texts, services, products, photos, and contacts) and linking your business to the website, a very important element for this type of platform is user reviews. The more reviews you have, the more credible your business will be in the eyes of the search engine and the people reading your profile.

More reviews mean higher rankings and greater visibility on the map that the search engine shows to users. Therefore, consider organizing a process that encourages the collection of positive reviews, as these will further boost your project.

Your goals remain the same: increase the visibility of your business to users with local search intent, increase traffic and therefore conversions, and gain positive reviews. This process, applied in a loop, fuels local SEO and allows you to stand out from your local competitors, capturing an ever-larger share of the market.

But as you may have noticed from the previous image, local SEO goes beyond just using a Google Business profile. Your website also plays an important role and needs to be optimized for local searches. *And how do you do that?*

First, you'll need to conduct keyword research focused on local search intent. Then, create content that makes effective use of the important keywords found and related to your area. Make extensive and proper use of "schema" tags, which are very useful for guiding crawlers to the local content of your pages. I don't even need to mention that your website must be perfectly optimized for mobile, as these searches are predominantly conducted on smartphones.

Since mobile search is currently dominant and closely linked to this type of search intent, it becomes essential for anyone with a local business to create and optimize their business profile to gain visibility and capture that search traffic. Try using the service yourself. Once you see the businesses on the map, ask yourself:

- Is there one particular business that catches your attention?
- Why?
- What do you see in that profile that works?
- Perhaps it's the images, the reviews, or the responses to user questions?

Explore, take notes, and apply what you think could work.

In simple terms, you've probably discovered that if your business or project has a physical presence rather than just a digital one and is thus suitable for this tool, you'll need to invest some of your resources in a local SEO strategy.

This involves working on your Google Business profile while also providing elements on your website that support local ranking.

Section 5: Links

A crucial ranking factor for resources on the web

The second most decisive ranking factor for search engines are *links*. Let's talk about it generally, and then we'll dive into the details.

You already know that, in Google's eyes, a website that is linked to by many other sites—meaning it has many inbound links—holds great value. However, unlike in the early days of search engines, the number of links is no longer the only factor to consider. Nowadays, what's decisive is not the quantity but the quality of the links a website receives.

Thus, a link from a highly authoritative website will carry more value to the search engine than 5, 10, or even 100 links from low-authority sites. Low-quality links from poor-quality websites can actually negatively impact your ranking.

The search engine algorithm that calculates the value of links is called "PageRank," often abbreviated as PR, which indicates the value assigned by the algorithm to a webpage. The higher the page's value, the higher its PR, also known as *link juice*. For example, a page with PR3 is less important than one with PR9.

> *'Pagerank'* is nothing more than the value that determines the "rank" position of "pages" in SERP results. PageRank, often called 'link juice', is transmitted from one page to another through links and measures the importance of a page in the eyes of Google.

As you explore this topic of page value, you will often read about the concept of *'link juice'*.

> *'Link juice'* is a term used to describe how much influence one link has over another. For example, a link from a PR7 website is said to have more 'juice' (value) than one from a PR2 site.

As a result, the links to your website should be of high quality, thematic (meaning connected to the topic), and from highly authoritative sites. When I talk about thematic links, I mean that if your website is about "paintings," a thematic link could come from an art gallery's website, an art magazine's website, an art and painting blog, or a website reviewing artworks. A link, for instance, from a website in South Africa, in Korean, discussing how to make a traditional dish from Madagascar, is clearly not a thematic link relevant to your website about "paintings."

Since the web universe, made up of websites, is built around links, and there are various types of links, we need to dive deeper into the specific categories of them.

The world wide web is built around links and made up of websites; since there are various types of links, we need to dive deeper into their specific categories.

Backlink

Backlinks, or *inbound links*, are extremely famous and a source of endless discussions. These are all the links from other websites that point to your website, directing visitors who click on them toward you.

Google has always considered the quantity of external links to be of primary importance. In fact, this was the innovative idea that set it apart from the competition and helped it become the most widely used search engine on the web.

But today, the search engine is increasingly focused on the quality of these links. In the past, to rank well in the SERP, it was enough to create 10,000 links (clearly using a bot and not manually) through forum comments, directories, or low-authority foreign sites, just to boost the numbers. This *modus operandi* was sufficient for an efficient SEO strategy.

However, with the development of various algorithms that improved the analysis of link origins, this practice has become not only ineffective but also potentially harmful to sites that used it.

Now, any link you receive is thoroughly analyzed by the search engine to understand its origin and authority and thus determine the "weight" it contributes to your ranking.

The theory behind the "link system" is quite simple: if a website includes a link to your website within its content, it means that it finds one of your pieces of content so interesting that it wants to share, cite, or reference it for its visitors. It's as if the website linking to you is giving your website a "vote."

For the search engine, the fact that one or many other sites "trust" your content and "vote" for it is an important quality indicator considered by its algorithms.

There are dozens of ways to perform *link building*, but the various techniques, despite their diversity, complexity, and cost, can be broadly divided into two categories.

- Purchased or exchanged links
- Free or organic links

"Link building" is the set of processes and techniques aimed at creating external links that point to the pages of another website to increase its authority.

Guess what? Those with a big budget, buy links. Here's how the system typically works:

First, you conduct research to understand your target audience. The target audience consists of the users who will read your content and whom you should already know from your market research. Once you identify who you want to reach—those interested in your topics—you're halfway there.

Next, with a clear understanding of your target, you look for the authoritative sites that are the most well-known, visited, and frequented by the people you want to reach.

You can approach this in terms of people and target demographics or by topics, seeking sites that cover topics complementary or similar to those on your site.

In simple terms, it's a new kind of market research. At this point, you need to contact the sites you've identified and propose a collaboration.

You could simply offer to write an article for free—something interesting and of great value for their site—in exchange for including a link to your website within the content of the article you write. In this case, it would be a fair exchange if the link's value is proportional to the quality of the article provided.

Alternatively, you might offer to do the same thing—provide a pre-written or ready-to-use article—but also pay a fee. This would be a paid guest post.

A small note on these link exchange practices:

Links have an attribute called "rel," which can have values such as "nofollow" or "follow," among others, to indicate to the search engine how to treat the link in terms of ranking calculations. We'll discuss this in more detail later, but it's good to introduce these concepts now.

For example, the "rel=nofollow" attribute tells Google that the link's destination page should not be considered for ranking, crawling, or inclusion in the index.

The rel="sponsored" attribute indicates to the search engine, with even more precision, that the link is a nofollow link and has been paid for or is a result of a sponsorship.

The rel="ugc" attribute signifies that the link was inserted by a user, such as in a comment.

The 'follow' link is clearly the most valuable. Not only does it bring referral traffic to your website, but it also indicates that the link was placed organically within the content, and that the destination is authoritative, thereby passing on *link juice* to the page and being considered for crawling and ranking purposes.

The second method for obtaining links is based on a different concept, and it's the one I use in most cases. I often can't afford to spend time on extensive link-building techniques, and, of course, I avoid black-hat tactics. Instead, I always rely on a foundation of "excellent content," and you'll understand why soon.

> The terms "*White Hat*" and "*Black Hat*" are used to describe, respectively, ethical and legitimate techniques or intentions (white) and their opposite (black). It's similar to referring to white magic and black magic.

The starting assumption is that you don't buy links. If a website links to you, it means they've found interesting content or a valuable resource for their audience; thus, they wanted to share it.

Therefore, according to this philosophy, the solution to obtaining links is simply to provide content and resources that are interesting and valuable to users. This ties back to the "content is king" concept regarding the importance of content. If you do a good job and create valuable content, it will naturally and passively attract links from other sites. In the vastness of the web, other website owners will find your content and link to you. Others will discover your content and share your pages on their blogs or social media. In all this, nothing is forced; everything is organic and natural.

The downside? Clearly, it's the time factor. This strategy is quite slow, and if you want to grow quickly, it may not be the best fit for your needs.

The upside? First of all, you don't pay for any links; thus, your link-building budget is zero, allowing you to allocate all of your resources to content creation. Secondly, since this technique is entirely "white hat," you're protected from potential penalties imposed by algorithms that detect unnaturally generated links. All your incoming links would be organic and therefore 100% safe.

Every link also consists of two different components beyond its technical characteristics: "link trust" and "link power." A link with high "link trust" comes from highly authoritative sites, such as university or government sites. On the other hand, a link with high "link power" comes from a very significant page within a website, such as a homepage.

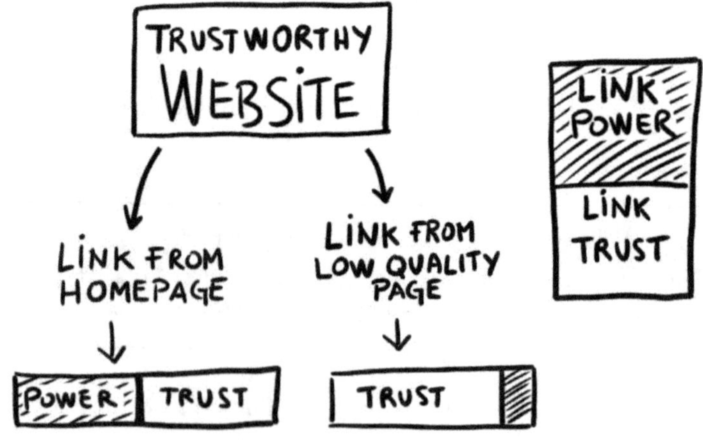

Keep these concepts in mind when someone sends you a link or when you create one yourself; they may appear irrelevant, but they are actually small pieces of knowledge that are important to understand.

How do I obtain links from sites with very high PR? I use a simple technique for this. I use Wikipedia, which is perhaps the most authoritative website for Google after Google itself (Wikipedia has a PR9 if I remember correctly).

So sign into Wikipedia as a user and get the permission to edit the published entries. Wikipedia is a free encyclopedia, so you can do this. Find a Wikipedia entry that you've also written about on your blog and dedicated an article or page to.

Read the content and identify something that can be expanded. Research the missing information, add it to your blog article, and then include it in the Wikipedia page. By doing this, your changes will likely be approved, as they add value and information (which should, of course, be accurate) to the original article and you can highlight the addition by including a link to the original source (your website). That is where your link will come from—the most authoritative source on the web.

If you're building a new website and don't know how to tackle the issue of authority, remember this: Google must consider small and new websites as well, so it does not only reward authoritative sites because authority is built over time with significant and consistent resources.

First and foremost, think of a link strategy based on creating high-quality content. Then you might use advertisements to drive traffic to this content while also retaining users by placing them in a funnel and allowing you to send them additional published content.

Now we'll talk about external links, including their functionality and weight. External links send visitors from your website to another site. In other words, they direct the visitor away from your site.

If your website is "A" and it has a page with a link directing users to website "B," that's an external link. If you link from "A" to "A1" on the same website, it's an internal link.

A link coming to your website "A" from website "B" is a backlink (or inbound link), which, in simple terms, is the opposite of external links.

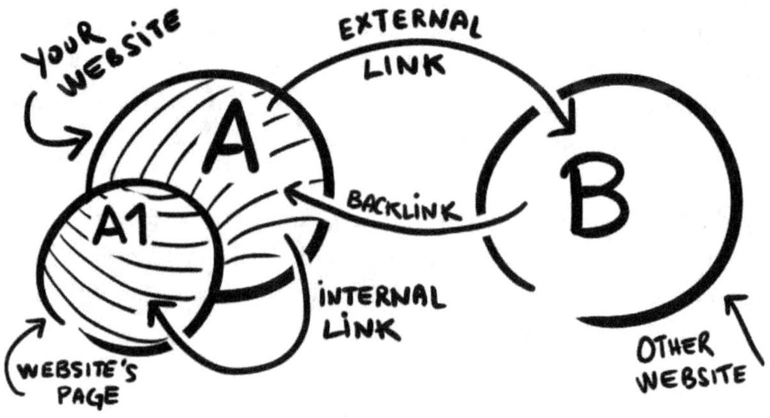

In the metaphor of the imaginary city, a user clicking an external link is like a person whom you direct to another place to find something specific that you don't have in your store.

Why use external links? These links are what created "the internet" and formed the structure of the web. They are simply the connections between different websites. External links are used in everyday life, specifically by those who write online content or create websites, to guide users to other resources.

Remember, we've said that linking externally should be a controlled practice to avoid risking your link juice. However, if we pause and consider this from a broader perspective, we can have some interesting thoughts.

What is important for the search engine? Definitely providing value to its users by helping them find the best content from the most authoritative sources. So, let's say a search engine user lands on your page, reads useful information, and then finds a link that you have intentionally placed, which leads them to another website where they can further explore the topic you've covered.

Maybe they find additional details, or perhaps you mentioned a regulation and provided a link to the full law on an official website. *Do you think this adds value to the user's experience?* I'd say yes. *Do you think you're improving their experience?* I'd say yes.

Therefore, from all this, it can be inferred that linking to external sites impacts ranking and thus the positioning of your pages. However, be cautious: linking to a highly authoritative institutional website is very different from linking to less reputable sites. Moreover, placing one external link in a 3,000-word article is different from placing one in a 200-word article (do you still write 200-word articles?) or adding 25 links in a single 3,000-word article.

The external links you include in your articles must make logical sense. They should be a natural extension of a topic and, of course, should be organically integrated into a context of original and valuable content.

External links increase the reputation of the sites they point to and provide search engines with significant clues about the content of the page they are present on.

In addition to establishing the relevance of your content, they can help identify the topic or precise niche. Let's say you're writing an article on "the best anti-cholesterol diet." In your content, you reference a recent scientific study and include an external link to the official website of the university that conducted the research. On that website, which is not yours, your user can find more details about the study. So, in addition to providing valuable content to your user, you're offering the search engine a clear signal to help understand the problem you're addressing in your article.

All of these actions build trust between your website and the search engine. The search engine sees that you're creating links to authoritative content and, as a result, trusts your content more.

Therefore, if you have the opportunity to organically include a link in your content that somehow supports the topic you're addressing and provides value to the reader, do it.

Also consider whether it's worth taking the resource you're linking to and using it as a reference for a dedicated page within your own website rather than linking externally. Perhaps you have the opportunity to improve that content and integrate it into the hierarchy of your website. This way, you can keep the user on your website, with all the associated benefits. Evaluate each case, as this solution isn't always feasible.

If you're linking to an external resource, consider setting the link to open in a new tab or window instead of loading over your site. This way, the user doesn't leave your website but opens another one while keeping yours open as well.

This practice can also encourage collaborations between different websites. When other sites notice external links coming from you, they might want to reciprocate (naturally, of course). It can create a loop of ranking benefits, as a user who was directed to a valuable resource by you and then returns to your website gives a strong signal of mutual trust to the search engine.

Internal Links

If external links play a significant role in determining a website's authority, *internal links* are just as important.

To approach the topic, let's define exactly what internal links are. An internal link is a link from one page of your website that directs the user to another page, also within your site.

In the city metaphor, a user clicking an internal link is like someone in your store being guided by you to another department or being directed down a hallway that leads to other rooms without leaving your store.

Often, you'll come across websites that don't have a clear strategy for using internal links. This aspect is frequently underestimated, which is a serious mistake. If you're investing a lot of energy into creating an external link strategy, you should put just as much effort into an internal link strategy, as the search engine's crawler relies on the internal link structure to determine the hierarchy of your pages.

Linking the pages of your website to other pages within the same website and doing so in a logical, intelligent, and useful way is first and foremost a great opportunity that you can't afford to miss. It enhances the accessibility of your content for users and clarifies your site's structure for search engines.

As you may have already realized, happier users will visit more pages, and the search engine will detect a lower *bounce rate*, which in turn boosts the ranking of your website and its individual pages.

Now, let's set aside the topic of users for a moment. The pages of a website with a well-thought-out and well-implemented internal linking strategy are indexed better and more frequently by search engine crawlers. You should always keep in mind that each link passes some *link juice* to the destination page, which contributes to determining the Page Rank (PR) of the pages.

For example, if page "A" links to page "B," for Google, "A" is passing some of its value to "B." But knowing this, *what is the best way to create and organize links?*

First, you need to think in terms of contextualization and user experience. Let's say you're writing an article on a topic and, within the text, you introduce another topic already covered in a separate article or page. In this case, you can create a link to that page, a contextualized link. A user interested in exploring the topic further would then have the opportunity to do so.

Secondly, when creating and organizing internal links, you should ask yourself: *What are the most important pages on my site? Which articles do I want my users to spend time reading, understanding, and perhaps taking further action on?*

Usually, these are the pages targeting the keywords with the highest search volume. Once you've identified them, you need to organize your internal links so that the most relevant pages receive a higher number of internal links compared to less important ones.

Do you think it is a good idea to link to your homepage from all your website pages? Usually, if you use Wordpress, you already have the image in the header (the logo, basically) pointing to the homepage, or at most you could put a 'home' button in the menu. The homepage is essential but not the most important page.

Moreover, the homepage is often not the most read page. It is usually not even the page where an organic user lands. An organic user should land on the article or on a landing page, any resource created specifically to answer his question. Linking to a page directly from the home page, on the other hand, is a simple way to get it indexed faster because the crawler landing on the home page first checks and follows all the links it finds on the home page.

Think instead of linking to the most relevant pages or even the most significant categories— pages we call HUBs. An article or page within a category must always have a link to its parent category. A category page, HUB content, must always link to the articles below it.

Be wary of links between articles in various categories. You must always maintain as much valuable PR as possible within the same category; otherwise, it will be dispersed.

So linking is fine, but not randomly. For further ways to control linking, the rel attribute we mentioned earlier can help. So, in theory, to link from page "A" to page "Z," I could use a 'nofollow' link to avoid passing link juice. Whereas to link from "A" to an "A2" page, I could use a normal 'follow'. This is a theory, because in practice the story is different.

There are two different schools of thought on this subject. Others believe that link juice should be free to flow throughout the site's pages, as opposed to those who believe it should be stored and maintained within certain closed categories. Personally, years ago, I was comfortable with the second method, which was a normal consequence of the 'Silo' strategy we will discuss in a moment. However, more recently, on some sites, I removed the link restrictions and noticed that despite letting the link juice flow freely inside (note that I wrote inside and not outside), the results were still very good.

Last note on internal links, from the perspective of user experience. If a user is on page "A" but wants to get to page "D," they should be able to find a link that takes them from A > D instead of a path like A>B>C>D. The less the user travels to find what they are looking for, the better.

Anchor Text

There are some standard concepts for creating effective and SEO-optimized links —links that are actually statistically more clicked by users and at the same time follow the guidelines of search engines. These standard rules apply to all types of links, both external and internal, which we will see in a moment.

One of the concepts to be explored is *anchor text*. Nothing complicated, anchor text is simply clickable text that once clicked on takes the user to another page or resource on the web. This text is usually underlined or coloured differently than the content text, so that it stands out from the surrounding content and makes the user realize that it is a clickable link. This is why it is also called 'link text'.

Why is anchor text important? From a user's point of view simply because if an anchor is done well, it informs the visitor in advance about what they will find after clicking on it. From a search engine's point of view, on the other hand, a well-made anchor helps the crawler understand the topic of the linked page.

So you have to consider the design and writing of anchor text among the top priorities when it comes to optimizing content for search engines. As previously said, any SEO expert must carefully evaluate the texts that form the content of web pages.

To create effective anchor text, you need a precise pattern to follow step by step every time you need to create a link to another page or resource within your content.

1) Before even creating the link, you must be sure you have established the context for the reader. Then write a sentence introducing the topic. (For example, 'Accessibility is an increasingly important aspect for websites.')
2) Then insert the anchor text, which must not only be relevant to the subject matter and context but must stimulate clicking without interrupting the flow of reading. (E.g., 'This insight into the "alt" attribute in images...')

3) Finally, you must close the sentence by ensuring that the link test is harmoniously integrated into the sentence and by providing, if possible, an additional 'benefit' for a clicker or crawler wanting even more information. (For example, '..explain how you can make your content more accessible to all users, including those with visual disabilities.')

Here is the full example where you find the anchor text within the [ ]:

- "Accessibility is an increasingly important aspect for websites; [This insight into the 'alt' attribute in images] explains how you can make your content more accessible to all users, including those with visual disabilities."

To summarize, the key concepts are that the anchor text should be relevant to the context, related to the target page's content, informative, brief and clear, and effectively integrated into the text so that it does not disrupt the reading flow.

Here is another different example with always the anchor text within the [ ].

- "With artificial intelligence, you can generate as many images as you want. But to understand how to make them more visible on search engines, I recommend reading this [guide on image optimization]; it will help you make your images more optimized in order to improve their ranking."

I hope what I intend to teach you is clear enough. Then, just as a matter of culture, you should know that anchor texts are categorized into different types. You don't have to focus on learning these categories by heart; you just have to focus on knowing the key concepts described earlier.

However, the categories are these:

- **Exact match**: it is an anchor text that corresponds exactly to the keyword that the landing page is targeting.
- **Partial match**: similar to the previous one but with more descriptive words to give more context.

- **'Related'** links to the target page using synonyms or related terms to the keyword on which the page is built.

- **Generic anchor texts** are the classic non-descriptive links such as "Click here" or "View more." They have low SEO value by not providing any kind of useful information.

- **Branded** anchor texts are texts that only contain the name of a brand and no other words. They are usually used to link to a resource on a corporate website.

- **Compound** anchor texts are similar to the previous one but also contain other words besides the brand in order to better describe the link.

- **Naked** anchor texts are texts that correspond to the URL of the page they link to.

- **'Image anchor text'** is simply the text written in the "alt" attribute of an image and which takes the place of the link text.

- **'Title anchors'** are the clickable texts that correspond exactly to the title of a page or article being linked to. They are common, e.g., when using plug-ins of the 'related content' type.

Therefore, as links are fundamental on the web and also a primary ranking factor, the text forming them is also fundamental for crawling, user experience, and accessibility to pages and content.

Links quality VS quantity

Have I already said that not all links carry equal weight in the eyes of Google? I think so. But in this case I am not talking about the 'rel' attribute, which we talked about a little while ago. I'm referring to another factor that was mentioned earlier: PR (page rank).

Getting one link from a high-PR website has a much greater effect than acquiring ten links from low-PR sites.

For example, let's say you get 2 links from a PR9 site. These are worth a lot more than 10 links from 10 PR1 sites. Considering this non-linear proportion, if you needed 500 incoming links to get PR3 on your website, it is likely that you would need not just 500 more links but many more links of equivalent value to get to PR4.

So, when you create a link, be aware that you are not only giving authority to the website you are linking to, but you are also passing some of the link juice from your page to the linked page.

When creating links to external sites, it is crucial to carefully consider the attribution of the 'follow' value, which, as you know, tells search engines to follow the link and transfer some of the authority of your page to the target page.

Therefore, use 'nofollow' for external links to sites you are not completely sure about or do not want to actively support. Conversely, internal links (within your own site) play a crucial role in the distribution of authority within your pages.

The more internal links point to a specific page, the more value search engines will assign to that page. When it comes to internal links, let the link juice flow freely within the website without any special attributes and rather focus on the number of internal links a page receives.

Section 6: Website structure

How to engineer a website properly

A fundamental part of engineering a website, which is very often underestimated, is organizing its structure.

I am talking about the structure of the website itself, i.e., how you structure the page hierarchy, organize the categories, and group the articles or pages. I am talking about how you lay the bricks that will form your castle according to a plan, not at random. Everything must be well planned and organized in a specific way, but above all, everything must be simple and understandable.

To make sure you understand it well and as quickly as possible, I should give you the classic example of jars full of colored balls (if you search the web, you will find it). I have modified it to make it even more specific by using geometric shapes.

In the first example, your website is one big jar containing many different shapes. There are triangles, squares, and circles, each different in shape and size. Each shape represents a page on a different topic and therefore with a different keyword. The different sizes, on the other hand, represent different keyword volumes. So, if one square is twice the size of another, it has twice the search volume.

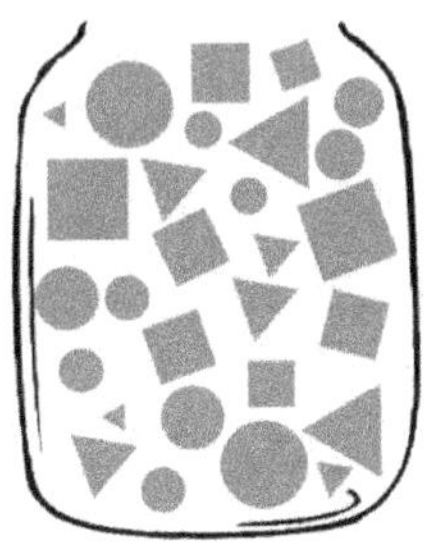

In the second example, your website is made up of multiple jars, each containing only shapes of a specific type.

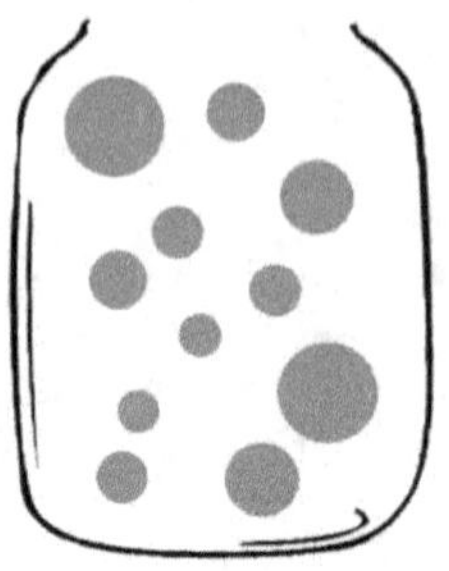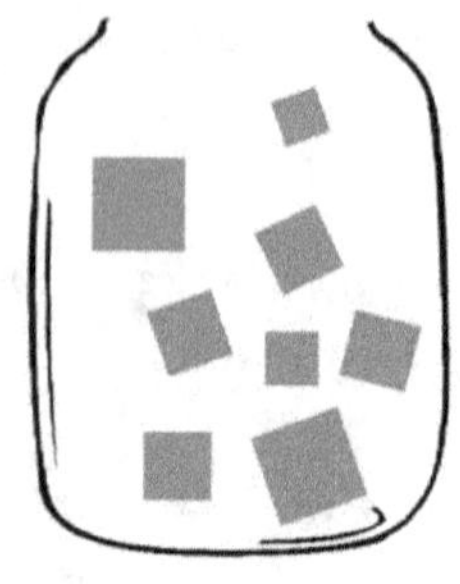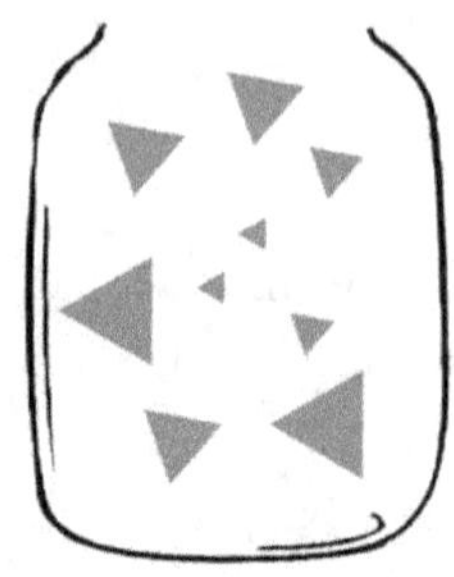

In this second example, pages or articles on the same topic are placed in the same jar, within the same category, which becomes a resource container that we can also call a *"hub."*

In the third example, however, each geometric shape of the same type is placed in the same jar but also arranged in a hierarchy, where the largest one is at the top. In other words, the pages with more volume (parent) will contain those with less volume beneath them (child).

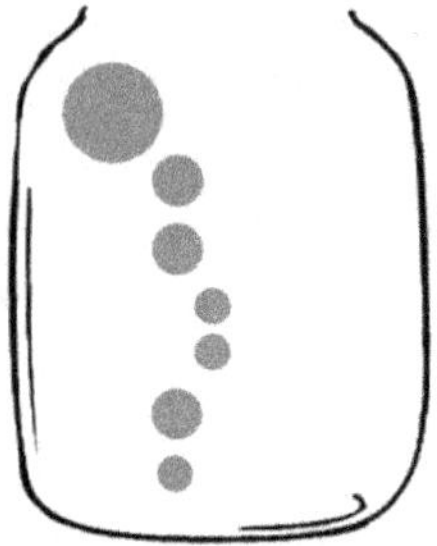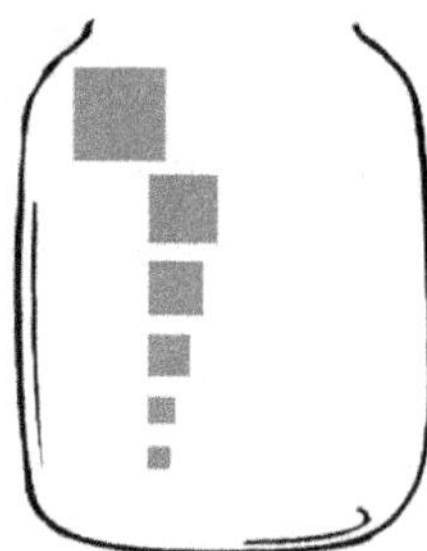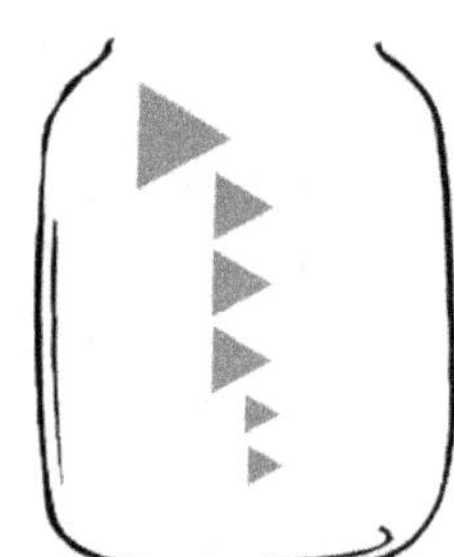

I think it's obvious that, in the first case, articles, pages, and resources will be thrown together without any clear order. It reminds me of my son's toy basket, where you can find everything from puzzles to toy cars to Lego pieces (I've actually taught him to organize his Lego in separate bins). Instead, in the second case, the articles are much better organized, divided into thematic categories, and with a clear hierarchy.

This structure, called a "SILO" structure, similar to the silos used to store grain, is optimal both from a user perspective, who quickly finds the information they're looking for, and from the perspective of a search engine crawler, who comes to analyze your website and finds it super organized.

The first thing the crawler will encounter is the website structure, which it may read from the sitemap. By analyzing it, the crawler will assess the entire structure, and if it finds it logical, clear, simple, and well-organized, it will have an easier time indexing pages, content, and topics, pushing your pages higher in the SERPs.

Moreover, such a clear structure from the start will help you maintain a precise organizational scheme. As time goes on and your website contains an increasing amount of content, it will be easier for you to keep everything in order and maintain a clear structure. You'll be able to organize numerous articles within the categories you've created. At first, there may be only a few, but later they could grow into dozens upon dozens of categories or subcategories.

The initial conditions of the site's structure are fundamental designing, and implementing before a project begins, especially if the project is complex.

If the initial conditions are not perfect and you haven't thoroughly studied the categories, structure, keywords, and their volumes, you'll face problems down the road.

The cause? The action of entropy, which, like everything else, operates in digital space, increases complexity, difficulties, chaos, and errors as time passes and the project grows. It's better to spend time planning well before starting a project than to spend twice as much time later solving problems. You wouldn't build a 50-floor skyscraper without a plan.

How should you organize the site's categories and pages? Check your market research file, the tab where you created all the keyword groups. You already have the entire website structure ready to be built.

Basic pages

Search engines give particular importance to certain key pages of your website. I'm not talking about the pages you create specifically for one or more keywords, which are crucial as they generate most of the traffic you receive.

Every website, whether it provides information or sells products or services, should mandatorily include some basic pages.

For example, consider the "About Us" page, which does not have necessarily to be called that. It's a page, which can be very simple, where you introduce the visitors to the people or company behind the domain or service being offered. This helps inform users about who "owns" the website they are visiting or who authored the articles they are reading. It's a matter of trust and transparency.

A "Privacy Policy" page, which describes the privacy policy in effect on the website, is also essential if you are asking for personal data from users, such as through a contact form.

A "Cookie" page, which could also be incorporated into the privacy policy, explains the types of cookies used on the website, what is installed on the user's browser, their purpose, expiration, and all the information that current regulations require to be disclosed.

A "Terms and Conditions" page is also essential, especially if your website includes an eCommerce platform where users input data or make purchases. This page should clearly outline the terms and conditions of using your service, including warranties, right of withdrawal, and other relevant details.

All these pages, when present, well-organized, and written in simple language, provide users with clear information and simultaneously reassure them by explaining who you are, how your service or product works, and what they can expect from you. The absence of these pages is a red flag for search engines, especially in the case of a manual review, and can lower the perceived quality of your site. If these pages are missing, users and visitors should be concerned, questioning the site's reliability, and may decide to visit more trustworthy or transparent sites with this kind of "basic" information.

Search engines are primarily focused on clarity and guarantees for users. So, you must always ensure that you provide this information, as it's good for both your visitors and the search engine.

Perhaps you don't yet have a "Privacy Policy" page, a "Contact" page, an "About Us" page, a "Disclaimer" page, or, if you run a store, a "Terms and Conditions" page. If that's the case, add them right away!

Location

We've discussed many factors that influence good rankings, and location is an interesting parameter, especially for certain types of searches. Location refers to the place from which a search is made.

By place, I don't mean whether the user performed the search from their kitchen or bathroom; I'm talking about the geographical location, the physical position of the user.

You've probably already noticed that when you search for "pizzeria" on Google, the search results show the pizzerias closest to you first. This search term is a classic example of a "VISIT IN PERSON QUERY," which we mentioned earlier, where location plays a significant role. In these cases, location often takes priority over other ranking factors like website content or backlinks. This type of search is also known as "search with local intent."

But how does the search engine determine which results to show based on your location? It uses several factors, with the primary one being the GPS localization of the search. You've likely encountered a prompt asking you to share your location for better results—that's exactly what this is for.

So, if I search for "Seafood restaurant Venice" and I'm currently located in Venice, Italy, the search results will indeed show restaurants from Venice.

Secondly, some on-page factors come into play—factors implemented directly on the website's pages, which we have more control over.

One of these factors is, of course, the content, specifically the location mentioned in it. If your page is optimized for the keyword "Seafood restaurant Venice," it means the title will contain the keyword, as will the content, headings, images, etc. The search engine will then detect a certain relevance between the content and the "location intent query."
The KPIs of the SERP itself will provide the search engine with useful information on whether the results and information associated with search intent queries are correct or not.

For example, if the mayor in your city is called 'Richard Cooper', the engine will see that results that actually relate to the mayor of your city will have a much better CTR and other KPIs (time on page, bounce rate) than other results that perhaps relate to a person with the same name but from another city. These KPIs will help the search engine understand the intention behind the user's search and provide it with better results when it realizes that location matters.

Speaking of KPIs, if you're working on a client's project, align your KPIs with theirs. That way, you are sure that you will consider the same things when measuring the success of your campaigns or your SEO strategy.

The other factors that the search engine considers will be fished from as many sources as possible. They can be, for example, the address on the contact page or in the footer of your website pages, if you have included it. Alternatively, consider your social media pages and the addresses you've associated with them. But also your business profile, which, as we've seen, you can create using the 'Google Business Profile' service and attach the address to your website. The engine will then simply cross-reference information until it decides the relevancy of your content to these specific keywords with 'location intent'.

In all this you can understand that if you are at point "A" in your city and you search for 'nearby hardware store', and the nearest hardware store is 60 meters away from your location, Google will put this result at the top of the SERP (or show it on a map in SERP) and it will be impossible for you to overtake it in SERP for that type of search.

This is clear, because distance matters enormously with a query of that kind, and therefore you cannot do anything about it, even if you have super-optimised pages for the keyword 'nearby hardware store'. To intercept this traffic, consider creating a properly optimized Google Business Profile.

Content quality VS quantity

Let's imagine we're going to write some content and want to optimize it for a specific keyword.

Of all the pages on the web that contain that keyword, *which ones are the most valuable in the eyes of the search engine? Which ones have the most relevant information and are most valuable in the search engine's view?* We know that Google takes users' queries and provides them with these pages by taking them from its ecosystem of services and proposing them to users in formats ideal to their search intent.

But how do I know if my content is good? The mantra is that content is good when it is tailored to your audience and solves their needs. The search engine can only assess the quality of the page according to its purpose.

Since there is 'audience' in this equation, it goes without saying that it is crucial to know your audience and speak their language. And remember how we spoke about creating the 'buyer persona' in the first part of the book?

What follows is a list of parameters that, in my opinion, are fundamental for establishing the quality of a page and its content. The following is a checklist to always keep in mind:

- ☐ Is the page fast?
- ☐ Does the writing style create interest?
- ☐ Does the page have a clear structure?
- ☐ Does it solve the audience problem?
- ☐ Does it speak to your target audience or to a buyer persona?
- ☐ Does it speak using the right language for your audience?
- ☐ Does it have links to other related content?
- ☐ Does it cite authoritative sources?
- ☐ Does it make the content usable in multiple formats?
- ☐ Is the website manicured?
- ☐ Is the content comprehensive, precise, clear, and SEO-optimized?

Most of these parameters are verifiable directly by Google and thus become of great importance to you as well.

Even more crucial are the contents of sites in specific categories, which Google refers to as YMYL (Your Money or Your Life). Google raises the bar even higher for sites or pages deemed to have a possible influence on people's security (financial or health), demanding greater quality in all aspects.

First, the search engine requires that the website be linked by a large number of other websites in order to be considered authoritative. It also requires authoritative content authors, including biographies, photographs, and links to LinkedIn pages or professional publications.

In these cases, Google will be even more finicky with only one objective: to increase the level of 'E-E-A-T' (experience, expertise, authoritativeness and trustworthiness) of the page it proposes to its users. This concept will be discussed later.

URLs

URLs, as you know, are nothing more than the address of the website or web pages. I could have mentioned them earlier, but I included them after the chapter on website structure because they are closely connected with the page hierarchy and, thus, with the "silo" structure.

This is an example URL with all its components:

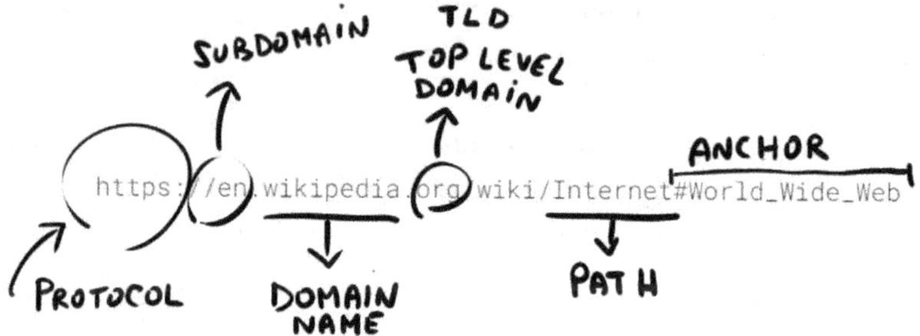

I have also already mentioned the importance the search engine attaches to web addresses containing the subject keyword.

The importance of writing URLs is true for the website address, but also applies to all internal pages, and to categories, including 'hubs', those containing a lot of content.

> 'URL' is short for "Universal Resource Locator" and is the address of a page on the web.

After reading the theory, the practice follows: the URLs of your entire website must be meticulously maintained. All of the addresses for the website's pages or categories must be selected and written with the understanding that they are vital for indexing and thus for SEO.

This is quite simple to do because all CMSs, including Wordpress, allow you to customize page URLs. Again, you will naturally optimize this over time because CMSs frequently create URLs that are nothing more than the title of the page or article you are creating.

Let's say you are writing an article about the 'Best beaches in Sardinia'. So, the string 'best beaches in Sardinia' is your *'long keyword'*.

The URL of your web page, in this case, must be:
`/best-beaches-in-sardinia`

It could also be a slightly shorter URL, such as:
`/best-beaches-sardinia`

Or it could be a URL to which you added the extension at the end, which is still a good solution:
`/best-beaches-in-sardinia.html`

Note that you can set up these URL settings, if you use Wordpress, in the permalink settings section.

It is not a bad thing to put the extension at the end because it is 'convenient' for the engine to know what type of page it is analyzing and offering to its users. By providing it with the information in the address, all you're doing is 'helping it understand' and increase the *trust* in your pages. You may, however, choose not to put the extension in for aesthetic reasons to keep the length to a minimum.

The theory and practice we are analyzing, which allows you to rename pages according to the keywords you are considering, also applies to categories.

The difference is that if each page deals with a single keyword, a category should 'contain' all the keywords in that category.

So, using the example from before, the category containing the article about the most beautiful beaches could be `/beaches-sardinia/`. This should be the category, the 'HUB' page. Inside, there should be a very long article of the type `/best-beaches-in-sardinia/` along with all the specific pages of the individual beaches throughout the island.

The thing you have to check is that the category name also corresponds to a keyword and that it is a keyword with very high volume. All this information should have been planned during the keyword research you have done.

Articles and pages handle the smaller volume; categories handle the larger ones. When I have grouped all the keywords into a group, as explained in the chapter on keyword analysis, I almost always select the keyword with the highest volume in the group and choose it as the category.

In fact, in the content of the category page `/beaches-sardinia/` (which focuses on a keyword with a high search volume), you can still use all the keywords with a lower volume related to the keyword 'beaches Sardinia'. You will then think about creating content specific to the individual beaches in articles contained within the category. In this way, you can intercept all the traffic volume in a transversal manner while maintaining the link juice within the HUB category.

In this way you create a hierarchy of content, and, later on, this hierarchy will also create a hierarchy of links, as I explained when we talked about internal website links.

When it comes to URLs, it's immediately clear what mistakes are being made because all you have to do is look at the address bar to see if a correct method has been used.

Surely a mistake is to leave the date in the URL, for instance:

`/2019/12/27/best-beaches-in-sardinia/`

Leaving the date may, unwillingly, confuse the engine's algorithm. In fact, you might think that the content refers to that date, whereas what you want to do is provide content that is always valid over time, possibly that is 'evergreen'. If you have to include a date, put it in the article.
Also, if you have dynamic URLs (e.g., `/page.php?id=32`), it is much better to turn them into static URLs so that you can include keywords as well as facilitate memorization, reading, and sharing by your audience.

In any case, a URL that's too long or filled with elements like dates isn't user-friendly, so it's best to avoid that.

One last interesting thing to mention about URLs: when Google scans pages it finds on the web, it doesn't take all the URLs it encounters. Some can be ignored because they are specifically discouraged by its guidelines.

These are the discouraged types of URLs:

1. URLs that use non-ASCII characters
2. URLs with special characters
3. URLs that use underscores (_)
4. URLs that contain long, unreadable ID numbers
5. URLs with words merged together (e.g., `/beachessardinia`)

Points 3 and 5 refer to a guideline that standardizes how pages are created. Stick to these standards as search engines rely on them and prefer them because they make their work easier.

Publishing new content

Let's say you've written all of the pages you needed to and finished the content creation part of your website. If you've done a good job building your online ecosystem, you're now in a phase of apparent calm.

When you have a blog with at least the first 40 perfectly written articles, designed according to the standards I've explained, you're in an ideal situation. I mentioned 40 articles, but it could even be fewer. Even 10 pages can be enough to generate a significant amount of traffic—it always depends on the topic's volume and competition.

While waiting for the search engines to index the hard work you've done in content creation (and we'll see later how to help the search engines with this), you can plan the creation of additional new content.

Keep in mind that the content of a brand-new blog usually takes months to be properly indexed and rank well in the SERPs. Knowing this, before investing time and resources into creating new content, you might want to take a moment to monitor the traffic performance of the current content on your site. Ask yourself some questions:

- How many visits is the website gaining every week?
- What behavior do the visitors exhibit?
- Are they finding what they're looking for?
- Do they stay and read, or leave immediately?
- Are they having a good overall experience?
- Are there already conversions?

All of this information, which you gather in the first few weeks or months after launching your website, is quite useful in determining if you're on the right track or if you need to make changes at various levels of your marketing approach.

Keep in mind that if everything is going well and you want to further improve your KPIs, you'll either need to enhance the existing content or write new content. For my websites, I publish at least one new piece of content every week, but everyone should design their editorial plan and publication rhythm based on their available resources.

If you have a larger budget for content creation, you could even have a higher publication frequency, like one article a day. The more content you publish while sticking to the frameworks and guidelines I've described, the more traffic you'll automatically gain, as your content will be indexed well.

However, if you're thinking of climbing the SERPs by publishing five 200-word articles per day, just know that it doesn't work like that.

Content Update and Removal

Another often underestimated aspect is content updating. In fact, more importance is usually placed on creating new content rather than improving the existing and already published material.

Search engines are happy when they find updated articles because they assume that fresh material and new, up-to-date content have been added.

Readers who land on the article are also pleased, as you may have expanded on a topic of interest to them or included the latest updates on the subject.

Updating an article takes very little effort. For example, you can add 1 or 2 paragraphs, perhaps along with 1 or 2 images, even just once a year. This is the bare minimum to consider an article "updated." From there, the more updated content you add, the better.

Users arriving on your pages from the search engine should always find the information they are looking for, which means the content must always be up-to-date. After all, user searches will change based on the latest trends in the sector, market, or niche you have chosen. As a result, the content they find must keep up with those changing searches.

Google can tell when a user doesn't find what they're looking for. For instance, if a visitor lands on your page and quickly hits the "back" button on their phone or browser to return to the search results, it's not a good sign for Google. The search engine will label your page as irrelevant for that particular query. Keep in mind that the phone you're using might be an Android device, and the browser might be Chrome, both of which are Google-owned products.

However, there are some types of content that, theoretically, don't require frequent updates. On the other hand, you'll need to update content more frequently if you've written about news, tech products, a guide on constantly updated software, or a process that changes over time—like an article on the best prompts to give an A.I., or similar topics.

The term *"prompt"* in the context of artificial intelligence applications refers to a question, command, or text input that you provide to the language model in order to receive a response or trigger an action.

If, on the other hand, you've written something about the sinking of the Titanic or the dimensions of the Pyramid of Cheops in Giza, those are things that don't change and should always have valid content. These are called *"evergreen"* content, and ideally, you'd want Google to consider all your articles in this way.

The term 'evergreen' conveys the idea of content with constant value.

For example, articles entitled 'Life of Leonardo da Vinci' or 'The Pythagorean Theorem' are evergreen articles because the content once written remains valid forever. The Pythagorean theorem does not change, nor does the story of Leonardo's life. On the other hand, if my article is titled 'The 10 fastest PCs' or 'Ranking the best smartphones under $500', it is obvious that these are articles that will always need to be revised and updated because they do not contain evergreen information.

What if I need to remove indexed content from the engines? It may often happen that you need to remove content, and Google provides a whole series of instructions on how not to show your content in Google searches and elsewhere on the internet. Here are some solutions:

- One way could be to simply remove the content from the website, causing a 404 error.
- Protect the file with a password.
- Use the "`noindex`" rule and put the 'noindex' meta tag (more on this soon) in the robot.txt file.

What about images and videos? Since Google only indexes videos and images that GoogleBot is authorized to crawl, blocking crawling of these resources via the robots.txt would solve the problem.

Section 7: Advanced Concepts

Advanced but necessary tools for building seo-optimized websites

Well, now you know a wide range of fundamental concepts for search engine optimization. As you have seen, SEO is not limited to simply choosing the right keywords. To achieve truly satisfactory results, it is essential to delve into a more complex world of codes, protocols, and specific tools.

In this chapter, we will explore some of the advanced concepts that every professional SEO should know in order to maximize the visibility of their website in search engine results. We will start by analyzing the "robots.txt," a file that acts as a guardian of your website, telling search engine bots which pages can be crawled and which cannot. We will discover how to use this powerful tool to control the indexing of your website and protect restricted areas.

Then we will look at meta tags, those little snippets of HTML code that provide important information to search engines and users. We will learn how to use meta tags to describe page content, manage titles and descriptions that appear in search results, and how the "rel" attribute can be used to specify the type of relationship between the current page and linked pages.

Another fundamental concept is the "canonical." We will understand how this attribute helps avoid duplicate content problems and indicates to search engines which version of a page they consider to be the original.

In addition, we will explore the importance of XML sitemaps, actual directories that guide search engine bots in discovering and indexing your site's pages, and TOCs, tables of content.
Finally, we will address the topic of redirects, explaining how to redirect users from one URL to another and how to use this tool to handle domain changes, website restructurings, and outdated pages.

Through this chapter, you will expand your knowledge even further and take it to a much higher level. Your work will improve accordingly.

Instructing bots

It is essential to know how to instruct bots if you want to manage certain aspects of SEO independently. Independent SEO management requires a solid understanding of the mechanisms that govern the indexing of content by search engines. To this end, you need to know that you can give instructions to bots on 3 different levels: at a **website level** with the Robots.txt file, at a **page level** with the 'Meta' tags, and at the **level of individual elements** within the page with certain parameters, e.g., nofollow.

- Website level (Robots.txt): The Robots.txt file is a standard protocol that allows you to tell search engines which parts of your website can be scanned and indexed and which resources should not be considered. It is like a road sign that tells robots which pages to visit and which to avoid. In this way, you can prevent duplicate content, development areas, or restricted pages from being indexed.

- Page level (meta tags): Meta tags are HTML elements that provide additional information about a page's content, such as title, description, and keywords. These tags offer more granular control than the Robots.txt file, allowing you to optimize each page for specific search queries. For instance, you can specify the most relevant title for a page, create optimized descriptions for snippets in search results, and block crawling with "noindex" tags as well.

- Element level (attributes): Within a page, you can use specific attributes to provide further instructions to search engines on how to treat certain elements. The 'nofollow' attribute, for instance, tells search engines not to follow links within an element, thus avoiding transferring authority to external pages that may potentially not be of quality. Other attributes, such as 'noindex' and 'noarchive', make it possible to prevent an element from being indexed or to prevent a page from being cached.

Let us look at all three of these levels of 'communication' with bots in more detail.

Robots.txt

At the website level, we can instruct the bots via a file called "robots.txt". The robots.txt file is also an official protocol that follows a precise standard, just as is the sitemap.xml file that we will see later.

The file is a simple text file in the '.txt' format and is accessible to everyone. It is placed in the root of the website, but if you have subdomains, you can place the "robots.txt" file in the root of each subdomain with any specific instructions.

It is a file that is always necessary to have, even if only containing two empty basic instructions, to avoid errors or problems in the case of a badly configured server.

The file is also included in the sitemap, but it is not necessary to report it to Google, which knows very well where to find it and reads it to understand whether we have communicated any particular rules to it.

For instance, it can be used to exclude indexing of the whole website or a part of it.

The basic instructions you can put in the file are 'User-agent', 'Disallow', and 'Allow':

- User-agent: (where we put the name of the crawler we want to inhibit access to). If we put User-agent:* (with an asterisk), we are talking to all engines.

- Disallow: here we indicate what we do not want to be picked up by the crawler. For example, if we put:
  `User-agent:* Disallow: /page-new.htm`

  We are telling all engines not to index the page "page-new.htm". You can use the same way to indicate a folder and all its included pages instead of a single page.

- **Allow**: allows certain combinations. For example, if we block all engines with (*), we can then give an instruction to Googlebot's user agent only and tell it to 'allow' a particular folder that we only want it to index instead.

- **Sitemap**: This is an additional instruction to put in the robots.txt file that simply indicates the sitemap address of the site.

Meta TAG

How can we communicate with search engines at a page level instead? We can give instructions to bots via 'meta tags', a code inserted right into the HTML code. Let's look at the main ones:

The `<meta name='robots' content='noindex'>` is a code to be inserted in the `<head>` part of the html code of the page and which transmits a series of instructions to the search engine.

It works like this: as soon as the search engine starts crawling, it extracts the meta tags and reads them, ready to follow their instructions. Let's look at the fundamental SEO-side commands that should be inserted in the meta tags supported by Google.

```
<meta name= "robots" content ="noindex">
```

The code that is written above tells the search engine and GoogleBot that it must remove the page from the results even if it finds other links leading to the page. In practice, if there is a 'noindex', it excludes the page from the search results, not putting it in Google's gigantic library.

Small note: if you decide to put the `meta noindex` on a page, the same page must not be blocked via robots.txt because otherwise the engine would not detect the rule and there would be conflicts. Here's another tag:

```
<meta name= "robots" content ="nofollow">
```

This tells the engine not to consider the links on a given page and thus not to pass it the PR (page strength or link juice). This meta tag is very useful in the case of pages full of links that cannot be checked.

This, on the other hand, is the so-called 'meta description' tag:
```
<meta name= "description" content ="...">
```

The <meta description> should always be filled in because it usually appears in search results and therefore has a high SEO value. Sometimes Google fills it in on its own, but you will always put it in and optimize it with the chosen keyword because it serves to describe the content of the page. As for the `<title>`, it is sometimes truncated if there is not enough space to display it.

```
<meta name="google" content= "nositelinkssearchbox">
```

This meta tag tells Google not to show a search bar inside the website in the SERPs along with the sitelinks that the engine sometimes automatically places in the SERPs.

```
<meta name="googlebot" content= "notranslate">
```
This is easy and avoids having the page translated.

```
<meta name="google-site-verification" content= "...">
```
This is a tag used to verify the ownership of the website in the Search Console.

There is another tag to check that is always on the pages, which is not technically a true 'meta tag' but is a closely related HTML tag:

```
<title></title>
```

The "title tag" represents the title of the page, which is displayed in the title bar of the browser and in search results. This is very important, as we have seen in the section about article content writing.

In short, these tags offer granular control over the content of each individual page, allowing you to give search engines precise indications of what they will find within them.

There are many more 'Meta TAGs' and you can find them on their own in the Google documentation, together with the rules for each of them.

REL

With the attribute called `"rel,"` we can give instructions to the search engine at the level of individual elements on the page. We've already discussed this when talking about links, but I want to list them here as well.

When we place a link within HTML using `<a href="...">`, we can add a REL attribute to define the relationship between the resource we are linking to and the page where our content resides.

The most important standard parameters for the REL attribute are the following:

- `rel="sponsored"` is used to avoid passing PageRank (PR) to links that point to sponsored content.
- `rel="ugc"` is used to mark links as user-generated content, such as links in forums or comments.
- `rel="nofollow"` is used to tell Google not to associate your website with the linked page and therefore not to pass any PageRank to it.
- `rel="canonical"` is used to specify to Google the canonical URL, meaning the "main" version of the page.

The introduction of the `"rel"` attribute in meta tags was a turning point in the SEO world, providing Google with clear indicators on how to interpret links within a page. This was particularly helpful in regulating the often-abused practice of link building, a fundamental element in search engine ranking.

Before `rel` was introduced, the uncontrolled proliferation of links, often without clear intent, made it difficult for Google's algorithms to accurately assess the importance of a page. The rel attribute, with values like `nofollow`, `sponsored`, and `ugc`, allowed for more precise indications of the relationship between the current page and the linked one.

However, it is important to note that these indicators are not absolute rules but rather guidelines that Google interprets with flexibility. For example, even if a link is marked as `nofollow`, Google may still decide to follow it and pass some authority. This more flexible approach was adopted to avoid excessively penalizing the web, as a strict application of `nofollow` would have resulted in the loss of many valid and useful links.

Why this flexibility? Imagine we've invested time and resources to build a page with a high PageRank. By systematically using `nofollow` for all external links, we would effectively limit the indexing of high-quality content on other sites. This would, in turn, restrict the search engine's ability to provide relevant results to users.

Canonical

When a website has pages with identical content but different URLs, it's a good practice to indicate to the search engine a preferred URL, called the "canonical URL."

The canonical tag is an HTML element, a parameter of the REL tag, that signals to search engines which version of a web page is the "original" or "main" one, among different versions that may exist.

In e-commerce sites, for instance, sorting products in different ways can generate distinct URLs compared to the product category's main URL. However, the content remains the same, just sorted differently (by price, size, color, etc.).

The canonical tag can also be used for identical content on desktop and mobile pages, or between variants of the HTTP and HTTPS protocols, when the same content appears on different domains, and in other scenarios.

To solve this issue and avoid confusing search engines, this code should be placed inside the page's `<head>` section:

```
<link rel ="canonical" href="..Preferred URL for
the current document.." >
```

In all variants of the main page, the canonical code should be included within the `<head>` section.

I wrote this short paragraph specifically about the canonical tag because duplicate content is a typical problem that search engines give significant weight to.

By applying the canonical tag in this way, you prevent search engines from treating these pages as duplicates, avoiding ranking penalties and improving the site's SEO.

Sitemap

It is always very important to let the search engine know that you have actually published new content or updated previously published content. If you don't tell it that your pages exist, *how will it put them in the SERPs?*

It could find them on its own by following links from other pages, but if the website is new, you will not have any incoming links, and so it will not be possible. If, on the other hand, the search engine already knows your website, its crawler will periodically check the pages.

However, if you send a notification to the search engine, telling it that you have published or updated content, it is much better and speeds up the whole process. This is done via the *sitemap*.

The sitemap of your website, which can also be more than one, is nothing more than a file that contains all the pages of your site. Specifically, it contains the addresses (URLs) and the structure of your website, consisting of pages, articles, categories, and more. It provides the engine with information such as the date the content was created, the type of content, and the address where to find it.

The format of the sitemap is ".xml" and is located in the root of the domain. It does not have to be in the root; it is just recommended by convention. It is not even recommended to use sitemaps for small sites under 500 URLs, but, especially for new sites, it is much better to make it easier for the crawler (especially if you have a lot of multimedia content on your site).

Another important thing to know is that sitemaps are an official protocol. There are therefore rules to follow, such as, for instance, not to exceed 50 mb in weight or 50,0000 URLs per sitemap. Using only absolute URLs is also standard.

If the sitemap exceeds the limits, you will have to create two sitemaps together with an index sitemap in which the crawlers take the addresses of the other various sitemaps.

But how is a sitemap created? Nowadays, every management system has an integrated system for creating sitemaps. These integrated systems are fine for most websites, but when dealing with complex sites, things change.

In general, preparing a sitemap is quite easy and is done via an internal plugin that can be installed on WordPress. Or also via free external services, which however have some limitations on the maximum number of pages that can be inserted or the parameters to be customized. I simply use the WordPress plug-in called Yoast.

Once the plugin has generated the sitemap file, it will contain all the links to categories, pages, and articles. The sitemap will always be accessible at an address like "www...../sitemap.xml" and should never change. If, for some reason, you change the sitemap address, you will have to communicate the new address to the search engine.

Once you have the sitemap address, you must pass it on to the search engine. With Google, there are several ways. The easiest is to go to the Google Search Console (GSC) panel, which used to be called Google Webmaster Tool (GWT), and enter the sitemap address in the appropriate section. With engines other than Google, such as Bing, the procedure is practically the same. Every time you publish or update content, the plug-in will automatically update the sitemap and, again automatically, send a signal to the engine (a ping), which will then be alerted and warned of the change. The engine will then send its crawler to analyze the page and then index it.

A practice that I often do, because I am now in the habit of doing it, is to report a new URL manually to the engine. This is also done via Google Search Console, with two clicks, and makes it possible to be sure that the engine scans the content with priority.

Another very good practice is to also create a sitemap for images. The concept is the same as the sitemap for pages, articles, and categories; only this time the file will contain the URLs of the images on your site. Since the images are also indexed, this makes it easier. When a user searches Google for a word and then goes to the 'images' tab, they will find your images, open them, and land on your site. Yoast automatically includes images in the sitemaps of articles or pages it generates.

The last practice to be taken into account, especially if you plan to publish daily content on the website you have created, or are creating, or in any case on a fairly frequent basis, is to create an additional sitemap dedicated to Google News.

This is a Google news aggregation service that creates a news feed taking into account only articles published in the last 24 hours. The feed is shown to users who then have access to the most recent news.

An evolution of the same concept is Google Discover, which includes in the feed the topics that most closely match your interests, creating a series of customized content that should therefore be more targeted to the needs of the reader.

Both services offer great visibility to the articles that appear in them, and thus great visibility to the website hosting the articles. You usually realize that an article has made it into the news feed or Discover because the traffic increases dramatically, and you can clearly see a spike in the graph on the Search Console. I often only realize this the next day when I look at the statistics.

Take into consideration that Google Discover is one of the first traffic sources for news sites these days; therefore, if your website falls into that niche, it is a source you cannot overlook. For instance, since Google Discover is the largest source of traffic for news blogs, the blog article should be designed before it is even written, specifically for inclusion on Discover.

However, each of these services has strict admission criteria, which must be met, and it is not enough to have a sitemap to be included in the service.

For instance, to get into Google News, you have to make a specific request and only provide articles that are actually current news. So often, evergreen articles are excluded from this service.

Furthermore, the reviewers are particularly concerned about the website's level of trust. The articles must be written by someone who is an expert in the field, in the subject they are actually talking about. As a result, both the author and the website must demonstrate trustworthiness and authority, with the only goal of informing people in a straightforward and accurate manner. An authority factor is also crucial for Google, especially when dealing with topics such as health or people's money, as we have seen in the chapter on content quality.

> Both 'authority' and 'authoritativeness' are important. The former indicates the degree of power you actually have; the latter indicates the degree of power others recognize in you.

But there is not only the classic sitemap; there is also the image sitemap and the news sitemap. There are many different types, and knowing them is a priority because we can go and insert specific instructions in each of them.

For example, in the video sitemap, one could enter the length of the video and thus add information useful to the crawlers. An example of information and parameters that can be added are the `<Priority>`, the `<changefreq>`, both ignored by Google at the moment, and the `<lastmod>`, which must be verifiable and consistent.

Simply put, if you state in the sitemap that the page was updated today, and then the page has no date visible to the crawler then there is inconsistency and the information will not be used. The mandatory parameters in the sitemap are `<urlset>`, `<url>` and `<loc>`.

The sitemap is an important component to facilitate crawler access to your website. Implemented correctly at the beginning, it will not need any more excessive maintenance.

This is not a particularly advanced SEO concept, but now that you are becoming a master at writing articles or pages full of useful and valuable resources for your future visitors, you should be aware of this. In fact, if your content is long, articulate, and complex, you need to find a way to make it more usable.

To do this, you must place a clickable 'table of contents' (TOC) at the beginning of the article. Each title is linked to an anchor link, i.e., an internal link that leads directly to the corresponding section of the page.

When the user arrives at the resource, one of the first things they will see is the table of contents, and they will be able to click on any topic and be taken to exactly that point on the page. To insert a TOC automatically, there are special plugins on WordPress.

The first step in creating an automatic table of contents is to properly structure the content with header tags. These tags (h1, h2, h3, etc.) define the hierarchy of the text and tell the crawlers which parts of the document should be included in the table of contents. Crawlers will also be pleasantly surprised to find a table of contents at the beginning of the resource.

Imagine a book: at the beginning you find a table of contents that shows you the chapters and the pages they refer to. An index within a website works in a similar way. It is a list of links pointing to specific sections of a very long page or an extended article.

Thanks to this single small detail, we can receive some interesting benefits. First, navigation is made easier because the user can quickly find the section that interests him without having to scroll through all the content. Then the user experience is improved because navigation is faster, more intuitive, and more pleasant. Finally, users are more likely to explore more parts of the content if they find it easy to move from one section to another.

All this works thanks to TOC anchor texts. When you create a table of contents, each element of it becomes an anchor text that, when clicked, takes the user directly to the corresponding section. In general, you won't have to worry about the code if you use an automatic plugin to generate the TOC. However, at the code level, the TOC works like this:

- To each title you wish to include in the table of contents, assign a unique ID. This ID will be used to create the link. For example: `<h2 id='about-us'>About us</h2>`.

- At the exact point on the page where you want the user to be taken when they click on the title in the TOC, create an anchor link using the href attribute and the # symbol followed by the title ID. For example: `<a href="#about-us">About us</a>`

Anchors are the words or phrases that describe the sections the links point to. *Guess what?* A well-formulated anchor clearly indicates to both users and crawlers the content the link is pointing to. Anchors help search engines understand the context of the link and evaluate its relevance. *Quite important, right?*

Knowing this, when creating headings and later the table of contents, it's essential to invest some time in designing the anchor text.

As we've already discussed in the section dedicated to anchor links, even in a TOC, each anchor should not only be representative of the content the link points to—concise and clear—but should also strategically use some semantic keywords. A well-organized index can help search engines better understand your content's structure and direct it correctly.

To conclude this chapter, an index with well-defined anchors is the perfect combination and a significant element for improving both the user experience and the SEO of a web resource. It helps users quickly find the information they are looking for and provides search engines with a clear indication of your content's structure. Use them for both long and short content.

Just a heads up: this chapter is quite boring. As you already know, when you request a webpage from your browser, the server sends an HTML document that the browser needs to interpret. In the HTML code, there will typically be a style.css to control the document's styles and a main.js for JavaScript operations. The browser interprets the code and generates the page. *But how does it do this?*

The browser starts by reading the HTML document (this reading process is called "parsing"), and every time it encounters an element (like `<body>`, `<div>`, etc.), it creates an object called a DOM node (Document Object Model).

Once all the nodes are created, the browser organizes them into a tree structure where the HTML elements are nested inside one another. Now, the browser needs to apply the CSS styles to the individual DOM elements. It reads the CSS and creates a new tree structure, the CSSOM (CSS Object Model), where each node contains information about the styles that need to be applied to the corresponding DOM elements. At this point, the DOM and CSSOM are combined into a structure called the "Render Tree," which represents all the elements that will be rendered on the screen.

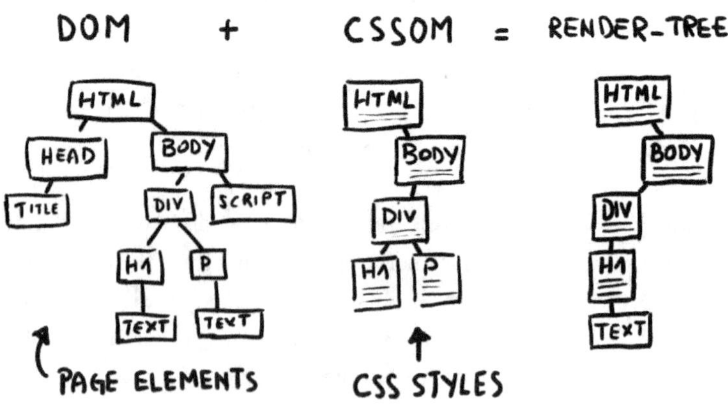

Note that some elements are not part of the Render Tree because they don't occupy space on the screen (such as elements with `display: none` or elements with "0px" dimensions).

We're halfway there. So, *how does the browser render the page now?* It starts displaying the elements on the screen in sequence through several stages:

1. **Layout**: For each node in the Render Tree, the browser calculates its size in pixels and its position on the screen.
2. **Paint**: The browser arranges the elements of the Render Tree into layers and applies all properties to individual pixels.
3. **Compositing**: The layers are passed to the GPU to be rendered on the screen.

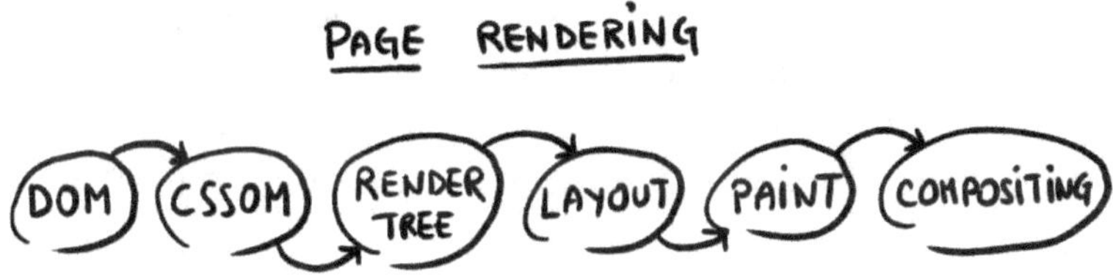

Now, if the browser encounters any external JavaScript or CSS resources, it must download that file in the background.

Regarding JavaScript, all scripts—whether embedded or external—block the parser and thus the construction of the DOM. Some scripts, such as those with the `async` attribute, do not block the parser until they are downloaded. The only non-blocking scripts are those marked with `defer`, which are downloaded in parallel and executed once the DOM is fully constructed.

CSS files, on the other hand, do not block the parsing process but do block the rendering process because the CSSOM is only updated after all the CSS rules have been processed. This is why it's recommended to load all external CSS files as early as possible in the page, ideally within the `<head>` block.

The dynamics between scripts and CSS within the rendering process need to be analyzed on a case-by-case basis because the JavaScript present can manipulate the DOM by modifying the content of the page. Understanding these processes will definitely help you solve common issues that prevent achieving sufficient "Core Web Vitals" scores, which directly impact the user experience. Here are the most common problems you'll encounter:

- CLS (Cumulative Layout Shift) refers to unexpected layout shifts.
- FP (First Paint) refers to the time the browser takes to begin rendering on the screen.
- FCP (First Contentful Paint) refers to the time it takes to render the first pixel of content.
- LCP (Largest Contentful Paint) refers to the time taken to render the largest element within the viewport.

I know these are complex topics. In fact, they could fill an entire book on their own, and this brief overview might leave you with more questions than answers. However, don't become overwhelmed by the technical details or examples of how to optimize these aspects.

You now understand how browsers interpret and render HTML, CSS, and JavaScript. You also see how this optimization benefits SEO. With this knowledge, you'll be able to solve the majority of these issues as soon as they arise. Just follow the advice of the PageSpeed tool. Trust me.

Redirect

A redirect is a mechanism that allows automatically sending a user from one web page (source URL) to another (destination URL). This happens "behind the scenes," most often without the user noticing. In simple terms, it's like telling the browser, "Instead of displaying this page, show another one."

It's an important tool because when a page's name—and therefore its URL—is changed, or when it is moved, a redirect to the new resource should always be set up.

For example, this type of redirect completely redirects one domain to a new domain.

```
Redirect 301 / http://www.example.com/
```

This, on the other hand, works on a single page, which is redirected to a different page (perhaps a new version).

```
Redirect 301 /oldpage/ http://www.example.com/newpage/
```

These URL changes happen more often than one might think, especially when working on an existing website. If the URL structure or page hierarchy is not well-designed, or if you need to relocate a website from one domain to another, you will almost certainly need to update them and create redirects.

Even if a page is removed from the website, it is best to redirect it to a similar page, or a page within the same category, or the category's root, as per the silo hierarchy.

There are different types of redirects, but the most common and relevant for SEO are the following:

- `HTTP 301 Moved Permanently`: It indicates that a resource has been permanently moved to a new URL. This is the most commonly used redirect for SEO, as it nearly fully transfers link authority from the old page to the new one.

- **HTTP 302 Found**: It indicates a temporary relocation of a resource and therefore does not transfer authority. It is not recommended for long-term SEO, as it can confuse search engines and dilute authority.

- **HTTP 307 moved temporarily**: It indicates a temporary move, and unlike the 301, which signals a permanent relocation, the 307 tells search engines that the resource will soon return to its original location.

From an SEO perspective, redirects are crucial because they not only prevent users from encountering "page not found" errors, enhancing their experience on the website, but in some cases (like the 301 redirect), they fully transfer the link authority and ranking power from the source page to the destination page. And we know how important link juice, or PageRank, is for ranking pages higher in the SERPs.

Imagine having five web pages covering similar topics. Instead of keeping them separate, you could choose to consolidate them into a single, more comprehensive page. To achieve this, you can use a 301 redirect. Essentially, you set each existing page to automatically redirect users and search engines to the new consolidated page. *The benefit?* All the authority (or 'link juice') built up by the five original pages will be transferred to the new one, making it more authoritative in the eyes of search engines. *Interesting, isn't it?*

Instead, to give you some guidance on how to implement redirects, here's how you can generally do it:

- Through the ".htaccess" file, which is a dedicated file for configuring redirects at the server level.

- Using plugins or built-in features to manage redirects that you find in CMS platforms like WordPress, Joomla, etc.

- Or by using server-level redirects for more complex configurations, which you don't need to worry about if you have a newly launched website or a resource with only a few pages.

There's also another special type of redirect, and that is:

- `HTTP Meta Refresh`

It's a somewhat crude method, less efficient and less supported by search engines, that uses a meta tag to redirect the user after a certain period of time. I recommend not using it except for specific cases, more in the context of particular marketing funnels than for search engine optimization.

For example, if you need to change a Call to Action or a banner link but can't modify the code or are in a hurry, you can use a meta refresh to take the user to the new page.

So you will undoubtedly hear about redirects and will most likely have to use them. Remember to pay attention to the details, always check that the URLs in the redirect are correct, and always test to see if the redirect works. It is possible that you will unintentionally create infinite redirect loops that redirect to themselves, which is a mistake.

When used correctly, redirects can help improve your site's ranking in search engines and provide a smoother user experience.

Section 8: AI and SEO

Artificial intelligence (AI), and specifically the evolution of language models (LLMs), is a topic that, during the months I'm writing this text, is revolutionizing the digital world. From hardware and software design to workflow optimization, search engines, and the development of online searches, AI has become ubiquitous across any industry.

AI technology and these "intelligent" response systems are also changing how users interact with search engines.

Instead of providing links that users must follow to arrive at a page they then have to read to find the answer to their problem, the search engine, through an assistant, will directly and simply provide the answer that the user is seeking right away.

One of the machine learning algorithms that Google uses is called RankBrain. *What is it for?* Essentially, the algorithm can understand more accurately what the intent and meaning of each query are. Thanks to its ability to learn patterns and search behaviors, RankBrain uses artificial intelligence to accurately infer the meanings of each word or phrase entered. *The result?* Simply put, it provides users with the most relevant results.

Moreover, like all language models, it continues to improve incessantly and gradually becomes an increasingly relevant ranking factor, rendering other factors less decisive.

How does this algorithm achieve such accuracy? To understand that, you need to grasp the general functioning of LLM technology and AI applications. There's no need to become an expert, so don't worry; rather, it's useful for broadening your SEO knowledge.

Embeddings e Rag

When discussing artificial intelligence, one must inevitably mention *"embeddings."*

Embeddings are not exactly a simple topic to tackle, but I'll try to explain it this way: they are numerical representations that enable machines to understand and manipulate human language with unprecedented precision.

In more technical terms, embeddings are the vectorization of a string of text. They are numerical representations of words that help the machine understand the relationships between the concepts expressed in those words, as if they were points on a map.

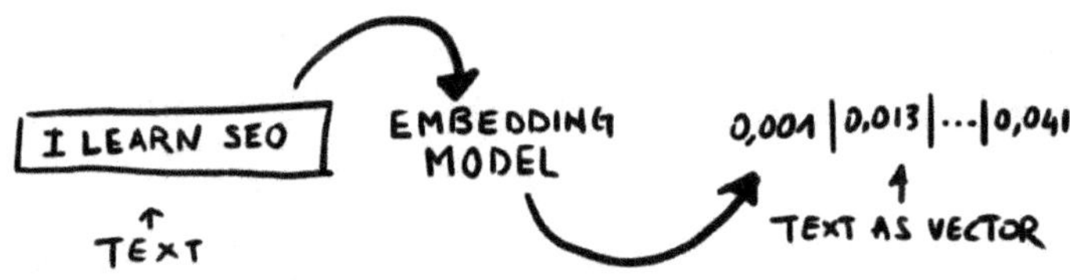

Companies developing these AI technologies provide models specifically designed to transform text into embeddings. At this stage, the numerical data is processed by machine learning algorithms in a kind of training to generate the embeddings and the relationships between them.

Here's how the process works: First, data is collected from a vast amount of text, such as books, articles, web pages, etc. This mass of data will then "feed" the AI.

In another phase, language models are created using neural networks that have the ability to learn from the data. Next, the model undergoes training. The model is "trained" on the collected data. Essentially, a large amount of text is shown to the model, and the relationships between the words are "taught." For example, it is demonstrated that the words "dog" and "cat" are often associated and should therefore have similar vector representations (*embeddings*).

During training, the model learns to create vector representations for each word. These representations capture the semantic meaning and relationships between the words.

Now we have the embeddings that can be used for a wide range of applications, such as:

- **Semantic search**: finding similar documents based on their meaning.
- **Automatic translation**: translating texts from one language to another.
- **Text generation**: creating new texts, such as poems or articles.
- **Chatbots**: developing chatbots capable of natural conversation.

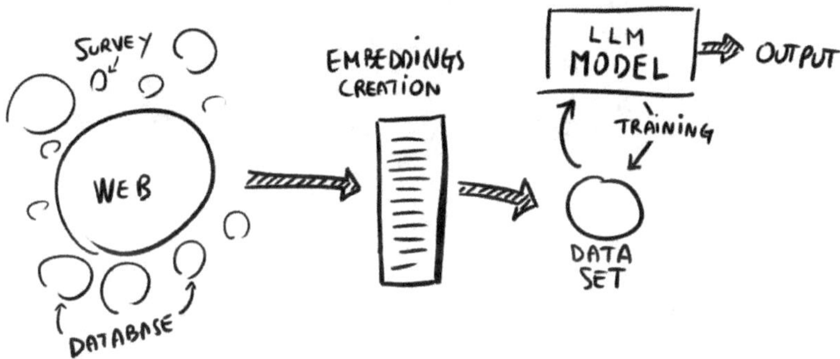

The performance of the model directly influences its ability to represent a string effectively. This is why a larger model produces more effective embeddings for searches; it incorporates a larger quantity of text during its training process.

As mentioned earlier, thanks to embedded systems, innovative applications such as intelligent chatbots, semantic search engines, and personalized recommendation systems can be developed.

But why should those of us studying SEO be interested in AI technologies and embeddings?
Embeddings are also highly relevant from an SEO perspective. The numerical sequences encapsulate the characteristics of texts, which are closely tied to one of the key factors for optimal search engine optimization: the texts that make up the content.

Think of it this way: if the values of the vectors containing the characteristics of certain texts are similar, then the concepts within those texts are also semantically similar.

However, vectors are not just simple numbers, as one might think. They contain thousands of dimensions, not just the two you see in the accompanying image (XY) or the three we are used to (XYZ). Visualization algorithms are used to reduce the number of dimensions, allowing us to represent them in the graphs we see.

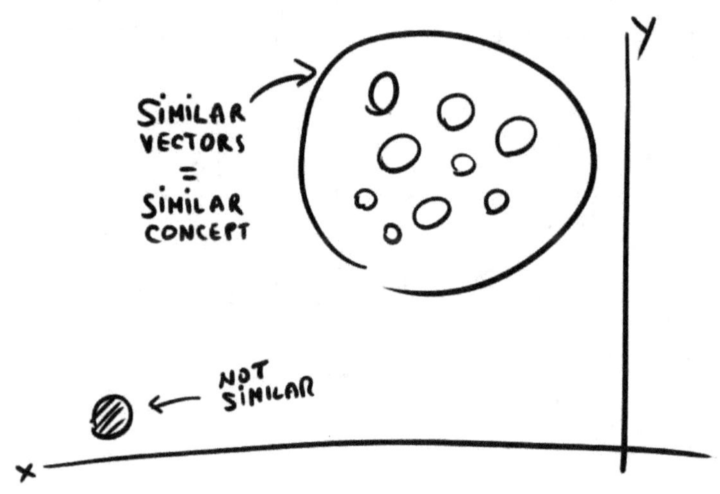

So, if a vector contains thousands of coordinates, we can reduce them to 2 for a 2D graph or 3 for a 3D graph.

All these concepts regarding the transformation of texts into numerical vectors have been known and developed for at least 20 years, but the real revolution today lies in how they are used. Previously, they were used solely to quickly determine how similar a user's query was to the content of a specific web page.

Now, embeddings can be used for various text operations, such as searching, calculating similarities, and classifications. It's also possible to summarize the meanings of multiple concepts into a single embedding to classify web pages while saving computational power.

Texts thus become coordinates in space, allowing for the identification of similarities by simply calculating the distance between points in that space.

The key concept that changes the work of search engines from now on is this one: since operations can be performed on embeddings to understand the content of a web page, instead of searching for numerous words in a text as was done previously, a search engine can take the text, calculate the embedding, and check how close the result is to other concepts, topics, or even competitors.

Now, there is another concept that needs to be introduced: *do you know what RAG is?*

RAG ("Retrieval Augmented Generation") allows you to insert all of a company's data into a vector database. Essentially, it divides the company's knowledge into parts and represents it in a structured and compact manner within the vector database, enabling more efficient searching.

Once the data is available, vector search is used to find any information. When I ask a question, my query is transformed into vectors, and the system searches for vectors similar to those I requested within the vector database. The found vectors are then passed through a language model that transforms them into natural language, a language that you and I can understand.

There is also another thing to note: the quality of the answer depends on the quality of the data and the model used. The answer will not always be perfect or exhaustive, at least for now.

AI application in SEO

You now understand at a basic level how these technologies based on machine learning models work. Now start thinking about how you may use these technologies in your SEO work.

Artificial intelligence applications and tools help you with certain processes that an SEO has to manage, making them less time-consuming. As a result of the time and energy saved, you can concentrate more on SEO strategy instead of other secondary aspects.

AI for keyword research and data analysis

One of the most important, but also most time-consuming, activities of the whole SEO strategy creation process is definitely keyword research. And a significant amount of time is spent cleaning up and organizing all of the keywords discovered throughout this activity.

This is a prime example of a process where AI can really come in handy. Not only can you use AI to help you with keyword research and ask it to provide you with lists of keywords or related searches, but you can also ask it to take all the lists and create "clusters" and keyword groups.

AI applications allow you to generate data files in various formats (.csv) and download them. But they also allow you to upload files containing the data. Then you can pass all the keyword research files of a particular project to AI and let AI do the dirty work of 'cleaning up' the data.

You could also ask an SEO tool with AI functions to generate a list of keywords for you by using one of your competitors as a source. Then you could ask it to filter all these keywords and eliminate those that are not suitable for your campaign or relevant to your strategy. After that, you could ask it to group the found keywords into clusters that have a semantic classification. And there you go; in 5 minutes, you already have a clear idea of the content you could create. Export the file, and off you go. Request a semantic classification or cluster of keywords so you know what types of content you need to create.

Then use AI to analyze and structure the data you collect which allows you to do so quickly with thousands of keys in minutes rather than weeks. However, even AI has limitations and may not be able to capture all the semantic nuances of some keywords. So, if AI cannot get there, you will have to do it.

AI for content creation

Generally speaking, whatever your process and workflow, you can use AI to speed it up or fill gaps that would otherwise have taken you longer. As a result, AI can be quite useful for finding inspiration and coming up with new ideas.

I know you're already thinking of giving the AI the keyword file and asking it to write a 1,000-word article for each keyword provided. But wait, it is not all that easy, at least for now.

Assuming I would not have the AI write the content entirely but rather use it to design the content based on the keywords it discovered, I would follow a process similar to this:

First, I would educate the AI about my audience. If I simply told it to create content, it would be difficult to establish the correct tone and style of writing immediately, and it would be even more difficult to maintain it for all of the required content. So I'd train and instruct the AI on the type of role it should play while writing (an expert, a consultant, a practitioner, etc.), the tone it should maintain (formal, informal, etc.), and the audience it should address. Furthermore, I would provide the AI with an example of content that I have already written in order to teach it to write like me. In the end, I can always review the material before publishing it to ensure that it is precisely what I want.

With this type of workflow, you can generate different content based on who you instruct the AI to interpret. As a result, you can generate content for a variety of audiences, ranging from a single generic piece to a large number of particular content aimed at specific buyer personas.

Once the content is created, use the AI to generate the description meta tags and the schema markup code. Always be aware that Google often changes the title and description meta tags; however, you can speed up the process by asking AI to generate these meta tags for a whole list of pages or articles you provide it with.

The same goes for "schema" markup code, which must always be checked via the schema.org markup validator or Google Search Console (I use both). Often the AI does not generate perfectly working code on the first attempt and you will more then likely have to consult the validator and ask the AI to fix errors or inaccuracies in the code when they occur. However, the overall process of writing markup code has been significantly sped up.

AI for audience definition

Artificial intelligence can help an SEO not only with data research and content writing, but also with audience definition.

An example? You could provide the AI with a description of your typical user by training the model on your buyer personas. Then you can ask the AI to put itself in the shoes of that particular user and envision which words it would search if it were that customer. Or you could ask the AI to act as one of the buyer personas; it will then be able to tell you what it expects to find in the page content and whether or not it actually found it. Then you can also ask what the best content format for a particular audience or person is.

This strategy helps you to create better content for users and is useful for highlighting any weaknesses in the content. As you continue training the AI model, you will find prompts that are more and more specific and useful for your objective.

Consequences

Now that you have a basic understanding of LLM technology and its applications in the field of SEO, it should be clear to you that today and in the future, SEO has to embrace AI technology.

But what are the current and future consequences of such technology? Well, I believe that it will completely revolutionize the search engine infrastructure as we have known it for years. Think of the crawling and indexing processes; both will certainly be impacted by AI technology and the algorithms that use it. We have seen how RankBrain uses machine learning technology to better understand user intent and search context, leading to more relevant search results.

Search engines are already and will increasingly become responsive systems through the use of vector database language models. Furthermore, AI could reduce the importance of website structure and favor more semantic search. Even now, we often start by searching for information with a traditional search engine, but then switch to an LLM simply because we require more speed.

For website managers and owners, there is a potential problem that impacts both traffic and visibility. If the user finds the answer immediately, they may not feel compelled to explore other search results. If you stop at the initial answer in SERPs, generated by an LLM, you lose a huge chunk of traditional organic traffic.

But even a search engine like Google faces problems that are not easy to solve. On the one hand, it would like to avoid requiring a user to open ten different sites when searching for information; therefore, it would like to use a more colloquial model to provide the same information.

On the other hand, it cannot give up the advertising revenue that users generate directly from sponsored links or when they visit websites through display ads. So, they will surely put sponsored content within the results given by the AI.

We can only imagine how content marketing strategies will have to change to adapt to a world dominated by AI and RAG.

High-quality, well-structured, and information-rich content will always be favored by search engines. Therefore, the standards we have already discussed remain the same:

- Focus on creating content that clearly and concisely answers users' questions, using natural, semantic language.

- Use schema markup to provide search engines with structured information on website content, making it easier to understand and extract data.

- Create FAQ pages and informational content that answers the most common user questions.

- Improve the overall user experience of the website, making it easy to navigate and quick to load.

If you can adapt to these new dynamics and offer high-quality content and an excellent user experience, your projects will have a better chance of success.

SEO tools such as Screaming Frog, which we will discuss in a separate chapter in the website management part of the book, already implement functions to query different AI models. You can then use these tools to regularly audit your websites and organize any optimizations necessary to make sure that the requirements of search engines are always met.

Technical SEO remains a fundamental pillar of an effective strategy, and factors such as website speed, mobile friendliness, and crawlability will always be immutable standard elements.

Section 9: How to ruin your ranking

The 3 weaknesses that can kill your project.

Once your website is online, you should always keep a close eye on its *ranking*.

Let me remind you that ranking refers to the positioning of your website's pages in search engine results pages (SERPs). You need to monitor the ranking to understand whether certain pages are moving up in SERPs, whether they are stable, or whether, unfortunately, they are losing positions.

Going down in SERPs is not ideal since it means losing organic traffic; thus, you should always try to prevent pages from losing their positions.

To accomplish this, you must not only understand and thoroughly study all the factors causing pages to improve their rankings in SERPs, but you also have to keep in mind what factors cause pages to suffer ranking deterioration.

Once you understand these negative factors, you will be able to take the right steps to remedy any drop in SERPs and recover your lost positions. The factors that kill a website in terms of organic traffic are these 3:

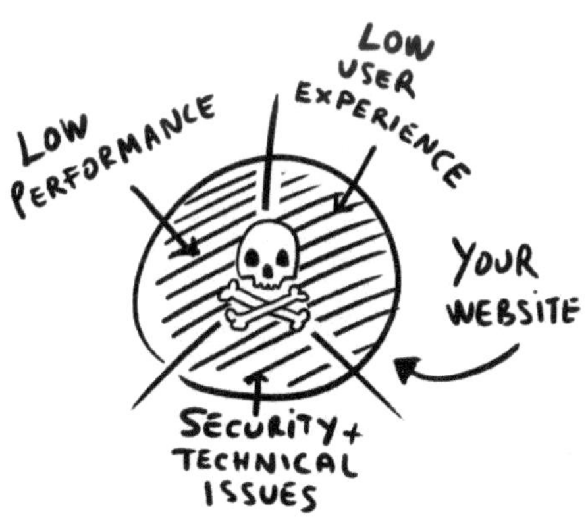

However, keep in mind that maintaining a fixed position in a SERP over time is extremely tough. Position volatility is common, and it generally increases when search engines update or add new features or algorithms.

In short, if you are a sailor; you have to know what keeps your boat afloat and what can make it sink; otherwise, you will never sail with confidence. Let's see what could make your website sink from an organic traffic perspective.

[1] Low Website Performance

How important is speed? Speed is one of the most important parameters Google takes into account when indexing the pages of your website. A page that loads slowly will result in users having a bad *user experience.* This will result in a worse ranking in SERPs.

Perhaps you weren't aware, but any minor improvement in speed performance results in a significant boost in conversion rate.

Slow Page Speed

Page speed refers to the speed at which the pages of your website open and is related to the idea of page-load, which is simply the time it takes for your website's pages to load.

Page speed refers to how long it takes the browser to completely load and display your entire web page. The higher the page load is, the slower the page speed. In practice, slower loading takes longer to complete and causes the website to load slowly.

A slow page or several slow pages not only cause problems for users, but also slow down the indexing of pages by the engines crawlers.

The most effective ways to boost the speed of your pages, and consequently your entire website, are as follows:

1. Optimising Images.
2. Optimize server response time.
3. Use a cache system.
4. Remove or compress javascript, CSS, and HTML.

There is a tool that is essential for analyzing website performance in terms of speed, and we talked about it at the beginning of this section: 'PageSpeed Insight'. It is a tool that allows us to accomplish a variety of things while also providing dozens of fascinating metrics for optimizing any website for SEO.

The tool not only provides an overview of the website's performance on desktop and mobile devices, but it also divides it into various categories.

But the great thing is that it also goes into great detail within each category and shows you through diagnostics what the errors are and also suggests optimizations to be made.

This tool can also be used to analyze competitors' websites and identify weak points to attack. In short, it is a tool that should always be at the top of any SEO expert's bookmark list.

I discussed CSS and Javascript earlier, and we also discussed how HTML works. Both CSS, an acronym for 'Cascading Style Sheet', and Javascript, a programming language used client-side to make pages more interactive (create dynamic menus, image carousels, etc.), are interesting topics to explore, but I cannot do so in this book.

In fact, CSS and Javascript optimization in the SEO sphere are advanced topics that would require their own book, and going into too much detail in this volume, with pages upon pages of code, is not possible. Therefore, I leave you with the curiosity to delve into these topics yourself.

Slow Server Time Response

Optimizing server response time is something to be done 'server-side' and depends very much on the performance of the server you have chosen to host your website.

Do not worry too much about this parameter, at least in the beginning. For a basic project, a hosting plan on a cheap server is more than sufficient. When the website has a constant and high flow of visitors, you can fix the problem by upgrading the server.

256

Caching is a system that saves weight and, therefore, time whenever a page is loaded. I won't go into detail about how it works, but I can tell you that it can be implemented via a WordPress plugin, which you can also set up depending on the features your server provides. Although every website is different and has specific settings it should be made to optimize performance; it is not a complicated thing to do.

Even the compression of javascript, CSS, and HTML can be done with plugins and thus with minimal effort. Keep in mind that all of this applies if you use WordPress. If you use another platform, however, you will need to do other types of server-side optimisation. On the other hand, some platforms already have 'closed' systems that are perfectly optimized and functioning, where you simply have to think about inserting content and that's it.

By using the Google Speed Insight tool, you can obtain important data in a few minutes to understand whether the server you are using is a bottleneck for your web project.

[2] Low User Experience

The user experience, or UX, is the set of perceptions and reactions of an individual resulting from the use or expectation of use of a product, system, or service. In other words, it is the set of all interactions a user has with a digital or physical product.

An excellent UX aims to make the interaction with a product intuitive, pleasant, and satisfying for the user, thus increasing user satisfaction and loyalty. If the user experience is poor on the website, you will find a high bounce rate in the statistics.

UX design focuses on understanding users, their needs, and their behavior to create products that are easy to use and offer a memorable experience. The UX of users is taken seriously by search engines, as you will read in a moment.

Low Quality Content

The first factor that destroys a site's ranking is low-quality content. We have already discussed content, its quality, its readability, formatting, structure, and relevance in Section 4. I don't think I have to repeat these concepts.

Duplicate Content

The second factor that destroys a site's ranking, which could be a subchapter of the preceding 'low quality content' chapter, is duplicate content. When we talk about content, we are referring to the key element for generating organic traffic. A website with poor content is a website that will never get organic traffic in the short, medium, or long term.

In terms of an online asset based on organic traffic, duplicate content is one of the most common problems your online ecosystem can encounter. These problems are, fortunately, also easy to eliminate. Duplicate content, as the word itself implies, is written content, i.e., text within your website, that has a duplicate on another page of the same website or even on another website.

The cases in which duplicate content can be found are usually these:

1) You copied some text from another website and put it on your own site.
2) You duplicated pages and did not change the content.
3) Someone copied your content.

As a result, I would strongly advise against copying text from other websites. Google and the other engines want original content, so make your peace with it and plan ahead of time in order to create it.

But hold on; it is not that you cannot copy. 'Copying', in the sense of taking reference, is in a way a good thing, and nobody forbids you from using other sites as a source of information. You can read them and take notes, but then it is mandatory to rework the concepts and information in your own style, using your own ideas and words, developing the concepts, and improving on what you have read, found, and learned. Before 'copying' something, make sure it is something that works because most people who write on the internet write things that do not work!

If you want to write an article about a campsite in the Dolomites in Italy, document yourself on 10 different websites, do a search, and organize the information, reviews, and pictures you find. You can also ask the A.I. to help you or even create a draft of the structure of the article. However, you will have to rework all of the acquired data. Rewrite everything to make your information unique, and strive to improve it. Become obsessed with creating a useful resource for users.

If a search engine discovers that one of your pages contains the exact same text as another website that has been online longer than you, you are in trouble. Google knows which website initially published the content, and therefore you can't get away with it. It is also not morally acceptable.

Don't even consider copying the text and changing two verbs and a few commas; the algorithms aren't stupid. In certain circumstances, you may want to copy content and quote it in your own article. For instance with quotations. In this case, you can do so, but you must include a reference to the original source from which you obtained the quote.

Are you wondering whether this duplicate content rule also applies to images? Let me reassure you. Google is very strict about the originality of texts, but images are a different matter.

In fact, the search engine is able to tell if an image is present on several different sites, but, for now, it does not use this as a ranking factor. Indeed, websites that use images from other sources are equally likely, if not more likely, to rank higher than the original sources. However, it would always be better to have original images for the sake of the *user experience*.

The problem with duplicate content that is caused by duplicate pages is common in e-commerce, where the same or very similar pages can exist due to extremely similar products. Or in eCommerce shops when the categories have so many products that they are divided into multiple numbered pages (page 1, page 2, etc.), each with the same title and description.

On the other hand, if someone has copied your content, Google will rank the 'copycat' website and reduce your organic traffic. This happens often, and having your website cloned, copied, or plagiarized is a serious problem.

If the website has been copied exactly, then you can make a request to remove it from all SERPs or you can even sue the owner. If, on the other hand, someone has copied your content and even slightly modifies it, you're doomed. You enter a maze where you have no power to do anything. With privacy laws in place, the only way to find out who is responsible is to report it to the appropriate authorities, although this process varies by nation.

There is no limit to indecency in these cases. Imagine that I have not only had entire websites copied but also tangible items and images with copyrights, all without shame. I've contacted the individuals responsible, warned them, reported them, and so on, but there is no quick and easy solution due to a complete absence of protection or intricate bureaucracy, at least in my country.

Although all the content you create is indeed copyrighted content, you still do everything to protect it. Put the name of your website and a logo or *watermark* on all images. There are special scripts or plugins to block copy-paste and right-click use by all visitors. Report plagiarism as soon as you become aware of it. Although these practices will not stop copying completely, at least you will make it a little more tedious to do.

To check whether content has been plagiarized, you can use some online tools that allow you to do so. I don't want to include all of the services I know right now because I'm not sure if they'll be available in the future. You only have to do an online search to find them. Using them is easy because you just have to paste the text you want to check or provide the URL directly to the tool of your choice.

They are useful tools to understand both how much other people are copying your content on the web and to do an internal analysis of duplicate content on the website itself. Ideally, a website should have a distribution of content like the image below, where the largest chunk is original content.

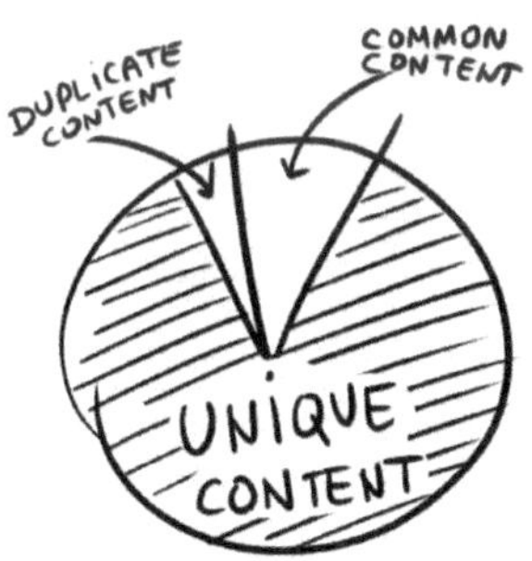

No Mobile Optimization

Another factor that destroys a site's ranking is the lack of mobile optimization. If you want to start an online business and use a website, you must now make sure it is compatible with mobile devices.

There is no escaping this; the days of using computers to navigate are long gone and unlikely to return. Today, everyone (or almost everyone) uses smartphones to surf the web, and in the future, we may even use watches, glasses, and other devices. As a result, your website must now be fully functional when viewed on a smartphone.

Furthermore, as we have seen, one of Google's crawlers is mobile-specific, and the search engine prioritizes smartphone-optimized content. So, be cautious that the mobile version of the website contains all of the same information and content as the desktop version; otherwise, Google may overlook information along the way. Structured data, for example, is frequently found in the desktop version but rarely in the mobile version, which is a problem.

What about adaptability between devices? The website must always be responsive and adapt to different devices, so the URL of each page will be the same for all versions.

The concept is simple and should be apparent to you. The engines will never place a website that does not work well on smartphones in the first positions of the SERPs.

Assume the absurd: the search engine unintentionally places one of your articles, taken from your website that does not work on mobile, on the front page for a day. The traffic you receive will probably be between 65% and 80% from smartphones and between 5% and 10% from tablets.

A mobile user who lands on a disastrous website that doesn't adapt to their device will leave immediately. Not only will you lose that visitor right away, but the high bounce rate will be detected by the search engine, which will promptly drop your website down to the bottom of the SERP. In five minutes, you'll lose the little traffic you had managed to gain—hypothetically.

The concept is what matters here. You must understand that today, most traffic comes from mobile devices. Maybe in the future, it will shift to smartwatches or augmented reality glasses—*who knows?*

You need to know who your user is, which platforms they use to search for information, and which devices they use.

Technically, you won't have trouble implementing a mobile website because all platforms are designed to natively create mobile-friendly websites, including WordPress.

However, building a mobile-friendly website isn't just about using a platform that allows it. As previously said, the concept must be applied throughout the board. The most typical example is the one about text. Text must be optimized with short paragraphs, white space, and well-structured headings to avoid long, uninterrupted content and make navigation easier.

Images must be lightweight, optimized, and quick to load. It's pointless to upload 2000px-wide images if the largest smartphone only has a screen width of 1125px. The loading speed we discussed is closely related to the topic of "optimization."

Lack of EEAT

The concept of E.E.A.T. (experience, expertise, authoritativeness, trustworthiness) is closely tied to user experience and is one of Google's fundamental parameters in its general guidelines. Low-quality content that lacks authority, reliability, and proper expertise negatively affects the user's experience and, consequently, their perception of the website's quality.

Google places great importance on EEAT, especially for YMYL (Your Money, Your Life) topics. Content that demonstrates a high level of EEAT is more likely to rank well in search results.

Navigation and Design

I will be brief because I'm sure you've already gotten the idea. The website must be easy to navigate. The content should be straightforward and easy to comprehend, with no distractions from banners or pop-ups. An intuitive and visually pleasing design also plays an important role.

Accessibility

The website should be accessible to all users, including people with disabilities. Links must be visually clear, the font size should be large enough to facilitate reading, contrasts between content should be sufficient to distinguish different elements, images should include alternative text, and so on.

When you use the "page speed insight" tool, it will point out all these things that need to be improved, and you will be surprised to see how many websites currently do not meet these standards.

[3] Security and Technical Issues

Security is another aspect that search engines take very seriously, and it's a factor that can severely impact a website's ranking. A website that isn't secure for users is simply not acceptable.

Consider this: traffic that reaches you is originally owned by the search engine, which then "forwards" it to you. As a result, the search engine requires that its visitors browse safely, with their data and devices protected. This is a crucial aspect that shouldn't be underestimated.

An "SSL" protocol on the domain is the bare minimum and is an easy system to implement, often included in most hosting plans.

Regular anti-malware checks are always recommended to keep security under control.

Clear information on privacy, cookies, collected data, and responsibilities should always be explained in the dedicated "basic" pages, as we previously discussed.

In another chapter, we will look at how to build an adequate level of security for your online assets.

Broken and Spam Links

Broken links can have a significant impact on a site's rating. Broken links are links that no longer work. For instance, if you link page "A" to page "B", but later, for any reason, you delete page "B," the link becomes broken.

In simple terms, page "A" can no longer find page "B." This often happens when pages are renamed, which should ideally never be done because pages should be properly named from the moment they're created.
If the search engine's crawler detects broken links on a page, it decreases that page's ranking. If multiple pages on the website have broken links, it leads to a drop in the ranking of the entire site.

It's like walking into a multi-story shopping mall and getting on an elevator to travel to the third floor, only to be met with a brick wall when the door opens. If this happens to users every time they use the elevator, they may decide to go to another mall or simply avoid using the elevator to get to the top floors.

Users waste time and don't find what they're looking for, which is a clear indicator of poor website quality. Consequently, Google will lower your site's position in the SERPs. As you can see, every consequence has an underlying cause.

How can you check for broken links? There are various free online services that allow you to input your domain's URL and will provide you with a full report on any "broken" links.

Once you have the report, you can download it and start correcting each link. This way, you can immediately take action and ensure that all the links on your pages lead users somewhere useful. You just need to change the link or its destination.

Earlier, I mentioned the 404 error that occurs when a page is no longer available at a certain URL. This is the type of error you encounter with broken links. As we've seen, it's not a major issue on its own, because you can edit the 404 page or update the URL to solve the problem.

However, if those 404 pages include external links or there are too many of them, the problem becomes more serious. In this case, just like with page moves via redirects, they must be controlled and resolved.

If a link from an external website leads to a 404 page because the page no longer exists, the PageRank (PR) that should have flowed through that link is lost, and Google isn't happy.

In that case, you should implement a 301 redirect to point the link and its valuable "link juice" to an existing page on your site.

Spam links, on the other hand, are hyperlinks inserted into a website with the primary intent of manipulating Google's search results. These links come from low-quality or irrelevant sites and are artificially created to try to boost the ranking of a page or an entire website.

Google considers this practice a violation of its guidelines and severely penalizes sites that overuse it. Spam links can take various forms, such as hidden links in HTML code, links in blog comments, purchased links from directories or forums, and links from websites with duplicated or low-quality content.

These are essentially shortcuts classified as "black hat" tactics for enhancing search engine ranks, but in the long run, they can drastically harm a website's online reputation.

Just remember this: no one is ever penalized for receiving a lot of links in a short period of time. The penalty comes when you receive a lot of low-quality links in a short period of time, as that is a clear indicator of spam.

Technique: How to make use of broken links

Speaking of broken links, I came up with a technique that you might want to know about. It will then be up to you to decide whether or not to use it in your journey. It all starts with a keyword that intrigues you and works like this:

1. You go to Google and search for the identified keyword. You look at the SERP and copy all of the URLs of the pages that are well positioned for that particular keyword into a .txt file. Obviously you have to skip the sponsored results because we are only interested in the organic ones. You can also use Chrome extensions made especially for extracting data from SERPs, so you save some time.

2. Once you have all of the URLs, you'll need to crawl each one to determine which pages link to a resource that no longer exists. You will have to automate this process and use free online tools to check for broken links or Screaming Frog.

3. If you find that one of the links leads to a page that no longer exists, check whether this is a resource that you could replace with your

current content or perhaps with new content that you can create.

4. Ask the owners of the pages to replace the link that leads to the resource that no longer exists with the one you created.

This entire process should be automated to the greatest extent possible, and instead of locating 1,000 low-quality resources and attempting to replace them, an ideal approach would be to find one high-quality resource that is missing and focus on that to restore a great value that was previously present.

Using the same technique, it is possible to find a single abandoned or expired domain that continues to receive links from other websites. In this situation, it is analyzed to determine how many incoming links it receives and whether it is worth attempting to restore it.

Section 10: Organic traffic pitfalls

The dangers that SEO experts must be able to face and overcome.

Organic traffic is the engine that fuels the growth of many online businesses. However, this valuable asset is exposed to a number of risks that can threaten stability and compromise results.

This type of traffic can be subject to volatility. Changes in search engine algorithms, core updates, manual penalties, and seasonal fluctuations are just some of the factors that can significantly affect the volume and quality of organic traffic. In short, all of these factors can trigger a sudden or prolonged drop in visits to your website.

Furthermore, the emergence of new trends and technologies may render previously effective SEO strategies obsolete, although standard principles will always remain intact in the future, as they are people-based.

To maintain your website's resilience in the face of these risks, in addition to constantly monitoring performance and taking a proactive approach to optimization, you need to be aware of these subtle, small threats and how to avoid them.

[1] Zero Click Search

The first threat that individuals seeking to create organic traffic should be aware of is the so-called *'zero-click search'*. You may have noticed that search engines increasingly tend to provide users with direct answers to their queries. A SEO expert must consider this behavior and assess the consequences it may have on a website's organic traffic.

Indeed, certain elements are becoming increasingly sophisticated and common in SERPs, providing users with clear and concise information, often without the need to click on traditional results.

These are the so-called 'rich snippets' and 'featured snippets' forms that Google suggests to users when it believes it will make it easier for them to find what they are looking for.

A click-free search occurs when a user types a query into the search engine and the engine returns the answer he or she was looking for within the SERP itself. The answer can be found at the beginning of the SERP before all the results and is displayed within a very visible and simple snippet.

So if the search engine already provides the answer to the user's query directly in the SERP, the likelihood of the user clicking on the link to your website is drastically reduced.

Since these elements are positioned high up in the SERP page, the competitiveness for the top positions increases because these elements occupy more space in the SERP itself and, being early and graphically different, attract more attention from users.

It is evident that the user, having found what they were seeking right away, has no need to search further and hence does not visit another website, including yours. They don't click anywhere.

No clicks = no users = no traffic = no sales, leads, or ad impressions.

In this case, the search engine plays against you. It wants to provide the customer with what they are seeking, which is fine. The problem with this is that it expects you to provide information to them as soon as possible, saving them the time spent clicking on a link and visiting a website.

Today, no-click searches are a big part of traffic. We also talked about the search results provided by LLMs, *remember?*

This feature is pitting the search engine against certain well-defined types of websites. For instance, if a user searches for information on weather, they will find the answer in the SERP. Similarly, if they search for information on flights from London to New York, tailored travel proposals will appear in the SERP without having to visit an airline's website. Restaurant sites, hotel sites, sports websites have the same problem.

So, how do we deal with the problem? There are two solutions.

The first solution is to try to optimize your content so that it appears as snippets in the search engine's results. In other words, it would correspond to position number 0 in the SERP.

In this case, you can think about optimizing the title and description of each article so that it already contains the answer the user is looking for, or at least a part of the answer. Some users will continue to click to refine their search.

The second solution is to continue creating valuable and highly optimized content (Schema, etc.). In fact, the search engine requires a diverse and clear response; a snippet is unlikely to provide it right away. As a result, the user will need to look for additional information on a website.

There is another recent tool that search engines make available to users to obtain information immediately and without going through the SERPs: *voice search*.

Voice search is currently not a problem because the first result provided by the voice assistant is virtually never what you are looking for. This type of search assistance is fine for simple searches and short and precise questions, but not for finding detailed information. All of these things are considerably easier to find if you look at the SERP titles and descriptions.

What can be done? First of all, if the SERP has to contain one of these rich snippets, it would be better if it was the one generated by your website. Then study the most suitable rich snippet formats for your industry and structure your content accordingly. Use schema.org markup to help Google better understand your content.

Then you should offer as much detailed content as possible to entice the user to continue exploring beyond the result found in SERPs. So in addition to textual content, consider creating videos, infographics, and other multimedia formats that can grab users' attention and try to adapt your strategy according to the changes imposed by search engines.

In conclusion, rich snippets and featured snippets are an increasing reality in SERPs and are changing the way users interact with search engines. Just as certain AI applications for search engines are transforming these tools into "response engines."

But there is another thing to consider: there must be a limit to this. If the engine does not direct the user to a website, the user will not click on any advertising banners that could possibly be found on that website. Since the banners run in Google Ads circuits, this is like shooting yourself in the foot. Even "sponsored" results in SERPs that are not clicked on imply that Google is giving away the largest portion of its revenue, which is unlikely.

So while we wait for these technologies to evolve, it is crucial to implement a SEO strategy that takes these elements into account and is always focused on creating high quality and highly relevant content for users.

[2] Deep Drop

Another big problem, perhaps the most insidious one, is what I call the '*Deep Drop*'.

'DD' is a catastrophic event that can occur when a website receives most of its traffic from a single key. I chose a catastrophic name since it appeared to be quite similar to 'Deep Impact', an old film that was quite catastrophic as well.

To visualize this scenario, let's create a hypothesis. Assume that your website's position in the SERP for the main keyword fluctuates and that it disappears from the first page, eventually landing on the 20th page. Undoubtedly, the website would lose all of its organic traffic.

Now, let's assume that fluctuations in SERPs are a normal, almost daily occurrence. If the website is new, it will have greater fluctuations. If the website already exists and a keyword has remained in second place for months, it might experience fluctuations, albeit to a lesser extent. For example, it might drop to third or even rise to first.

The truth is that if you've only worked on one keyword and Google drops you, you're doomed. It could be a temporary fluctuation, *but what if it's not?*

New articles published in accordance with the guidelines I've outlined are often indexed instantly on the first page, at the fourth or fifth position. Then, after a few days, they experience a dramatic drop that drops them to as low as 50th place, and after a few days, they are permanently fixed in first, second, or third place. Here is an example:

The image refers to an article that was in the 6th position in SERPs but fell beyond the 94th position in just one day. After another day, it will consolidate its position around 4th or 5th place. These things happen all the time.

This position consolidation occurs when articles are written in a specific way, but only if there is a framework behind them to support them, such as external links, internal links, keywords that complement each other, and so on.

To have one website with only one page and one keyword driving all traffic is a situation you don't want to be in; it has a limited future. It is like building a castle using a single shaky column as a foundation.

Having a website with 100 articles but receiving traffic from only one of them is a time bomb. If the keyword that holds the article drops, the article loses visibility, and you can say goodbye to all traffic from the web.

In this case, prevention is preferable to remediation, so the solution involves effective editorial preparation of keywords and related content, supported by an appropriate structure.

Conclusions on Organic Traffic

We have covered many different topics in this very long and central part of the book, which has now come to its conclusion. All of the topics we discussed are complementary to one another; each is important in its own way. These elements, when well combined, guarantee long-lasting results.

It is true that some aspects are not intuitive or easy to implement with a single 'click' of the mouse, but there are many topics, and if you are experiencing a feeling of 'information overdose', know that this is normal.

I understand that managing organic traffic may seem like a complex undertaking, especially when faced with the sheer volume of information available. In reality, the basic concepts are simpler than you might imagine. Although some technical aspects require time and effort, there is no need to complicate your life with unnecessary anxieties.

With each step you have read about, you will find that in the end, it all boils down to these three simple steps:

1) A technical component to create a solid foundation: building a trustworthy, healthy and well-structured website. A website that includes 'Trust', for both users and search engines.

2) A human component: enriching the website with valuable resources and content and putting users first in order to help them solve their problems.

3) An authority component: obtaining relevant links from credible sources to improve your online reputation.

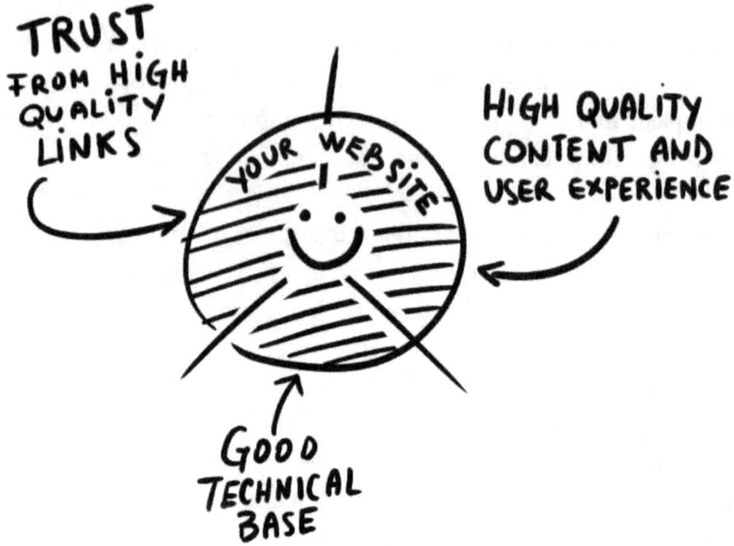

The recipe for an effective SEO and for attracting organic traffic is surprisingly simple: it is built on three fundamental and related components.
Building a trustworthy website, creating valuable content and earning the trust of other websites are the keys to long-term success, regardless of the platform.

I hope this is clear now.

GENERATING MORE TRAFFIC

Section 1: Generating Paid Traffic

Tips for Acquiring the Most Scalable Traffic Source

Paid traffic is the easiest type of traffic to acquire among all those we will analyze because, as the term itself suggests, you only need to pay to have it.

It consists of users who are brought to your website after clicking on a banner, an advertisement, or a paid link. To generate paid traffic, you need money and must have a budget set aside for campaigns.

It doesn't necessarily mean that those with a larger budget will generate more paid traffic in the same amount of time. While purchasing traffic is simple, optimizing the campaigns that drive it is rarely straightforward and often requires very specific skills and knowledge.

There are many factors to consider when deciding which paid traffic source to use, and I will discuss a few of them below.

The Volume of Traffic

Often, when the available traffic volume is large, you can acquire the traffic at a lower cost because the competition is less intense, being spread across a broader audience. The risk in this case is that the traffic quality may decrease.

For example, if you're selling "iPhone cases" and you bid on that keyword, you'll end up paying significantly more compared to bidding on the keyword "smartphone cases." This is because the first keyword is highly specific, while the second one is broader, and its search volume audience isn't specifically segmented for iPhone users. To take the example even further, you could specify a specific iPhone model.

The ideal scenario would be to find a traffic source that offers large volumes of traffic specifically interested in your niche, with low CPC (cost per click), and therefore, low costs. This was the case with Google AdWords and Facebook ads in their early days.

As mentioned in the smartphone case example, if you pay too little for visitors, you risk lowering the quality of the traffic you receive. It's important to also consider the amount of available volume in relation to the chosen niche or vertical, as well as the geotargeting.

The word "geo" refers to a geographic area. For example, Italy would be "geo IT," and the United States would be "geo US." The term is used to refer to groupings of different geos, such as "tier 1 geo," "tier 2 geo," and so on.

For example, if your typical customer is Italian, you will only seek a traffic source that has a large volume of traffic available in Italy (geo IT). At the least, you might consider a non-IT geo but limit the ads to Italian speakers.

Traffic cost

Cost is clearly one of the main factors to consider when discussing paid traffic campaigns.

The cost itself is a variable that depends on many factors. It usually depends on the country of origin of the traffic (geo), the type of traffic, and its quality. Buying traffic from Tier 1 countries is generally always more expensive than from tier 2 and tier 3 countries.

> *"Tier"* indicates the level of difficulty of different geos. The wealthiest and most competitive countries are classified as "tier 1." Developing countries, where purchasing power is negligible or very low, are classified as "tier 3."

There are formulas and rules that need to be memorized when you start buying traffic. CTR is one of them, but by now, you should already know what it is.

A fundamental formula is ROI, or *"Return on Investment,"* which is the parameter that allows you to determine whether you're making or losing money by purchasing from a particular traffic source. The formula to calculate it is simple:

$$\text{ROI: [(revenue - expenses) / expenses]} * 100$$

The cost of the campaign over time is also crucial. When you run ad campaigns, you'll need to monitor your KPIs daily. You may think that if your Facebook advertisements generate a lead for \$0.10 with a daily budget of \$50, you can simply invest \$500 per day to get ten times as many leads. It is not easy; especially with Facebook, your cost per lead will increase with time, so you will always need to optimize the campaign or cancel it and start over.

The more you narrow down people's interests when displaying ads, the higher your cost per click or CPL (cost per lead), will be. This is because by defining your buyer persona more specifically, you're increasing the targeting precision of the traffic.

Traffic Quality

When buying traffic, it is possible that a certain percentage of the traffic purchased on specific platforms is not legitimate.

Here's what happens: after analyzing the data and your analytics, you may find that some of the traffic originates from bots generating fake traffic, as these are not real people visiting the website. This lowers the overall quality of the traffic source.

Unless you're highly confident and familiar with the traffic source you're using, it's always a smart move to use a tool that allows you to analyze the data and determine how much of the traffic you're paying for is actually valuable and how much is not.

To verify this, you can cross-reference traffic source data with the website's *analytics* or use *trackers*—specialized tools that precisely track every single click from the ad banners to your website.

For instance, a high number of visits with short durations and unusual behavior, such as repetitive meaningless scrolling or quick entries and exits from a page, are red flags that may indicate bot traffic at work.

These fake clicks and visits are sometimes generated through "click farms," which are actual companies made up of groups of people who intentionally click on ads. These companies may even be hired by your competitors, who use this unethical tactic to inflate your acquisition costs and worsen the KPIs of your ad campaigns.

Traffic source rules

All the platforms from which you purchase traffic have rules that you must follow. Some of these platforms have strict regulations and do not approve banners or ads of a certain type or level of aggressiveness. Simply put, if you don't follow the rules outlined in their respective "advertising policies," you risk being banned from the platform. Once banned, you will no longer be able to use their system to purchase traffic.

Facebook, for example, is one of these platforms with very strict rules. Images referencing sexual content, nudity, or semi-nude bodies are prohibited on this social network, as they should be. It is also forbidden to sponsor or use advertisements to promote harmful products (e.g., drugs, pharmaceuticals, alcohol, gambling). There are also dozens of regulations and limits governing content, image layout, word choice, and targeting guidelines, all of which are necessary.

These are just the restrictions related to ads on the platform, each of which you need to be familiar with if you're buying traffic there. There are also rules for the landing page, which is the page on your website where the user arrives after clicking the ad. These pages must also follow strict guidelines aimed at protecting the user.

Like Google, Facebook wants its users to have a great user experience and land on trustworthy websites that sell reliable products. Otherwise, there would be a negative impact on the platform's reputation. However, the rules for traffic sources must always be studied, regardless of the platform you want to utilize for traffic.

If you purchase traffic from these sources, you must adhere to their rules and be familiar with their regulations. Clearly, you can't afford to be banned, especially if your traffic relies on a single paid source.

The traffic source will review your ads both automatically and manually, with reviewers responsible for ensuring the quality of all of your ad campaigns.

Targeting

Platforms that allow you to precisely identify your target audience are often the best. One of the most fascinating in this regard is Facebook, which allows you to choose the age, gender, interests, and other characteristics of the individuals who will view your ads.

Targeting, as a general topic, is an incredibly powerful tool, and it's worth writing an entire book just on that. Since I can't do that here, it's enough to say that targeting options allow you to precisely segment the audience that will view your ads. *Do you remember when we talked about knowing your audience?* If you know them well, you can target them precisely and focus your budget like a laser beam on them.

This not only allows you to optimize the campaign's budget by spending money solely on the people who are most valuable to you but also allows you to improve performance across all KPIs. A targeted audience will always respond better to campaigns compared to a generic audience.

All of these targeting possibilities, together with the platform's tracking system, which functions via the *pixel*, allow you to track all of the user's actions on the website and collect a large amount of data.

> The word *"pixel"* refers to a tracking tool that is implemented on a website by installing a code, which records visitors' activity and converts it into useful data for optimizing ad campaigns.

The data collected on your website will then be processed by the platform's algorithms, cross-referenced with existing data in the system, and used to optimize your campaigns in terms of targeting. Essentially, the platform will be able to determine which users are most likely to be interested in your specific offer and will direct your budget towards that particular audience.

I've simply given you a brief and simplified overview of the platform's targeting capabilities, as it currently has the best system. There are many platforms available, each with its own methods for tracking and optimizing campaigns. It's not necessarily true that Facebook will be the best for your website—perhaps Google Ads, YouTube, or TikTok will work better for you. You should always test and base your decisions on the data you've gathered.

When and if you venture into the world of paid advertising, or even if you're simply optimizing banners, buttons, or flows, you'll encounter the concept of "split tests."

A/B testing, or split testing, is a common technique in digital marketing that involves comparing two (or more) versions of an element to determine which one delivers better results.

Ideally, you should only use this type of test when you have a dominant version of an element. *But what does it mean for an element to be dominant?* It means that the element is generating a positive ROI. Only then should you develop a variant to test the results. Split testing is pointless if the system has not yet reached ROI, which is the evaluation standard.

It's not the opt-in rate or the CTR that matters—it's the sale, the conversion. Whenever you change something, it always affects the final outcome. Even if you manage to increase the opt-in rate, sales could decrease. Just because you double the open rate doesn't mean sales will double, as there's no direct mathematical correlation.

Therefore, avoid making changes without understanding the impact, and remember that split tests need to run long enough to gather statistically valid data. This means that these tests can be long and expensive.

Paid sources

At the time I am writing this, most traffic is purchased from Facebook, Google Ads (including YouTube), TikTok, and other sources such as native ads, PPV traffic, push notifications, etc.

To buy traffic, you need to create a campaign that targets a specific audience, showing them tailored content.

This is essentially how your *marketing* strategy works: showing your message to the right user through the right platform. The user sees your campaign content, clicks on the link leading to your website, and becomes part of your (paid) website traffic.

Imagine creating a Facebook post showcasing the rooms of your beautiful Bed & Breakfast House, with a description highlighting its features and a link to your website. Now imagine promoting this post on Facebook with a $20 daily budget.

Let's assume Facebook shows your ad to 2,000 people, and 10% click your link. That would mean 200 users landing on your website, resulting in a 10% CTR. Metrics such as reach, impressions, and CTR are all variables.

On Google, however, paid traffic is also purchased by creating campaigns, which can vary, such as video campaigns or universal campaigns that display ads in various formats.

These campaigns compete with your organic results in the SERP. Technically, they don't compete directly with organic results, but they do compete for SERP positions, as paid ads are shown before the organic ones.

Your task will be to create an ad and choose the keywords that will trigger that ad to appear. Once a user searches for the keyword you've selected, your ad will appear in the SERP. Like the topic of targeting, paid traffic is such a vast and fascinating subject that it would take another four books to cover it all. If this is the traffic source you decide to use for your website, there's nothing wrong with that.

As you know, in this book, I've had to focus solely on organic traffic and SEO optimizations, but I want to leave you with two key pieces of advice regarding paid traffic sources:

- The first is that if something is working, don't change it. If a campaign, a target, an ad, a copy, or an image is performing well, don't modify it until it no longer works.

- The second point is that once you've discovered a successful platform or medium, you should never replace it. Continue to examine other channels and alternatives, but do not abandon the one that works until it no longer produces results.

I deem these to be simple yet invaluable pieces of advice.

Section 2: Generating direct traffic

Tips for obtaining the most prestigious traffic source

Direct traffic refers to the specific type of traffic you get when a user types your website's address directly into the browser's address bar.

	29.811	100%
① ORGANIC SEARCH	26846	89,41%
② DIRECT	2164	7,21%
③ REFERRAL	551	1,84%
④ SOCIAL	465	1,55%

Direct traffic is another valuable and welcomed type of traffic. Here's why. If your website receives a lot of direct traffic, especially when compared to a competitor, it could indicate that you're doing a good job of positioning.

Think about all the major websites or companies you know. When you want to access their content, you generally don't look up their name on Google.

Instead, you're likely to type their brand name and domain directly into the address bar (e.g., apple.com for Apple, instagram.com for Instagram, or pinterest.com for Pinterest). The same is often true if you're visiting an airline's website.

Even for search engines like Google, their homepage receives a massive amount of direct traffic (at least theoretically, since no one should be searching for "Google" on Google, right?).
Checking direct traffic is one of the simplest ways to determine whether a website or brand has value.

Another small variation of direct traffic occurs when a user saves a bookmark in their browser and accesses the website by clicking it. This process is essentially the same as typing the URL directly into the address bar, except the bookmark saves you the trouble of typing. Clicking the bookmark icon connects directly to the website, and that traffic will also appear as direct traffic in your analytics.

There are other scenarios that can generate direct traffic, but they are secondary. For example, links embedded in PDFs (which Google can index) or in Word documents can also contribute to direct traffic.

In short, it should be clear that this type of traffic is valuable. *But how do you get it?* You're not Apple, Google, or Facebook, and you don't spend billions of dollars on marketing to attract these visitors. *So, how do you do it?*

To get this traffic, a big branding effort is required, both online and offline.

This is because the user must already know your website or brand name beforehand. They need to come directly to you without going through any intermediaries. There is no social media, search engines, or links in emails; otherwise, we'd be talking about other forms of traffic.

Those who arrive through direct traffic are users who already know you. They've already paid you a visit or obtained your address from someone else. These are people who are already interested in and enjoy your content and are also familiar with your website.

If a website has a lot of direct traffic, it means it is regarded as authoritative by its users, with content of such value that they decide to visit it directly and regularly (since this is likely at least the second time they've visited).
As a result, Google receives a positive signal and improves your ranking. The search engine receives the signal even if the user does not go through it directly, because you most likely have Google Analytics or Search Console linked to your website, so all of the data is in their databases. Alternatively, the user types your brand into Google's search bar, and the search engine just needs to put two and two together (2+2).

Online and offline branding

In case you weren't already familiar with it, it would be very useful, especially now that we are discussing this specific topic and type of traffic, to briefly talk about the meaning of *"branding."*

"Branding" is the work done to ensure that your brand's message is immediately recognized by a customer. It's the process of creating and defining the identity of a brand. It includes elements such as the logo, design, tone of voice, values, and the brand's personality. It encompasses everything that builds the brand's image and identity in the eyes of your audience.

The concept of branding goes hand in hand with that of brand positioning; they are not the same thing, though they are closely connected.

Brand positioning is how a brand is perceived by consumers in relation to its competitors. It's about the mental space the brand occupies in people's minds and its uniqueness compared to others.

It has nothing to do with SEO positioning in the SERPs. Branding creates identity, while brand positioning establishes how that identity stands out and competes in the market.

To explain positioning better, let me give you an example. Let's say your website is about the weather conditions in your area. Users ask themselves, *"Where do I go to check tomorrow's weather forecast?"* If they think of you immediately, then you've done a great job with positioning.

Building a brand is essential, as it is what attracts direct traffic to a website. In the end, users type the name of your website (or your company), which should be catchy, easy to remember, and easy to spell.

If your plan involves investing more in offline marketing, you will definitely receive more direct traffic than someone who doesn't. For instance, a sudden word of mouth can trigger a spike in direct traffic. An event in which someone says, "I found this thing on website Y," where "Y" is your website, will result in an increase in direct traffic. A mention in a newspaper or a magazine article will generate direct traffic.

Just last week, for example, in a question on a popular TV quiz show, they mentioned a topic that immediately caused an increase in views on one of my websites, as well as earnings.

If you have the budget and want to work in this direction, you can organize branding campaigns online or offline. Online campaigns are mostly Google or Facebook ads with the goal of *"awareness,"* which, as the word suggests, are optimized to increase the awareness of your website/brand, etc., among the target audience.

Offline campaigns are the traditional advertising efforts that involve the use of print media, ads, billboards, posters, etc. However, they are not limited to these; for instance, using TV or radio is also a part of offline branding strategies.

Niching down

If you don't have the budget but you still want to develop your brand, one thing you can do is conduct more meticulous niche research, a process known as *"niching down."*

I'll put it like this: You need to find a niche...within a niche... of a niche. *Sounds interesting, right?* Look for something extremely specific, starting from a generalist niche and diving deeper and deeper into subsections until you reach a point where you look around and realize that you can create the best website in that field.

Starting with this mindset and a super-specific niche, it will be easier for you to stand out from the crowd, and, more importantly, you can become a reference point for users interested in the sub-topic you've chosen.

Naturally, your content will be very focused on that niche. For example, take the vast niche of "photography." Begin by narrowing down to certain sub-niches, such as "astrophotography." Check to see if the ground in that sub-niche is fertile, the competition is minimal, and the volumes are interesting. If you've found fertile ground, stop there and start building your asset. If not, keep searching in other sub-niches or different markets.

Influencers

Another effective strategy to generate direct traffic is "influence marketing."

> *"Influence marketing"* is a marketing strategy that relies on individuals (influencers) who have an influence on a potential customer base.

It involves relying on an influencer that is active on social media, typically Instagram or TikTok, to promote your website or products to an audience that is as similar to your target audience as possible.

It's simply a way to implement a "word-of-mouth" technique by using the online tools available. One or more well-known individuals recommending your website can lead to a significant increase in direct traffic, as people hearing the name of the website will type it directly into their browser. Many will still search for it on Google, *but does it really matter?* They are still valuable visits.

If you want to contact influencers, there are dedicated platforms that serve as aggregators.

Here's how it works: if you have a website selling fishing rods, you can search for accounts in the "fishing" niche and filter them by followers. Again, you should do some "niching down" to find the individual whose audience is most identical to your own.

Have you been told that having more followers is better than having fewer? Remember, that's often not true. More followers does not always mean a better performance. There are many parameters for assessing the quality of a social account, and the most important one is called the *engagement rate.*

> The "engagement rate" is the ratio between the number of followers and the number of people interacting with the content.

Once you find an influencer's account with a good engagement rate and a cost that fits your budget, you can contact them and agree on creating sponsored content.

You may ask them to publish one or two posts, a story, a reel, or a video, or to link to your website in their Instagram bio. In any scenario, there will be a cost to pay, and the outcome will determine whether it was worthwhile.

This technique is applicable to all platforms that feature influencers. I am referring to YouTube, Facebook, Instagram, TikTok, and many others.

Clearly, you need to choose the right influencer and, first and foremost, the right platform to invest in. How do you do this? Choose the platform where the majority of your audience is present, and then choose the influencer with the most similar audience to yours.

Theoretically, the platforms I mention in this book may not exist in a few years, but new ones will emerge.

Section 3: Generating referral traffic

How to obtain the most relevant traffic source for Google.

Referral traffic is primarily a type of traffic that comes from other websites. It is generated through links to your website found in articles, pages, or banners on other websites.

> *Referral traffic* is called this because the traffic source, meaning the originating website, is called the "referrer," as it sends part of its visitors to your website.

The image below shows how Google Analytics displays referral traffic among the traffic channels that reach your website.

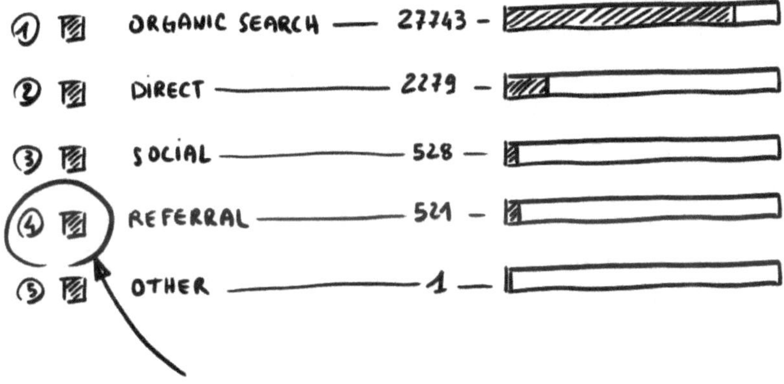

Taking into account the source of referral traffic, which, as we've mentioned, comes from other websites, it's clear that to obtain this type of traffic, you need to do some "external" work outside your online asset. In simple terms, you must actively or passively create links on other websites that will send visitors to your asset.

I mentioned "actively" because you can create these links using techniques such as guest blogging, which I will cover shortly. You can also generate them passively by providing exceptional content that is so valuable and interesting that it generates links organically and spontaneously.

Clearly, as with "link building," choosing the first or second option depends on your budget, goals, and timeline.

Monitoring referral traffic is essential to understand which websites are driving the most traffic to you. Once identified, it's a good idea to build a relationship with these sources, nurturing and improving it over time.

Google Analytics can occasionally miss things when tracking referral traffic. If you specifically open the "referral" tab in your statistics, you'll likely find traffic from social networks like Facebook, YouTube, or others, or even email traffic within the referral channel. In short, when studying referral traffic statistics in detail, you may find inaccurate data or a mix of other types of traffic in that channel due to imprecise tracking.

To resolve this issue, you would need to create filters or rules in Google Analytics that accurately and correctly group email traffic into the "email channel," social traffic into the "social channel," etc., leaving the "referral channel" with more accurate data.

All of this would be part of a more extensive setup of the tool, which you probably don't need right now. Ultimately, when you open the referral channel page, you'll discover which websites are actually referring traffic to you, and you can simply ignore the data that you know is incorrect.

Guest posts

One of the simplest and most commonly used ways to obtain referral traffic is through the *"guest post"* technique.

It works like this: you contact websites in your vertical and niche and offer to produce content for them to publish on their site. This way, you aim to attract visitors and people already connected to your niche in some way.

> A *"guest post"* is the practice of publishing a post as a guest on another website. Essentially, you write content and publish it on another website. You get a link on a website that targets your audience, and the website receives original content and compensation.

In this way, since you will insert a link to your website in the post, you will receive traffic from the article; *easy peasy, right?* The people who click on the link will land on your website. Another advantage of this technique is that you will receive a valuable link to your website.

However, be careful where you publish the articles, as you don't want to risk being penalized by Google by acquiring links from low-trust websites.

By creating valuable content on your own website and consistently maintaining high-quality content, you will always generate a magnetic effect. Your content will catch the attention of some bloggers, who may use it as a reference for an article and include a link to you.

There are two ways to implement this technique. The first one requires you to do everything yourself, including searching for websites where you can submit your articles for publication. You will need to conduct thorough research and record all the data in a spreadsheet.

To start, you can note the URL of the website you're considering, its category (niche), and the contact email of its editorial team.

Conduct more research and include additional relevant data in your file, such as the quantity of traffic the website receives, its domain authority (DA), and even a note about their social media following (which you could use if they share your content on their platforms). It would be like killing two birds with one stone.

Then, contact all of the websites in your file to see if they are interested in collaborating with you through guest posts. They will likely ask for a fee, which you should always note in your file. After that, you can make all your evaluations, keeping the value of the article, the cost, and your budget in mind.

The second method for implementing this technique is to contact an intermediary who already has a database with all of the details you would otherwise have to find yourself. These intermediaries have a list of websites where they can publish articles. Sometimes this list contains thousands of entries (URLs) sorted by category, with all the data regarding DA, traffic, etc. readily available. You will pay them directly and provide them, if requested, with the article written and packaged, ready to be published. Clearly, this is the fastest and most convenient solution.

The risks of this technique are doubled. The first is that, if you're not careful, it can drain your entire budget. Consider that a single guest post on a trustworthy website can easily cost $250, excluding the content itself. The second issue is that you risk the possibility of receiving penalties from Google, which is already monitoring this method, which is frequently used to get links in dishonest ways.

An additional improvement or change in the algorithm that monitors this aspect of links could lead to difficult-to-resolve penalties. Honestly, I can't imagine how a search engine could tell if a blog post is organic or paid (unless it's explicitly marked *"sponsored"* in the post or in the "rel" attribute of its link), but you never know.

Infographics

Another technique that I have used on occasion is to create distinctive and interesting *infographics*. I include them in articles and make sure they are easy to share.

An *infographic* is a visual representation of information. It is a technique for gathering various types of data into tables, concept maps, diagrams, graphs, and histograms, making the information easily readable.

Infographics provide originality to your articles and can easily capture the attention of content creators or those who share them.

People love images, especially original images that summarize concepts or data. That's precisely what infographics do. This type of content can generate shares, links, comments, and consequently referral traffic to your website. Furthermore, if the multimedia content is in ".pdf" format, search engines can index it regardless of which page it is on.

If you need to explain a difficult concept within a highly specific article, you could use an infographic. If you need to present data from a table or make comparisons, you might consider presenting this information to the reader in a simpler, more original, and more visual way with an infographic. Alternatively, if you simply want to summarize the topic or key concepts of an article, you can create an infographic and possibly add it as the first image in the content or as a cover image.

To create infographics, I hand-make them with Photoshop or vector software. I have a graphic background, and using graphic software is enjoyable for me. If you are unable to do this manual work, which requires some knowledge of graphic software, you can use AI support or online tools that simplify the process and provide you with pre-made templates that you can insert your data into.

The infographic is a technique you can test on your blog, but you need to evaluate it carefully. It's possible that infographics are a good fit for your specific niche, writing style, or blog's graphic style and generate a lot of engagement and traffic.

Alternatively, it is possible that your target audience does not respond well to this form of graphic content or that it does not complement your text or stylistic content. It will be up to you to test, analyze the data, and determine whether or not it is worth adopting this technique.

Push Notification

Another form of traffic that is highly intriguing for certain GEOs is "push notifications." Push notifications are services that send automatic messages or notifications to a user's device without them doing anything other than subscribing to the service.

This type of traffic, unless you have created specific filters within your analytics tracking system, will likely end up in the referral traffic channel.

Having a list of users subscribed to a push notification service is like having a list of users subscribed to your newsletter. It's like creating your own traffic source from which you can draw at minimal costs whenever you want.

We will discuss this in detail later in the book, where we will cover the topic of how to manage traffic.

Section 4: Generating social traffic

How to Obtain the Potentially Most Viral Traffic Source

Social media, as we've seen, can be an excellent source of *paid* traffic, but it can also be a massive source of free traffic.

If you've just launched a website, keep in mind that you'll probably need to wait a few months to get indexed and well ranked in the search engine results pages. If you're in a rush and don't have the funds to invest in paid traffic, social media can provide you with a quick boost of traffic, allowing you to blast off like a rocket. You can use it to attract traffic long before you're ready to receive organic traffic.

To do this, you need to give users what they want (*strange, huh?*). For every piece of content you provide to users on a social media platform, there should always be corresponding content on your website. So if you create a post on Facebook, that post should link to an article on your website. If you create a video on YouTube, there should be an accompanying article, and so on. You need to leverage social media to increase your reach.

The social media algorithms, applicable to all these platforms, prioritize user interactions, shares, and comments from friends. These are the most significant factors that will be taken into account when the algorithm decides whether a piece of content will have broad or, conversely, limited organic reach. Whether your post is seen by many people or none at all depends on these parameters.

Social media also applies the rules of print publishing, particularly those of magazines and newspapers. The "headlines" of posts are crucial, as is the sensationalism of the news being published. It's essential to create content of general interest that can attract the attention of a broad demographic with high viral potential, or content that is highly targeted to the niche you're focusing on. It largely depends on the market in which you operate. Let's look at some practical examples of how to generate traffic from social media.

If you publish a particular post on Facebook and it goes "viral," it will generate significant traffic (there must be a link in the post directing users to your website). This is the case with typical sensational posts that link to a blog article and explore or publish the news in full.

The more the post touches on a hot, popular, or sensational topic, the more likely it is to attract users' attention and, consequently, clicks. It's similar to why the front pages of newspapers always have sensational or frightful headlines; this is how a user's curiosity is piqued.

Facebook, like Google, monitors everything and has specific algorithms that calculate the engagement level of each post. If the algorithm detects that a post is getting a lot of clicks and therefore has a high CTR, it increases the post's organic reach. This means the post will be shown to more people.

In truth, you may be unaware that the posts you publish on your Facebook page are not seen by all of your page's followers. This is because the platform expects you to pay to display your content to the audience it hosts. So, it simply implies advertising and sponsoring your content through paid campaigns. It's also possible that a post is widely shared and thus has a high organic reach, but Facebook limits its reach and requires you to sponsor the material. *Funny, isn't it?*

The same concept applies to other social networks like Pinterest, Instagram, YouTube, or TikTok. Comments, likes, saving images, watching videos, or shares are all KPIs that contribute to increasing a post's reach and making it visible to more people.

All of this traffic, resulting from the viral content, will be free. Some might say it's low-quality traffic, but it depends. If the traffic originates from your page's followers or those already familiar with you, it will be easy to attract them with the appropriate offers. On the other hand, if the traffic comes from a broader audience, it could still be worthwhile to implement copywriting and marketing techniques to warm it up a bit and make it convert. By warming up the audience, I don't mean turning on the heaters, but rather starting an educational process to help them understand who you are, what you do, and how you can help them.

Now, let's look at how to generate traffic using the most popular social platforms, but first, remember these two important factors:

1. It is not certain that a social platform that works for one of your friends' businesses will work for yours. Every business operates in a particular market segment with a specific demographic, and the social platform you use should first and foremost consider this factor.

2. The quickest way to generate traffic from social media is to buy it by creating paid ad campaigns on the platform. So, if you don't want to invest time in studying, organizing, and implementing an organic social traffic strategy, the only option left is to buy traffic.

I'd like to conclude this discussion about generating traffic via social media with my personal opinion: social media is destructive. However, it is a tool, and if it is part of your lead acquisition funnel or strategy, it is acceptable to use it.

However, there is a significant distinction between utilizing social media to receive content and using it to create it or for marketing purposes.

Pinterest

This is one of my favorite sources of social traffic, and in fact, I use it on all my web projects, where possible.

With over 200 million users worldwide, it's a key platform for those seeking visual inspiration. It works like a giant image search engine where users explore themed boards to discover new content.

If your website falls within the "food" niche—covering recipes, diets, etc.—you'll find Pinterest to be fertile ground for generating excellent social traffic. Keep in mind that the majority of users on this platform are women, so niches like beauty, fashion, recipes, design, accessories, jewelry, hairstyles, travel, home decor, and many others can be ideal to implement on this social platform.

If you've positively evaluated this platform, carefully considering your content, niche, and audience, then open a profile and start organizing it. Once you've filled out the profile with all the details, info, logo, and everything else, organize your boards. Create one board for each category of your website, or if you have fewer categories, create one for each subcategory.

Then, go to your browser and install a plugin that allows you to "pin" images directly from your website, and begin adding all of the images to the board under the appropriate category. Use high-quality, original, attractive, sharp, and vertical images. The images on your website should already have these characteristics—*remember when we previously talked about the SEO features of images?*

Carefully curate the title and description of the image, keeping in mind that both the copy and especially the keywords are important. Therefore, apply the SEO techniques for content that you already know. Include the keyword from the article from which you're "pinning" the image, as well as the category keyword, in the title and description. Use this concept and arrangement for all of your boards until you've pinned images from all of your articles on your website.

By organizing everything in this way, not only will you get plenty of links to your website pages, but people who open the pins will be able to click directly on the link and access your content.

Remember that, like other social platforms, Pinterest's main goal is to keep users on the platform by offering them fresh and interesting content and giving them what they're looking for. This way, users regularly return to discover new ideas and inspiration.

The platform wants to reward their users. So if you create images that users can easily save while they continue to scroll through the feed, you initiate an ideal process: "Scroll > save > scroll > save..."

The user will stay on the platform because they are constantly finding content to save. They will then return to the platform to review the content that they have saved and will eventually land on your website. In this way, you may not immediately receive clicks and traffic, but you first need to satisfy the platform and its algorithms, which will then reward your content and enhance its organic reach. By working this way, with the right content, you can reach a lot of users and generate substantial traffic.

> The *feed* is the "board" of the social platform, the section where notifications or new content appear when they are published.

Instagram

Let's assume that your ideal audience is on Instagram. *What do you do?* Well, you need to find a way to generate traffic from this social platform.

The advertising campaigns you could run from Instagram are managed through Facebook's advertising platform, which owns Instagram. So, you'll have access to all the powerful advanced targeting tools and tracking that Facebook provides.

When it comes to generating organic traffic on Instagram, the process is much broader and more complex. First, you need a profile on the platform and this profile must be crafted in a certain way. It should be engaging, clean, and reflect a cohesive communication strategy. Additionally, it must feature content aimed at attracting the specific user you're targeting.

Content is crucial, and on Instagram, it mainly consists of images and videos, including short clips or reels. If you're unable to produce a large quantity of high-quality images and post them daily, Instagram may not be for you. Posting a picture once a week won't turn your profile into a traffic-generating machine.

Ultimately, the traffic that flows from Instagram to your website almost always passes through your Instagram profile. Whether you place the link to your website in your bio or include it in your *stories*, these must be consistently viewed on the platform.

The goal of your content is to capture the user's attention, encouraging them to visit your profile and decide to click on the link in your bio. Alternatively, users might choose to follow you and later view your stories, where they can click on a link. In short, the process involves multiple steps and is more complicated than simply "show an ad > click the link."

Regarding the link in your bio, of course, you'll want to direct users to a landing page rather than a random page on your website. The landing page should be optimized for visitors coming from Instagram, perhaps including a prominent email capture form. Similarly, your profile bio should be crafted to give users the best possible "first impression" of you, your brand, or your website.

To generate traffic, you need a significant organic reach, and you can only achieve that by understanding what your ideal customers want to see. Once you've identified what resonates with your audience, commit to delivering this content daily. Post 3 to 4 times a day and use hashtags strategically to expand your reach organically. There are many strategies for leveraging hashtags effectively—feel free to research them further.

If you're a photographer, Instagram is a platform you can't afford to ignore. Even if you're in a niche like clothing or run a jewelry store, Instagram provides fertile ground, and you shouldn't have trouble creating and sharing 3 or 4 images (or more) daily. Aim for highly original and creative content, and always post high-quality images.

While today's smartphones can produce excellent photos, it might be worth taking a short photography course to learn more about framing, composition, lighting, and so on. Investing in yourself always pays off. You might even buy a basic lighting kit, which can be found at reasonable prices. Anything that helps your images stand out from the vast sea of competition on Instagram is a worthwhile investment.

We've talked about photos and images, but your content should, and ideally must, include videos. You could personally appear in videos to answer questions from your followers, perhaps directing them to your website for complete content. Plan your videos in a way that they can be repurposed for other platforms like Facebook, YouTube, or TikTok, or even embedded in articles on your website.

Another option is to post exclusive content on Instagram that isn't available on your Facebook page or website. This way, users will have a reason to follow you on Instagram since they won't find that particular content anywhere else.

Persistence and consistency are crucial and should be an integral part of your strategy on this social platform, just as on any other. Engagement is equally essential, as it is one of the key metrics used to determine the value of an

Instagram account. As you now understand, increased engagement directly contributes to greater reach for your posts.

Before diving into a strategy that might later turn out to be ineffective, it's important to conduct research and gather platform-specific statistics to see which formats perform best. For instance, at the time of writing, reels tend to have much higher organic reach compared to other formats. Take these factors into account.

Instagram also provides detailed analytics for business profiles, which you can use to extract valuable insights and improve and optimize your strategy accordingly.

Generating organic traffic on Facebook is not an easy task. Before allocating a budget to this goal, it's wise to conduct a thorough cost-benefit analysis.

Given the high level of competition and the ever-changing platform algorithms, organic competition on Facebook is quite intense. The organic reach of posts is drastically limited, both for profiles and pages, usually between 1% and 3%. However, groups remain a valuable tool for building communities, which could be crucial for your online asset or brand.

Keep in mind that growing and managing a group requires time, and you or someone on your behalf will need to spend time on the platform. The approach remains the same: post a lot of content, as specific to your niche or audience as possible. Provide free information, help users, inform them, and then direct them to your website for more content or details. You should use all the content formats the platform offers, including videos, images, live videos, and more.

However, this system also has some critical flaws. For example, let's say you sell a product and create a community, such as a free Facebook group where users join without paying. If you don't educate these users from the start about the fact that you'll eventually be selling them a product, it can hurt your business because these people receive free content while your management costs increase as the community grows.

If you've correctly implemented the Open Graph protocol on your website, as we discussed earlier, you'll be able to quickly share any content from your website on this social platform, whether it's a page or an article. Of course, everything you do needs to be tested and tested again, focusing on what converts best or is most suitable for your audience. When making decisions, always rely on the data you see from the statistics. For this platform, pay close attention to KPIs like the engagement rate or CTR.

YouTube

YouTube is one of my favorite platforms, and I gladly spend some time each day studying, updating myself professionally, or watching videos that inspire me.

This platform has billions of users, including those interested in your business and prospective customers. YouTube also generates billions of video views every day, and each user spends an average of 60 minutes a day on the platform.

The interesting fact is that people type in keywords and conduct searches through YouTube's search bar. This makes the platform a massive search engine, the second largest after Google, which also owns YouTube and includes YouTube videos in its search results.

Essentially, users visit the platform, type something in the search bar, then view a video search result page; a SERP made of videos. They select a result by reading the snippet (which also provides a preview) and click on it. They select a result by reading the snippet (which also provides a preview) and clicking on it. They watch the video and, on average, spend 60 minutes on the platform consuming content. They may not even be watching the initial video anymore, having moved on to something completely different that piqued their interest or that they simply discovered.

However, users come to YouTube because they are looking for a specific video, a solution to a problem they have. This behavior differs from that of TikTok, where visitors are drawn in by algorithmic suggestions that keep them glued to the platform, presenting them with a constant flow of content.

On YouTube, people are searching for information or "inspiration." Observe the behavior of YouTube users carefully; they potentially want to do the following three things:

1. Know: they search for information on a topic they want to learn more about.

2. Do: they look for tutorials, guides, or instructions to accomplish what they need to do.
3. Buy: they search for reviews, product tests, or additional information about a product they're considering purchasing.

All of this makes YouTube a vast and fertile ground for those, like you, who are looking for traffic sources for your online assets. It's all tied to the video SEO strategy of your project, where YouTube becomes your main tool.

There are three ways to generate traffic from YouTube.

The first and simplest way is to purchase traffic from the platform. Since it's fully integrated with Google's advertising platform, you'll be able to create various types of ad campaigns through their system. You can leverage the power and effectiveness of videos to deliver your message to your audience. You can use *remarketing* techniques to re-engage traffic that has already visited your website and bring them back once they are on YouTube. Alternatively, you can target searches, keywords, and terms that users input, honing in on people using keywords related to your niche. You can also target users based on their interests, just like on Facebook.

> *Remarketing* means carrying out a marketing operation on someone who has already performed a tracked action, such as watching one of your videos or visiting your website.

A remarketing strategy allows you to re-engage those users by showing them relevant ads on platforms like YouTube or Google, reminding them of your content, products, or services, and encouraging them to return to your website or complete a desired action. It's an effective way to capture the interest of potential customers who have previously shown interest but didn't fully convert.

The second way is more complicated and expensive, but also potentially the most beneficial. It involves becoming a content creator on the platform, meaning you will physically produce videos to publish on YouTube.

You will need to create your own channel on the platform and develop a precise editorial plan for content publication. However, be cautious since you need to understand what you're doing. *Do you want to create a channel to entertain people or to sell something?* Here, factors like originality, creativity, communication, video and channel SEO optimization, branding, and all those elements that can help your channel and video content stand out come into play. Each piece of content, every video you post, will undoubtedly need to link back to your website.

Many people do not have a website and instead focus all of their content and marketing efforts on the YouTube platform. However, since you do have a website and need to drive traffic to it, you should use the platform as a new traffic source. The goal of your channel must be clear (selling vs. entertaining), and the strategy should be tailored accordingly. The KPIs will differ as well: for a sales channel, sales will be the measure of success, while for an entertainment channel, views or average watch time will be the key metrics.

It's a big task, but maybe you're tackling a niche where creating videos works well. For example, people who engage in recipes, DIY, arts and crafts, and so on—already have creative skills and can simply combine those skills with the possibilities, technology, and reach that today's digital tools provide.

Keep in mind that by doing this, you're building an additional asset, separate and independent from your website. A YouTube channel will generate subscribers and traffic, giving it significant value. In contrast to a video posted on Facebook, the videos you post on YouTube will always be your content and remain visible in search results.

Also, consider the following: every video you publish can be consumed passively by users. A blog doesn't have this feature. YouTube, and even a podcast (which is essentially a spoken blog), offer this great advantage from a marketing perspective.

And finally, once you reach basic requirements in terms of the number of subscribers and watch time, you can activate the internal monetization of your YouTube channel, producing an additional stream of income for your business.

The third way to get traffic from YouTube is to act as a "commentator." Search for videos that are relevant to your niche or the topic of a certain post in which you have presented a solution to a problem. In the videos you find, insert comments in the comments section that can help users solve their problems. In the comments, you can direct users to your website, for example, by stating that you presented a possible solution in an article that can be accessed via the link you provided.

This is a task that should be done while maintaining a certain morality without becoming spam. It should also be developed on a broad scale, with numerous comments on many videos, before it can generate a significant amount of traffic.

YouTube is the video version of Google, perfect for your online assets, and thanks to its passive consumption combined with organic reach, it is an exceptional tool. Make the most of it within your strategy.

TikTok

TikTok has managed to revolutionize the way users consume content online, thanks to its short and engaging format. While Instagram kept people glued to scrolling through its endless feeds of images, TikTok now achieves the same for videos, engaging users across increasingly diverse age groups. Setting aside the social consequences and the level of attention that these platforms produce, we need to focus on understanding their functionality. So, *how do we leverage this platform to drive traffic to your website?*

First of all, it's essential to understand the dynamics of TikTok. Unlike platforms like YouTube, where videos can be longer and more in-depth, TikTok rewards creativity, immediacy, and the ability to capture attention within the first few seconds. The platform's algorithms are designed to show the most engaging content to users, regardless of the number of followers.

To generate traffic from TikTok, the usual rules and standard principles we've already discussed are essential: identify your target audience and create content tailored to their interests.

First, consider the video formats; if your user expects to see long videos, then the horizontal format is ideal, and consequently, the right platform is YouTube. However, if they want to see short videos that are completely accessible in vertical format, TikTok could be the perfect solution.

TikTok favors short and engaging videos, while YouTube allows for longer and more in-depth content. The audience on TikTok is generally younger and looking for fun and trending content, while the audience on YouTube is more heterogeneous and interested in informative and niche content.

You'll have understood that the choice between TikTok and YouTube depends on your goals and your audience. If you want to reach a young audience looking for short and entertaining content, TikTok is the ideal platform. On the other hand, if you have longer and more in-depth content, YouTube could be a better choice.

Additionally, it's important to consider which stage of the customer journey people are at on TikTok. *What does the user want to see?*

Utilize trends, challenges, and popular hashtags to increase the visibility of your videos. Remember to include clear calls to action in your videos that indicate what you want visitors to do after watching them, such as visiting your website or landing page. Currently, tracking visitors from TikTok to your website is a bit problematic because you can't put links in videos, but I am sure in the future they will add this feature; for now you can still generate traffic and track it by placing a link in your profile.

Collaborations with other creators are another effective tool for reaching a wider audience. Involve other users on the platform in duets, challenges, or shared projects. Furthermore, don't limit yourself to TikTok; share your best-performing videos on other social platforms to expand your reach.

TikTok represents another opportunity to generate traffic to your website and increase your brand's visibility. However, in order to achieve significant results, it is necessary to create high-quality content, understand the platform's dynamics, and utilize the most effective marketing strategies, first checking statistical data on platform usage and your audience's needs, and then conducting various tests to determine what works best.

Not everyone has the same goals or the same audience, so run tests and make data-driven decisions.

Communities

Forums are an internet tool that has always fascinated me. They were extremely popular, particularly in the years preceding social media; nonetheless, they experienced a crisis as a result of the rise of social networks. I myself created various online forums, one of which had thousands of users.

Forums (the word comes from the Latin "forum," meaning public place) are online platforms that host discussions divided into groups or sections, where users can post messages to share common interests, and these messages remain permanently accessible.

The interface of forums, often text-based and less intuitive, has struggled to keep pace with the more visual and interactive interfaces of social media. In fact, the rise of mobile devices has favored the use of apps and platforms optimized for smartphones, while many forums have not been able to adapt quickly enough to this change.

Today, there are huge communities where people are united by common interests and generate vast amounts of content and information. Platforms like Reddit have billions of monthly users, while others like Twitch, Discord, and Quora have hundreds of millions.

All these users spend time on these different platforms because they are seeking information and answers to their questions. If there are communities among these services that are truly relevant to your niche, consider investing in these platforms as part of your strategy.

Sign up, create a profile, and start "feeding" the community. Provide comprehensive answers to users and try to help them, then direct them to more in-depth content on your website. Not only would this generate targeted traffic, but it could also yield a few links, usually of low value, with little additional effort.

Section 5: Generating email traffic

How to Use Letters and Postcards in the Digital Age

Email traffic consists of individuals who land on your website after clicking a link included in an email they have received.

I define this type of traffic as "very valuable," and the reason is simple: the people reading your emails are likely interested in the content you write. After all, they have voluntarily registered for your email list or newsletter, *right*? Therefore, they are much more inclined to click on the links you include in your emails, as long as they find value in the content and the topic interesting.

Email traffic is also one of the best converters of visitors into customers and, in general, one of the easiest to convert. In fact, it's no coincidence that emails and newsletters have been used in marketing since the dawn of the internet and continue to be widely utilized today.

Another essential positive aspect of this type of traffic is that it is almost entirely automatable. The process of generating email traffic and managing the email marketing system can be summarized as follows:

First, you need to obtain the user's email address. *How can you get it?* You could do this with a form on your website, a lead generation campaign on Facebook, or a pop-up with an offer in exchange for the email that appears on your homepage. There are a thousand ways to do this, which you'll need to explore on your own because it's not the focus of this book.

Once you have someone's email address, you enter it into a list managed through a CRM (customer relationship management) service. Email lists are organized collections of email addresses, often enriched with other personal information such as names and phone numbers, voluntarily provided by users. These lists, which can be quite extensive, are usually managed within CRM systems, which are often broader tools used to manage customer relationships, sales, and marketing activities.

Let's outline, in general terms, some of the most important concepts when it comes to email marketing. Your goal in this specific case is to generate traffic to your website from an email list.

How to make lists

If, after careful evaluation of your strategy, you have chosen email marketing as the primary channel to reach your audience, it is essential to understand its mechanisms.

Remember that building a list is always a smart thing to do. If you have a blog or a website with a good amount of traffic, asking interested people for their email addresses is a useful practice for building a valuable asset at a low cost. Asking for an email from a user who is reading your website doesn't cost you anything. Maybe the user is organic, so attracting them to your website didn't cost you anything either. Or the user comes through paid traffic, and since you paid for it, not asking for their email at this point would be foolish, *don't you think?*

There are two techniques for creating or implementing an automated email system in your ecosystem:

The first method, which I usually use, is to build your own email list. This will take time, especially if the traffic is low or inconsistent. However, don't forget that this would be a cost-free process if the traffic were organic.

The second method, on the other hand, is to find people who already have established email lists and obtain their permission to use them. You can find them by contacting those who launch or sell products similar to yours. In this case, you have to pay the user who owns the list and provide them with the content of the email you intend to send. A smart move at this point since you are paying for the traffic is to convert this traffic, which is not yours, into traffic that you own by using a *"squeeze page"* or a form.

A *"squeeze page"* is a short landing page with minimal content, perhaps just a title, a brief text, and a form, designed solely to capture contact information.

Let's assume you pay $200 to send an email to 5,000 people on a list interested in electric bicycles, and in the email, you include a link to a product you're selling. Perhaps the email has a 20% open rate (meaning 1,000 people open the email) and a 40% CTR (which means 400 people click the link and land on your product page). Let's say your sales page has a 2% conversion rate, and your product gives you a net profit of $25.

Let's do the math: you would sell 8 products, generating a profit of $200, and since you spent the same amount, the campaign is at breakeven.

However, say you include a popup on the product page that offers users a discount in exchange for their email address right before they leave the page. If this popup has a 50% conversion rate, you would collect 200 email addresses from people who have already viewed your product and are likely interested in the discount you offered.

You then send an email containing the discount code and achieve a 20% conversion rate. This means that, with a list you built at no cost, you now have a conversion rate ten times higher because the traffic is "warmer." You could generate $1,000 in revenue with a simple email. This list of 200 people whom you invited to provide their contact information becomes one of your assets. The list is now a source of traffic that you own, and you can send them emails until they unsubscribe.

This simple example demonstrates how important it is to persuade people to subscribe to your list, as well as the value of maintaining one or more lists while keeping things as simple as possible.

How to use lists

Let's assume you have successfully implemented a form, a widget, a landing page, or a squeeze page on your website to capture email addresses from visitors every day. Let's say you have a list of 10,000 email addresses (a nice-sized list).

Do you want to use the list to drive traffic or to sell? Your objective will determine which technique to apply to your list. The technique should be used to achieve your goal.

To drive traffic to your website, you'll need to generate interesting content and publish it, and then share this content with your list subscribers. A smart way to redirect traffic is to write an engaging blog article and then notify the entire list that the new article has been published.

In the email you send, you'll write an appropriate subject line that grabs your reader's attention, along with a few lines of text to preview the topic and, most importantly, pique the user's curiosity. Once the user clicks the link, they'll land on your website and will be able to read the full article.

Make sure to always check the email statistics, especially the deliverability rates, and verify that your emails are not flagged as spam or have any other issues that lower their quality score. Emails with low scores are often flagged as spam and thus may not be delivered to subscribers' inboxes.

This will result in a typical flow in which you provide value to the user while the user generates traffic for your website. Essentially, both sides benefit, with the exception of your list management expenses.

How to automate lists

One of the most wonderful aspects of email marketing, in addition to generating high-quality traffic at a low cost, is that it is almost completely automated.

What does automatable mean? It means that if you have been thinking about sending individual emails to each of your subscribers manually, you've made a big mistake. And that's good news, *right?*

Current email marketing systems, along with user event tracking technologies, allow you to fully automate the entire email sending process.

The simplest example is when you enter an online shop and a banner appears saying, "Get 10% off for free." *Do you think the shop gives you 10% off for free?* Of course not; they give it to you because you provide them with something valuable... your email.

Every email on a list has an economic value that corresponds to $1, $5, $10, or even $50, depending on the list and the market. Now that your email is in their list, the system recognizes that you are a new user and automatically sends you a first email, typically referred to as a "welcome email." Inside this email, you will find your 10% discount code. All of this happens automatically, without the person who set up the system needing to do anything.

But it doesn't stop there; in fact, it's just the beginning. If the shop's marketing system is even minimally decent, you will have been inserted into a sequence of emails that will arrive periodically, aiming to convince you to make a purchase. These are the famous "follow-up" sequences.

> *Follow-up sequences* are called this because the succession of emails "follows" the user, aiming to inform, educate, and persuade them to take the action you want them to take.

All the emails that make up the follow-up sequence, which can be hundreds, are written once. You then decide when the user will receive them, including the frequency, timing, the action that triggers them, the action that stops them, and what happens if the user takes action "A" or action "B."

Everything is then sent automatically, in a loop for every new subscriber, along with the automations and rules you've set. This way, you can create truly complex and effective email marketing systems.

Social Proof

Social proof is an effective marketing technique that leverages the psychological principle of imitation to enhance the credibility of an offer and encourage purchases. It can be applied across various channels, including email marketing and online sales.

> *"Social proof"* is the element that shows the user that what they are viewing has been valuable to many other people before them.

This is a very important psychological principle, especially in marketing and online sales. Essentially, it is based on the idea that people tend to imitate the actions and opinions of others, especially when they find themselves in uncertain situations.

In the banner or pop-up you use to ask visitors for their email on your website, include an element that conveys to the visitor that many others have already taken the same action you are asking them to take now.

For example, in your email subscription invitation, you could say something like, "Join our newsletter along with over 40,000 subscribers like you."

This small detail—the number, a social proof—is often all it takes to trigger the visitor's desire to join the "group," tapping into their social nature. As a result, the user ends up providing their email.

If you think about it, even the number of "likes" you see on social media, the number of views on a YouTube video, the number of shares on Facebook, or star ratings of products on Amazon are all forms of social proof.

Sometimes, on landing pages—especially well-designed ones—you'll find reviews from users who have already purchased the product. You may also see testimonials or logos indicating the product's mention in a magazine. All of these are forms of social proof.

I suggest you delve deeper into this concept, along with other persuasion techniques, because you will undoubtedly find incredibly useful information. By learning to leverage the psychological mechanisms that guide people's decisions, you can enhance your authority, credibility, and conversion rates.

As a result, your online assets will benefit, both visually—such as on landing pages—and in terms of content quality and effectiveness.

Giveaways

Giveaways are another interesting technique worth mentioning, often used in email marketing to increase subscriber engagement and encourage them to visit your website or purchase your product.

> The term *"giveaway"* often refers to a type of contest where something is "given away" to users to capture their attention and stimulate their interaction.

The ultimate goal of giveaways is not just to distribute the prize but to convert the user. The organizer of a giveaway, where the latest iPhone is offered as a prize, isn't merely giving away the phone; rather, they aim to collect the email addresses of all participants to potentially sell them a phone later.

Giveaways have an irresistible appeal. Simply mentioning a giveaway, contest, or a chance to win triggers an immediate reaction in many people, prompting them to actively share the content and participate without thoroughly reading the terms.

For example, let's say you have an eCommerce website selling bracelets. Each bracelet costs the customer $25. You post a giveaway on your social page, announcing that everyone can enter to win one of three bracelets. To participate, users must click *"this link"* and sign up on a registration page (which is essentially a landing page with a form to capture emails).

The entries for the contest close 10 days after the announcement, and within three days, you already have 500 entries. The news attracts attention, leading some users to post about it, which results in increased sharing and viral reach. By the end of the contest, you have a list of 3,000 subscribers.

The contest concludes, and you randomly select the three winners from all participants. You ship the bracelets to the winners. Up to this point, you have given away $75 worth of products for free. *What have you gained instead?*

Now you have 3,000 email subscribers who are interested in your product and who could potentially purchase it.

You can activate your marketing system on this list over the following weeks, months, and years. Immediately after the contest, while the topic is still fresh, you can offer them a discount, telling them that even though they didn't win, they can still purchase the bracelet at a 20% discount. Assuming this discount yields a conversion rate of 4%, you would sell 90 discounted bracelets, earning $1,800. *What was your investment?* The cost of the three bracelets given away.

Keep in mind that giveaways are subject to certain restrictions on different social platforms, so it's essential to familiarize yourself with the platform's regulations before implementing these techniques. Also, check if the value of the prize requires additional permissions to conduct the giveaway, as this can vary by country and regulatory frameworks.

MANAGE THE TRAFFIC

If you've made it this far, it means that you might have already set the right strategies in motion to grow your website. Your efforts to attract organic traffic are paying off thanks to the SEO optimizations you've implemented. Or perhaps you're receiving another type of traffic from those we've discussed, but either way, your work is bearing fruit. Congratulations! You've gone beyond merely creating a website. Now you're part of that small circle of people who can boast a strategic vision and consistent dedication.

If organic traffic still hasn't arrived, it might indicate that you made an error in the market research phase, that you haven't implemented all of the strategies we discussed in the third part of the book, or simply that not enough time has passed. After months of work, you'll have finally finished building your online ecosystem (your website). The ecosystem will be made up of two main elements, which we can summarize as follows:

1. The **front-end** is the version of your website that users and visitors see. The tip of the iceberg for your work, consisting of pages, articles, content, and so forth.

2. The **back-end**, the underlying system, consists of various platforms and tools, each with its own function (CMS, autoresponders, follow-up sequences, upsell, cross-sell emails, redirects, tracking, payment systems, monetization systems, and so on).

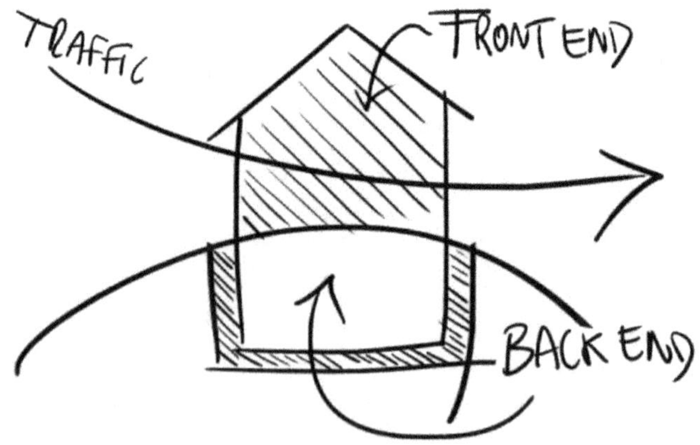

At this point, with your online ecosystem in place, your main task will be to generate traffic to the front end while the back end does the rest.

Section 1: Elements of your ecosystem

The three ingredients that make up your online business

In the numerous pages you've read up to this point, I've discussed several concepts relating to traffic generation, as well as web marketing and the creation of online assets.

These are the three fundamental components that form the foundation of everything:

1. **Traffic**, which is generated through SEO techniques or other systems.
2. **The website**, which we've called the "ecosystem," consists of a frontend and a backend.
3. **The marketing strategy** is aimed at achieving conversions, whether it's product purchases, contacts, clicks on an offer, banner views, or information views—it is anything that generates revenue.

There are three basic elements needed to make the whole system work. Visitor traffic, as you can see, is just one piece of the puzzle, a part of the formula.

Without the last ingredient, your website, and therefore your business, won't work.

- If you have a lot of traffic but no website, where do you send it?
- If you have a website but no traffic, what's the purpose of the website?
- How can you make money if you have traffic on your website but no product or revenue strategy?
- If you have a product and a website but no conversions, sales, or interested leads, how do you make money?

[1] The traffic

In this journey, we've thoroughly explored the concept of web traffic. You've understood how SEO techniques, as well as other strategies, can generate a steady flow of visitors to your website. Now, it's crucial to realize that traffic is the fuel that powers your online business.

Imagine traffic as a water source: the more water that flows, the greater your ability to irrigate your garden, grow your plants, and harvest the fruits of your labor. Similarly, the more traffic your website receives, the more opportunities you have to convert visitors into customers and achieve your business goals.

Traffic sources, as the name suggests, are the origins of this valuable flow. They are the starting point for every action that takes place on your website; they are the seed from which everything else grows.

[2] The website

If traffic is the seed, then the website is the fertile ground where this seed is planted.

If you want to generate organic traffic, I recommend using WordPress. Keep in mind that a huge percentage of all websites are built on this platform. When WordPress was launched in 2003, it was a game-changer, especially for people who didn't know how to code to create a website. It was like witnessing a miracle, making website creation accessible to everyone.

Prior to WordPress, creating a website required knowledge of HTML coding, and even then, you could create simple websites. Building a dynamic one was even more challenging. And creating a website that also looked aesthetically pleasing was another story entirely—you'd have to create a graphic layout. Wow!

WordPress simplified things and made it possible for people without a technical background to create their own website. If you want to write, you can; if you want a stylish website, you can upload a premade theme; if you want special features, you can install a plugin, and so on.

With its subsequent evolutions and integrations, it has become one of the fastest, simplest, and most affordable ways to develop online assets. WordPress is the best free tool for creating websites and blogs that can generate and get organic traffic because of its high level of customization and versatility, which is aided by the numerous plugins available.

But that's not all—this free platform can also be used to build single-page websites (or one-page websites), as well as any kind of landing pages.

[3] The Marketing and funnel

We said that "marketing" is the strategy and process you use to satisfy and retain customers over time, *right?*

The first rule of marketing is that if there is no market, there can be no "marketing." That's why all the market research we did at the beginning of the book is so crucial. You need to be sure that the topic you want to discuss, the information or product you want to sell, has a market.

The second rule of marketing is that it always consists of three phases: attraction (or profiling), education (nurturing), and sales.

1. **Attraction or profiling phase.** This is the phase where the customer sees that "you exist" and you declare, "I am here." This is where SEO does its job, capturing site traffic, but it might also be ads on Facebook or Google Ads that make you known to a visitor who will later become a subscriber.

    The question you need to ask yourself during this phase is: *who is my audience?*

2. **Education or nurturing phase:** This is the phase in which you define who you are and what you do not desire. Here, you educate your subscribers and explain how you can help them in detail, as well as the services you provide to do so, with the goal of converting them into leads and ultimately prospects via an extra profiling funnel. You can accomplish this with a series of emails, articles, or even videos on YouTube, among other techniques. You need to demonstrate to potential clients that they have a "possibility" of solving their problem. This is the phase in which copywriting is vital because you will have to address and resolve any of the objections the lead may have. The question you need to ask yourself during this phase is: *How do I educate my audience?*

3. **Sales phase of a product or service:** The question you need to ask
    yourself in this phase is: *What am I selling to my audience?*

The *funnel,* on the other hand, is a subpart of the marketing system. There
can be various funnels within each part of your marketing system, or funnels
that span across all three phases. For example, in the attraction phase, there
could be an acquisition funnel that shows a Facebook ad, prompts the user to
fill out a form, sends a chat message, and signs the user up for a list by sending
them content. In practice, it moves the user from phase 1 to phase 2.

Alternatively, there could be a nurturing funnel in phase 2 that invites the user
to a webinar, educates them with informative emails, and then offers them a
product, moving them to phase 3.

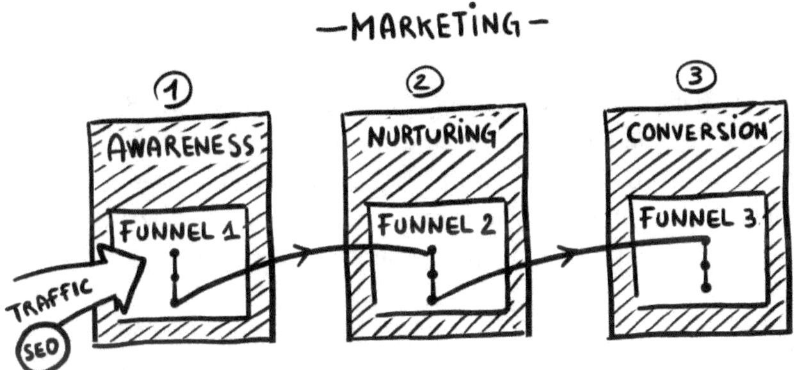

Funnels are the part of your marketing strategy that focuses on customer
conversion. However, conversion can occur each time a user transitions
between the different marketing phases (1, 2, and 3) until the final sale.

The concept of a funnel is often misunderstood because it's depicted as a
funnel, but in reality, it's a sieve; its purpose is to filter out the people you
don't want and perfectly profile your ideal customer, your buyer persona.

As we covered when discussing the audience, you must clearly identify your
buyer persona.
So, a funnel within the educational phase of your marketing system must
exclude all the people who are not a good fit for you, your product, or service.
Why is this important?

For example, imagine that at the end of your marketing process, there's an operator who calls people to close the sale. If you don't profile the people, the operator will end up making many calls that turn out to be useless. *Why?*

The people receiving the call are not perfectly profiled for you, or you're not a good match for them, meaning they probably won't be interested. This leads to a huge waste of time and resources, which could be automatically avoided by using a profiling funnel.

Is the funnel the most important part of the system? Every single part is important. However, the sales funnel is the beating heart of any online business. It's the pathway that guides a potential customer from their first contact with your company to the final purchase. Every stage of the funnel is interconnected and contributes to overall success: from lead generation to lead qualification and finally to customer conversion.

Without traffic, the funnel stops at the starting line. But even a well-structured and optimized funnel needs high-quality traffic to work effectively. It's important to note, however, that not all businesses require a traditional sales funnel. For instance, if your core business revolves around selling advertising space on your pages, your needs may differ.

Despite this, a funnel, in one form or another, is always present. Whether you aim to generate leads, educate your audience, or sell products or services, a structured pathway is essential to achieving your goals. Keep an open mind.

There's not just one single funnel; the funnel you'll use depends on the specific project. Some purchasing processes use models that differ from the standard funnel structure, resembling more of a loop—a circular path that the user takes until something triggers a conversion behavior, prompting them to do the desired action.

Sezione 2: How to get the traffic back

The main elements that keep visitors coming back.

In this case, your ultimate goal is to cultivate a lasting relationship with your visitors. By meeting their needs and providing an exceptional user experience, you'll greatly increase the chances that they'll return.

It's all about "closing the loop"—actualizing and completing all of the steps that allow your ecosystem to self-sustain and thrive (or nearly so).

Whether you own a physical store or a website, once you've acquired a customer or visitor, making them return should be one of your top priorities. *Why?*

Simple... It usually costs much more to acquire a new customer than to retain an old one.

But how do you get a visitor to come back to your website? First of all, keep in mind that by providing the user with what they're looking for, you're building a relationship with them. You create trust and increase the likelihood that the next time they're searching for similar information, they'll remember your website and visit again.

If this user had a very positive experience on your website, they are more likely to return. Let's go through the processes you can implement to bring the same visitor back repeatedly.

Make new content

One of the "secrets" to getting people to return is to provide them with new and valuable content in an environment that consistently offers a pleasant experience.

Write new content and serve it to your audience. People always need fresh content. They're hungry for new information. Create information and content that genuinely add value to the reader, and make sure visitors consume this content on your website.

Once the visitor has "consumed" your valuable content, it's time to guide them towards the action you want them to take. *And what do you want them to do?*

Perhaps buy a product, subscribe to your newsletter, leave a comment—anything that is valuable to you. After all, you're asking for a minimal effort, and you've already provided a lot of content without expecting anything in return (so far).

Generating interesting and unique content is the most logical way to attract a user back. It will become automatic for the user to return to you, where they know they can find clear, interesting, and unique content—exactly what they're looking for. On blogs, this content is usually informational. Other types of websites may offer discounts, coupons, advice, offers, contests, free content, and more.

You can't just hope the visitor will remember you and come back one day. You need to have a strategy, a point of contact, or a method that allows you to stay in communication with the user.

User Experience

Making the user experience simple and useful should always be one of the first things to design.

As mentioned earlier, it's crucial to ensure that the place where the user lands is orderly, simple, and as effective as possible for achieving the intended purpose.

I once heard a rule that stated that a user should be able to find what they're looking for in a maximum of three clicks. The rule is not incorrect, but it should be adapted to the type of website you've created.

If the user lands through organic traffic, they will likely arrive directly at the page with the content or information they were searching for. Perhaps a single click on the table of contents, which we provided on the first page, and they've found what they're looking for. The user reaches the information they need with just one click.

Assume the user discovers what they are looking for, receiving information that helps them make a decision or learn something, which satisfies their search purpose. *What do you think happens next?*

The page is seen by Google as a quality page, making it a preferred resource compared to others that are less useful or don't have a beneficial purpose.

Provide variety

When a user is reading your content, if it's engaging and you've placed the information they were seeking at strategic points throughout the content, they'll likely scroll down to the end of the page.

When they reach the bottom, it's not ideal for their experience on your website to end there, *right?*

To keep them engaged, propose fresh articles that are related to the one they were just reading. On WordPress, this is simple to accomplish with a plugin that automatically adds "related content" to the bottom of articles. Some themes have this feature built-in, so you may not even need to install a plugin.

These articles can complement, expand upon, or even be completely different from the original article where the user landed. Either way, the purpose of related content is to retain the user and encourage them to continue browsing by offering them more information.

It's a quick and easy method to boost various website KPIs, as well as internal link building, if the plugin is set up correctly.

Website speed

As we discussed, how quickly your website responds to user requests is a key factor in their decision to stay.

Patience, as we know, is a virtue, but on the internet, it's a rare commodity. If a user has to wait more than three seconds to view a page's content, it's highly likely they'll leave your website and turn to a competitor. It's like walking into a store: if they take too long to serve you, you leave.

When I worked as a graphic designer, I'd ask clients, "When do you need it for?" Often and predictably, the answer would be, "I needed it yesterday."

On one of my websites, it's clearly stated that delivery takes 20 business days. And every week, there's someone who wants to place an order but "needs it in two days."

So, I think you get my point. People are impatient; they want everything, and they want it immediately. Often, they don't even read because they're in such a hurry, or they simply don't care.

This is why website speed should be one of your top priorities—not just from a SEO standpoint but also from a user experience perspective. Every second of delay in loading a page results in 15% less user experience and 10% fewer page views.

Let me give you another example of why speed is crucial. In this example, actual money is at stake, and on your website, it will probably be your money.

CAMPAIGN NAME	SPENT	CPC	CLICK	LANDING PAGE VIEWS
FC-04-EN	30,71	0,27	162	118

This Facebook campaign spent $30 and generated 180 link clicks from the ads. However, the visits to the landing page recorded are significantly lower, around 118.

Since we don't fully trust Facebook's stats, which are collected by the pixel installed on the website, we will perform a double-check by verifying through Google Analytics how many visits the landing page received during that time frame.

PAGE	PAGE VIEWS
LANDING PAGE	112

We see that the data from Google Analytics matches fairly well with Facebook's, confirming the reliability of the information we've collected.

What do these numbers tell you? That 44 visitors were lost between the ad (on Facebook) and the landing page (on your website).

Why? The reasons could vary, but in this case, the cause was the website's slow loading time. Since the landing page was slow to load, you lost 28% of the visits. Economically speaking, you basically burned almost $8.

Multi-language

If you're designing a multilingual website, there are several aspects and scenarios to carefully consider. For example, what happens if a user lands on your website but on a page in the wrong language? *How do you handle that?*

Instead of using a redirect, you might opt for a pop-up banner that opens and suggests the user change the language, leaving the choice up to them. This seems like a softer approach that simultaneously enhances the user experience.

Be mindful of the translations for these types of websites. In terms of SEO, they shouldn't be mere literal translations but rather contextualized for the specific geo-cultural audience.

It's also important to differentiate between multilingual and multiregional websites, a distinction that Google explains in its guidelines:

- A multilingual website provides content in multiple languages.
- A multiregional website is specifically designed and targeted at users from different countries.

Then, there are choices regarding domains, which partly affect positioning, as we've seen. You can either choose country-specific domains (e.g., .de, .co.uk, etc.), use subdomains of the main website, or even use subfolders for each language, such as /de, /it, etc.

Each solution has its pros and cons, from the perspective of cost, maintenance, resources, and branding.

To determine the primary language of a website, Google checks both the top-level domain name and the server's location through the IP address. It also considers the instructions from `<hreflang>` tags or the sitemap.

It is also important to tell Google that we have pages available in other languages, and to do so with HTML, the "alternate" tag is used.

```
<link rel="alternate" hreflang="en-gb" href="..." >
```

Of all these technical details I'm writing, it will be your responsibility to check the official pages to see all the commands, exceptions, and best practices.

I'm only introducing the topic. Remember that the SEO field, especially for multilingual websites, is broad, and there are particular cases where the right solution for each specific case will need to be found.

Above the fold

A particular significance, when talking about user experience, is given to the part of the page called "Above the fold."

This strange name simply refers to the portion of the page visible on your device without the need to scroll.

It's an essential part of your landing page or any content because it's the first thing the user sees when the page loads. Consequently, it should always be the first thing that loads and is fully displayed.

Poorly optimized websites often load everything except the most essential part, which gets loaded last. This lack of optimization clearly results in the loss of users, as people quickly leave.

In any case, this section not only needs to load quickly but should also contain those few, yet crucial, pieces of information that capture the visitor's attention and convince them they are in the right place.

The above-the-fold section is responsible for convincing the user to continue navigating the page. The person viewing this part should naturally flow toward the subsequent content.

Therefore, it is an integral part of a system that provides a pleasant user experience on the website.

Social Subscriptions

Another way to bring traffic back is by diverting it to a social media platform. Essentially, you are directing traffic to where you're more likely to reconnect with it in the future.

This operation should be done, of course, while the user is still on your website or just before they leave. Capture users before they exit: invite them to follow you on social media to keep the contact alive.

Remember, you are providing content for free that users can freely consume. So it is not wrong to ask for something in exchange.

The goal is to create a smooth and engaging user experience. Once you've captured the visitor's attention with valuable content, offer them a next step that feels so natural it almost seems like the logical next move.

If it's too early in their customer journey to convert them, make sure they take another action anyway, whether it's visiting another page, signing up for your newsletter, or sending a request. Find a way to make this additional step or new action easy and natural.

> *"Customer journey"* is the path a customer takes during their relationship with a company. It's the story of the relationship between the customer and the brand, representing the interactions and experiences a customer goes through during all phases of the marketing process.

A classic example is redirecting the user to a Facebook page, YouTube channel, TikTok or Instagram page. Telegram or Discord groups are even better.

This way, when a user subscribes to your page or joins your group, they will receive notifications of your posts. When you publish a new article on your blog or website, you will also share it on your social pages to reach people through these platforms.

By doing so, you not only attract organic traffic generated by the article (which we know it will take time to build) but also activate "social" traffic, which is more immediate and has the potential to go viral.

You can also automate this process by using plugins that will automatically distribute your new content on your social media pages after it is published. And that's not all.

When users browse their Facebook or Instagram feeds, they'll also see your posts, including older ones. And it just so happens that all your posts always link back to your website. If the user finds a post interesting and wants to learn more or read it, they'll click on the link and land on your article, thus generating a *"returning visitor."*

To redirect users to social platforms, there are various "badges" you can add to the *footer* or *sidebar* of your website. A badge is, for example, the classic Facebook "like" box.

> The *"footer"* is an HTML element of any web page that delimits the lower part of a page.

Other more original and effective methods can include "pop-ups," which are simply banners that occasionally appear and place themselves in the middle of the page you're viewing. They can be set to appear after "x" seconds and grab the user's attention, leaving them with only two options: take action or close the popup. So, they provide an A or B option and a 50% chance to convert.

There are more advanced features with the same technology, such as "Exit popups," which detect when a user is about to leave the website and appear just before they do, possibly asking them to continue following your unique content on your social media profile.

Of course, you should also consider things from the perspective of your audience. *Which social platform is most suitable for communicating with your niche? Which platform does your audience use?* These are questions you must ask yourself when deciding where to direct traffic. The general rule is to use the platform that best fits your niche and audience and where you already know people are interested in consuming your content.

It's also worth noting that all these methods are constantly evolving, adapting to ever-changing needs. Plus, it's always important to stay flexible: social platforms can act as traffic sources, bringing traffic from them to your website, or as a repository where you direct traffic from your website and can reuse it later.

The Content Plan

A content plan (or editorial plan) is a strategic document that defines what content will be produced and published on a channel or platform (blog, social media, website, etc.), always in relation to the buyer personas. It is essentially a roadmap, an action plan that guides you in creating and distributing your content throughout the customer journey.

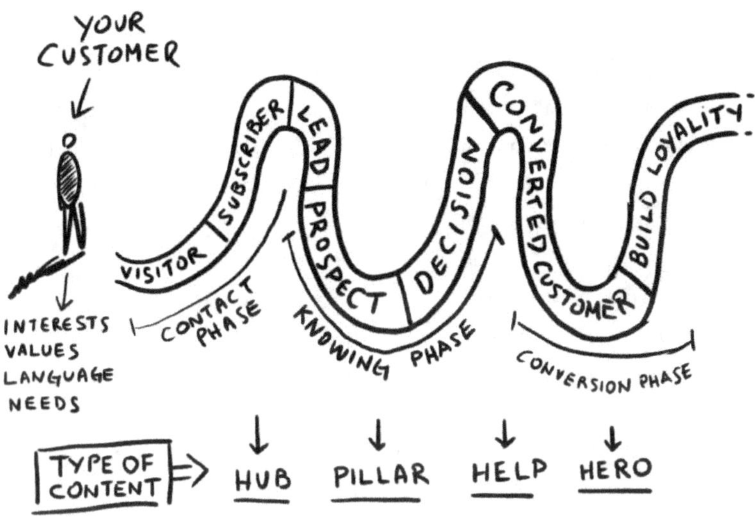

The image above should give you an idea of what I mean. Now, you should know that most websites focus only on a single phase of the content plan and overlook the rest. So after a while, something unpleasant happens: visitors get bored.

A content plan varies from project to project, but in general, it should include the following elements:

- Your mission, your values, your vision—in short, the identity and positioning of your brand.
- Definition of your audience, the language they use, and their interests.

- Every stage of the project's customer journey (visit, contact, awareness, decision, conversion, retention).
- The objective of the content is to increase traffic, generate subscribers, strengthen brand awareness, boost engagement, educate, entertain, inform, etc.
- The definition of content types, topics covered, and formatting. Will the content be independent and informational, a hub with multiple resources, "pillar" content that is extensive and comprehensive, or hero content? Will it be in the form of an article, video, podcast, infographic, etc.?

Today, a simple blog cannot keep up with the times, which is why a broader strategy and a more elaborate plan are necessary. Combining the content plan with an editorial calendar and an iconic example of your funnel's most significant KPIs will allow you to better plan and organize your content creation activities.

A plan prevents wasting time and resources on producing random or irrelevant content. Any content that focuses on a keyword based on search volume should also be consistent with your content plan.

Why? This way, you avoid straying off course and create quality content that is relevant and consistent with your objectives.

Section 3: Knowing your traffic

Techniques for collecting data on your traffic

Imagine owning a shoe store, and a person walks in. You can deduce that, most likely, they need shoes, *right?*

Imagine knowing in advance, before the person enters the store or just after they've entered, what specific thing they are looking for.

With this information ahead of time, a knowledgeable and well-prepared sales assistant could immediately guide the user to the most appropriate section of the store. Alternatively, they could already prepare one or two models for the customer to try on, saving time and providing better service.

Knowing in advance what someone wants is valuable information both offline and online. Let's consider another scenario.

This time you own a website that is about "chainsaws." A user lands on a page of your website and leaves after a few seconds.

They were looking for chainsaw reviews or tutorials, possibly of a specific brand, such as "Stihl chainsaws."

When developing the website, you should have recognized this query and a keyword linked to the brand the user is now looking for. This is accurate unless it was a query with a low volume that you neglected or a query that came up after your keyword research.

As a side note, Google identifies new keywords and searches every day. Did you know that one in seven searches is something that has never been entered into Google's search box before?

Fourteen percent of daily Google searches have never been typed into the search box. So, the search engine's index needs continuous updates to organize information in real time.

However, even though the visitor landed on your website through the generic keyword "chainsaws," there is no article optimized for that more specific keyword (Stihl chainsaws). Therefore, the user finds no useful, specific information.

This lack of relevant information leads them to leave. The visitor will click the "back" button on their browser or smartphone, returning to the Google search results to choose another website suggested by the search engine.

One thing is clear: if you had known beforehand what the user was specifically looking for, you could have acted differently and kept the user engaged on your website, reading your pages or clicking on your banners. And perhaps, by the end of their visit, you would have achieved a conversion.

But how can you understand what users expect to find on your website? A great help in solving this dilemma comes from the internal search system on the website.

Studying website searches

By using Google Analytics tracking on your website and setting the tool up correctly, you will be able to access user search data on your website.

Websites typically have a "search" button or an icon where you can search for something on the website; *do you know what I mean*? Essentially, every query that users enter into the search box on your website gets recorded in a database.

In the table below, I have put some random data just to give you an idea. If you check your Google Analytics, what you will see in the "Search Term" column are exactly the phrases and words that users enter and search for on your website.

Search Term	Total Unique Searches	%
term 01	5	25%
term 02	2	10%
term 03	1	5%

What are these search terms? Simple! They contain the exact information you seek: what people are looking for and what they want to find.

This is a valid reason to always have a search box on your website. It's a feature that is usually found in the sidebar or header; and it will give you a lot of useful info.

By analyzing the searches made by users on your website, you can identify specific gaps in your content offerings. By creating targeted content to fill these gaps, you will meet your visitors' needs and encourage them to stay longer on your website. A user who finds what they're looking for is more likely to return and engage with your content.

Users' searches on your website can lead you to fresh and exciting discoveries, such as terms you hadn't considered, new trends, and new article ideas, among other things.

It is up to you to analyze and study all of the search data on your website, perhaps comparing it to new keyword research and volume, before deciding which content to include in your articles and pages.

Behavioral analysis

There is another class of tools that allows you to obtain useful and valuable information about user behavior on your website.

These are referred to as "product experience insight platforms," and if implemented on your website, they can track user behavior in a much more advanced manner and provide you with visual feedback to help you better understand your users and improve their user experience.

In practice, with these tools—which I strongly recommend you implement—you will be able to record users' actions on your website as if you had a camera recording what they do.

You can see where they click, when they scroll, what they read, the content they skip, and what they pay more attention to, as if you were right next to them while they navigate through the pages.

You can also record heatmaps, which show the points of greatest attention on your pages, a feature we've already discussed. This is particularly useful if you need to optimize landing pages.

Of course, you won't see other windows that users have open, what they type, or any private information; you'll only see navigation on your website.

Additionally, you can easily and intuitively launch surveys on the website. You can make a small popup appear and ask visitors questions of your choosing, gathering valuable information about your users and their needs.

You have the opportunity to interact with your visitors and actually ask them something. For example, you could ask whether they found what they were searching for, if their experience was enjoyable, what they believe is lacking, how they would improve the content, and much more. In essence, you can understand how your users feel or get their opinion regarding something specific.

By analyzing the videos produced by the tool, you can understand why a certain page isn't converting, why users abandon their carts, how they behave in certain situations, or why they get stuck at a certain point in the funnel without progressing.

In short, if you want to maximize the optimization and enhancement of your pages and content, you can gain access to a variety of genuinely helpful information.

The danger of distractions

We have seen how to analyze searches to understand what your visitors want. *But what makes people leave a website? What do they not want to find?*

The answer is simple: frustration. A slow, confusing, or difficult-to-navigate website generates frustration and drives users to look elsewhere. It's like a crowded and messy store: you enter, take a quick look, and exit immediately.

Users don't want to waste time or be confronted with so much information that it confuses them and discourages them from proceeding.

A typical example is the old homepages of web portals from the '90s, which were filled with links, images, and content. Once you opened the website, you found yourself in such confusion and a myriad of distractions that you had to spend 10 minutes reading everything and trying to figure out what to click on.

However, even modern websites still face the same issue. In fact, the distractions for users are far greater now because there are new tools, new features, and new functions that are often overused.

The main idea is that having too much information is bad. But as every piece of information is also a stimulus, too many stimuli can tire the reader if presented in the wrong way. Distracting information can include texts, titles, images, banners, icons, pop-ups, notifications, and any other visual or audio components that pique the user's attention and divert them from their main goal: finding what they're looking for.

If a user lands on a website like this, filled with clutter, they might refuse to continue and could return to the search results to enter a different website, one that is more "relaxing" and less aggressive.

So, their journey would be: Google > Your website > Back to Google.
The search engine detects that the user has returned from the suggested website after only a few seconds, and regrettably, it draws conclusions. The

website's content is probably not relevant to users searching for that specific keyword. This situation will therefore affect the website's ranking.

If you're lucky, during a specific planetary alignment, the user may still proceed. This is the case for users who are genuinely interested in finding what they are looking for—those that need a solution and do not have time to look elsewhere. Users who are accustomed to blocking out all distractions and completing their navigation, or desperate users familiar with "suffering."

The problem would merely be postponed because, eventually, on the second page, the user would confront the same overwhelming amount of "too much" information, causing them to leave. They will find it difficult to return. People don't have time to waste (some do).

The trick to solving this kind of inconvenience caused by distractions is to maintain a simple structure. The German designer Ludwig Mies van der Rohe said, "*Less is more,*" and he was right.

A simple, clean, orderly, and bright website layout is often the best presentation for a new user. Look at the homepage of Google as an example. Does it contain distractions, *or does it only serve the basic function useful to the user?*

Imagine a person strolling down the sidewalk, looking at the shops and windows around them. They have the opportunity to find what they are looking for in two different stores right next to each other.

They glance at the first store and find it unorganized, with so much stuff that they can't even walk inside. The other store is an Apple Store—spacious, clean, bright, with comfortable chairs and fragrant flowers. In both stores, they would find what they were looking for (or the same information). *Which one do you think they would enter and purchase from?* Definitely the second.

Then there are distractions that appear as soon as you open a website. Nowadays, it appears that we are flooded with this type of content, alerts that frequently contain irrelevant information.

I refer to these as "blockers" (because they block the user); below are some examples:

1. The Facebook chat that appears as soon as you enter, taking up half of your mobile device's screen and asking if you require assistance (obviously, you haven't had the chance to view anything yet, but they believe you already need assistance).

2. The banner that asks you to subscribe to push notifications, which usually appears at the top left of the browser when you're browsing from a desktop.

3. The central banner that interrupts your view to request a subscription to the newsletter (maybe offering a 10% discount for new subscribers even though you haven't seen what products are available yet).

4. The cookie law notification banner, with an accompanying link to the cookie policy, which no one has ever read and no one will ever read, but you have to accept.

5. The privacy and GDPR banner, which, along with the cookie law notification, pops up for visitors in European countries.

6. An exit pop-up banner that appears not when you're about to leave but when your mouse moves too much.

7. An advertising video that starts playing automatically with audio turned on, and before it finishes, another one starts overlapping with the previous one.

Imagine that a website has all these blockers active on its pages or on the homepage. So, the user has to click five times just to close all those distractions before accessing the content.

People's attention has a limit, and these types of activities waste it unnecessarily. Their abuse or improper implementation significantly worsens the user experience.

The right balance

When analyzing your website traffic, one of the first questions to ask is: *How is the flow of visitors distributed across different traffic sources?* Understanding this distribution is crucial for anticipating potential traffic declines and taking preventive measures.

Using data extracted from analytics, you can quickly see the percentage of traffic received from various sources.

In a hypothetical situation, the statistics might look something like this:

- 70%   Organic Traffic
- 5%   Direct Traffic
- 10%   Referral Traffic
- 15%   Social Traffic

The mistake, which should never be made, is to rely on a single traffic source for the majority of your users:

- 90% Organic Traffic
- 10% Social Traffic

If your organic traffic disappears, either due to a Google penalty or an aggressive competitor surpassing you in the SERPs, you're in trouble.

Another situation that is dangerous is:

- 80% Referral Traffic (with a single referral accounting has the majority).
- 10% Organic Traffic
- 10% Social Traffic

If all of your traffic originates from other websites that have placed a link or banner pointing towards your website and then they remove it, you will lose the majority of your visitors in one fell swoop.

In a previous chapter, we talked about the "DD" (deep drop), *remember?* Imagine what would happen if the source of the majority of your traffic stopped generating visitors. *What would happen?*

The website would die.

As a result, analysis becomes critical for predicting difficulties like these, particularly those involving traffic distribution. Analyzing helps identify weak points and address them before irreparable disasters occur that could compromise the website in the short, medium, or long term.

You cannot, and do not want to, be dependent on a single source of traffic. Your business needs stability. It's like having only one major client for your company. If that client leaves one day, it would spell trouble for you as well. It is like having a table supported by only one leg. It is not safe.

Diversifying is always a good strategy; it strengthens the foundations of your business and makes it more resilient and adaptable to sudden market changes.

Section 4: How to manage your leads

Contacts are one of the most important aspects of an online asset. A contact is much more than just a piece of data. Every contact represents a person, a potential sale, a strategic partnership, or a growth opportunity. Each email and phone number is a chance to create authentic and meaningful connections with your audience. They serve as a direct communication channel.

Therefore, contacts form the foundation of any successful marketing strategy. The resulting contact lists are one of the secrets to generating qualified traffic at a low cost and increasing sales. In fact, these lists can influence both incoming traffic to the website and a portion of the revenue. In this context, it's crucial to understand the difference between subscribers, prospects, and leads.

Subscriber = General Interest

A subscriber is a visitor who has agreed to be contacted by you through your website. You may know their name and email because they downloaded some free content you offered and provided their details in a contact form. They might have subscribed to a newsletter to receive periodic content but do not show an immediate intent to purchase.

Lead = Specific Interest

A lead is a person whose existence you are aware of and who fits your ideal target audience. A lead has shown some interest in you and your services, indicating that they could convert now or in the future if educated properly. They are therefore a potential customer who requires more attention.

Prospect = Ready to Buy

Prospects are the advanced stages that follow the lead. It is a lead who has taken the next step, showing their interest in your product or offer by completing a specific action. They have a problem and have shown strong interest in solving it now. They may be waiting for a commercial proposal. This state ideally precedes the customer who converts and makes a purchase.

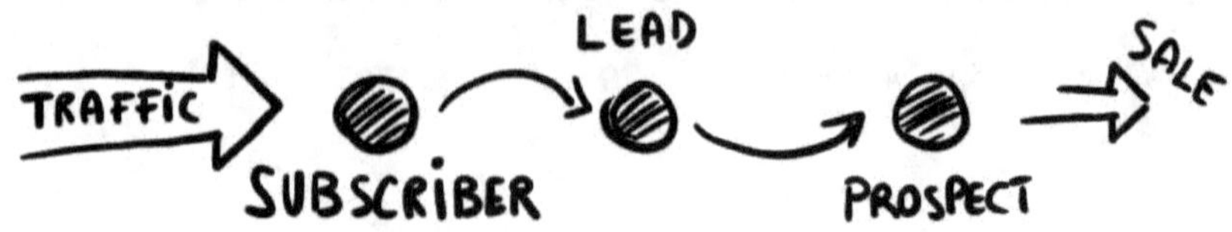

But why is it important to distinguish the different stages of contact qualification? Because it allows you to personalize your communications and target your marketing actions more effectively.

For instance, you'll send different content to a subscriber compared to a prospect simply because they are at different points in the customer journey.

The main tools for contact management are mailing lists and push notifications. There are indeed many different methods to collect and retain users, such as webinars, online courses, YouTube streaming, contests, chatbots, landing pages, and many others. This topic leans too much toward online marketing than SEO; you'll need to investigate these methods on your own.

The Mailing List

The simplest and most common way to stay in touch with visitors is to ask for their email addresses and convert them into subscribers.

This is accomplished by requesting a subscription to the classic newsletter, which, via scheduled email campaigns, will offer various information to those who have previously visited the website and are thus familiar with you, initiating a long-term relationship.

The trust you have already created, the email copy, and the information contained inside them will take care of the rest. Thanks to personalized emails, you can strengthen your connection with your audience and guide them towards specific actions, such as purchasing your products or services. Alternatively, you can simply direct them back to your new online content.

The newsletter will generate a low-cost traffic percentage that could potentially convert into high-value traffic. The goal will be to guide the subscriber to the next step in their customer journey. If you intend to monetize the website in the future—perhaps with your own products or by leveraging your brand—you must first create lists.

In short, you should always encourage users to leave their email addresses, and there are many ways to do this.

However, you'll need a third-party email management service; this is not expensive, at least until you manage a few hundred emails. Many services are free up to over 1,000 subscribers, allowing you to have a good starting audience at virtually no cost.

One of the most popular ways to obtain email addresses is to offer something for free in return. This could be a discount, an ebook, a limited-time offer, or access to a private group.

Once you have collected 10,000 or 20,000 email addresses, you have another source of traffic at your disposal. This source has two significant advantages: first, you control it. Second, these are all people who already know you.

So, start nurturing these contacts with weekly content. Send them engaging emails filled with valuable information. Users should be excited to open your emails and look forward to seeing your name in their inbox. Surprise your subscribers. It won't be a burden for them to open your emails, read them, and click on the links you include once they are confident that they will find what they want in your content and be amazed by the "free" value you are providing.

Remember to personalize the emails you send. To do this, simply request the user's name in addition to their email address. This is an excellent practice when it comes to emails, newsletters, and email marketing in general.

When you receive an email with a generic subject line, that's one thing. When you receive a similar email that speaks directly to you and includes your name in the subject line, it is unique since it is addressed to you personally.

Emails with personalized subject lines, for example, containing the recipient's name, significantly increase open rates. And if, within the body of the email, you continue to refer to the person by their name, the user experience changes dramatically. The email feels more personal, more intimate, and generates greater trust. Think about this the next time you check your email.

Which emails do you open more often or find more interesting? Probably those that speak directly to you.

Automate

Email marketing is much more effective when it's automated. Once you've captured a visitor's contact information, it's essential to set up automatic flows to provide personalized information and offers.

If you receive 50 new sign-ups each day, you certainly can't manually copy the emails into the system that manages them, nor can you send individual emails to each of the 50 subscribers. You can't even do this if only one person signs up per day, because you'd still be spending valuable time on it, and your job might not be writing emails but selling something.

Adopt the mindset of automating everything. Email management systems allow you to do this. They capture the email for you and add it to a "list." Once you have the email address, you can set up automations that trigger on that "list."

For example, you can activate a standard auto-response thanking the user for signing up. Alternatively, you might send an email immediately after sign-up with the discount voucher you promised.

You can activate follow-up sequences, which are simply multiple emails designed to educate the customer.

You can do some truly incredible things. I use various tools depending on the function I need; if I need to create interconnected sequences, customize forms, implement "if/else" or "loop" instructions, insert variables in emails, guide users through different flows, send messages to their phones or notifications to me, I use advanced paid tools.

If I only need to manage lists and a regular newsletter without specific automations, I implement an internal system using "phpList," an open-source software for managing email lists. The upside of phpList is that you have no user limits, no monthly costs, and the ability to customize templates. The downside is that it lacks the advanced features found in paid tools.

Regardless of the system you choose, you'll need to improve the user experience and, consequently, the conversion rate. The idea is to set up all the tools and functions once and then let them run automatically.

Over time, based on the data and results obtained, you can make necessary adjustments to enhance your automations.

Push Notifications

I previously mentioned how certain features can distract users, and I included push notifications among them.

However, it's important to consider things from a different perspective and recognize that some distractions can be beneficial, especially if they add value to the visitor and lead to conversions for you.

Push notifications are a way to stay in touch with visitors, and they have become evergreen among marketing practices, increasingly used due to their simplicity and effectiveness.

This service allows you to display a notification directly to visitors on their browser or mobile device. The tools available online for push notification services are usually paid, but there are free plans with limited features that you can try at no cost.

An opt-in banner for notifications immediately grabs the attention of visitors who have just entered the website, asking for their permission to send them notifications in the future until they decide to unsubscribe.

If the visitor closes the notification or responds negatively, they can continue browsing. However, if they click "yes," giving consent, they are added to a list similar to the mailing lists we've discussed. Now that they are subscribers, you can send them notifications at any time via the service, which will appear straight in their browser while they're using it.

This type of service has an opt-in rate of 5% and a click rate of 10%. These are excellent figures, considering the minimal costs involved. For instance, managing a list of 10,000 subscribers can cost you less than $20 per month, allowing you to send notifications as often as you like.

Of course, you shouldn't send notifications every day. Keep in mind that each time you send a notification, the average unsubscribe rate is about 10%.

The *opt-in rate* in this case is simply the conversion rate (CR) of the notification asking the visitor to subscribe to the push service.

With this type of notification, you can personalize based on the interests and behavior of each user. These factors help make the notifications more targeted and effective.

In conclusion, now you know that push notifications represent another powerful tool for increasing user engagement and retention. When used strategically and with respect for privacy, they can generate significant results.

Section 5: Manage the website

How to make your web-ecosystem work best

Your website is not just a container for information, text, words, and phrases that people read; it is not merely a design object or a digital business card. It is, instead, a complex computer organism—a true digital ecosystem that functions thanks to a series of software elements (platforms, funnel systems, templates, plugins, automations, etc.) supported by hardware elements (servers, networks, virtual storage, etc.).

All this complexity, of which a visitor is unaware, must be controlled, monitored, managed, and protected.

If you already have the technical skills to manage your website yourself, great; you have an additional advantage. Your knowledge will allow you to have complete control over your digital project. However, remember that as time goes on and your activities increase, you may find yourself needing to delegate certain tasks to optimize your time.

If you lack specific technical skills in website management but are digitally savvy and have a dynamic mind that adapts quickly, you can get started with minimal effort and testing.

If you're starting from scratch without a budget, keep in mind that you'll need to learn how to manage your website—or websites—yourself, particularly for the first few projects. You can't immediately rely on a technician to help you; otherwise, you'd face serious budget issues.

Learn on your own, buy a domain, and create some test websites. Experiment and acquire skills and techniques. Installing WordPress is free, takes about 5 minutes, and a domain is inexpensive. You could even start testing on the free web space that WordPress provides. This way, you wouldn't need to buy a domain for your initial tests. You could create a test project on this free platform, on a free WordPress subdomain, and then eventually migrate everything to your own domain.

This is a solution I generally do not recommend, but it is still an option. And above all, avoid using other pre-packaged website creation services; they are not as flexible as WordPress.

Regardless of your situation, here are some tips that will allow your web machine, once you have a functioning one, to operate efficiently and continue to do so for years.

Your own personal crawler

Let's start by discussing how to ensure that everything on your website is functioning as it should. You might want to check the structure, individual pages, meta tags, images, and everything else to verify that the work has been done properly. *How do you go through all this?*

An excellent tool for checking indexing and SEO quality that analyzes any website effectively is Screaming Frog, which offers a free version with some limitations. This "frog" acts as your personal crawler, providing useful and clear graphs along with an intuitive interface. You can instruct this trusted crawler to scan your website or any competitor's web project to analyze valuable data and identify strategies or opportunities.

The software not only provides indexing errors and website structure but also allows you to dive into the details, similar to how a search engine crawler operates. It can generate reports on page titles or descriptions, individual headings, page errors, inbound and outbound links for each page, and other genuinely useful information.

You can also visualize the website's structure and use its filters and sorting options to drill down into each individual element, helping you prioritize which issues to address first. The tool offers many options to customize its crawler, allowing you to configure the user- agent and access external APIs (like Google Analytics or Search Console) to extract data. By cross-referencing the data, you can feed the tool with traffic statistics for individual pages, making its analyses even more comprehensive.

Using such a tool gives you capabilities similar to those employed by a search engine crawler during the crawling phase. Moreover, it saves you a significant amount of time when analyzing a website by extracting pages from individual sitemaps or lists or by scanning entire domains and their subfolders.

Security

Protecting your website is akin to putting a lock on your front door. When you create a website, you're building a digital environment where valuable information is hosted. Just like a home, your website can be a target for intruders. Therefore, it's crucial to implement security measures to protect your data and that of your users.

Consider the costs associated with this aspect as an investment, an insurance policy against the damages that can always occur in the digital environment. I'm referring to physical damages, such as data loss caused by failures, errors, or other people's actions, such as data theft, sabotage, content copying, hacker attacks, spam, and so on.

Rely on an experienced technician to implement the 20% of operations that will boost your website's security by 80%.

If you're unable to do this yourself, I will explain what these operations are so that you can delegate the task to the technical person assisting you.

1)   Setting up a backup system

An automatic and always operational backup system can protect you from the most serious unexpected events and save you if you need to restore a prior version of the website due to an error or a problem that was not your responsibility.

It's a security protocol that can be a lifesaver. Many hosting providers already include a free backup plan, usually daily, in the plans you can purchase. I can assure you that sooner or later, you will need to restore a backup copy of your website, and you'll thank me for having read these lines.

2)   Protecting access to the WordPress backend

This is done by implementing an additional login layer to access the WordPress backend. It adds an extra layer of security to your assets. The password for this additional layer should obviously not be your child's name or their birthdate. Make the access truly secure.

3) Keep plugins updated to the latest version

This is very important because outdated plugins may have vulnerabilities and be subject to higher security risks.

For this reason, developers update plugins, and you should do the same. You don't need a technician for this; you can accomplish it right from the WordPress backend. An additional step is to automate all updates so you don't have to think about them every time you enter your website's dashboard. You can set up a weekly backup that activates by first taking a preventive backup of all files and the database, allowing you to restore the previous version if necessary.

4) Always use the latest version of PHP.

This operation is significant for both security and website performance. The only rule is that you should ensure that all of the plugins you use are compatible with the PHP version you intend to activate to avoid conflicts or malfunctions.

5) Use hard-to-guess usernames/passwords.

Clearly, long, alphanumeric passwords with symbols are harder to guess or decrypt than short and simple ones. You can increase the effectiveness of this security protocol by changing the password every 5 months to make things even more secure. Additionally, you might consider enforcing the use of SSL across the entire website. Never share your login and passwords at the same time via messages online.

6) Move the wp-config.php file outside the document root.

This adds an extra layer of security by preventing unauthorized access to this crucial configuration file, which contains sensitive information like database credentials.

7) Disable calls to the xmlrpc.php file, which is often exploited for DoS attacks or vulnerabilities.

By disabling this file, you reduce the risk of attacks that take advantage of its functionality.

8) Disable direct editing of files from the WordPress backend, requiring all files to be modified via FTP or SSH.

This prevents unauthorized users from altering your website's files directly through the dashboard.

9) Disable hotlinking: prevent others from including images or other content from your website (e.g., href).

This protects your bandwidth and ensures that your content is not being used without your permission.

10) Disable right-clicking and keyboard commands that copy text to minimally protect your original content.

That being said, if you already have a product to sell, you may want to explore using an "all-in-one" platform. This way, instead of spending time on these security measures, you can focus solely on your main objective: building traffic and selling your product.

Monetizing Traffic

The purpose of this book is to teach you SEO optimization techniques to drive traffic to your website and help you understand how to attract the ideal visitor. However, I would also like to provide you with valuable tips on how to monetize your website and generate income from your online asset.

Of course, all the work you do to create a web asset is intended with the ultimate goal of earning a profit. Sure, you might create a website for passion, and I understand that. But if your passion could bring in an extra paycheck every month in a passive and automatic way, *would you mind?* I don't think so.

Sooner or later, you'll need to monetize your traffic. It's a good idea to start a project with a clear understanding of how you plan to monetize it later on.

Monetizing as soon as possible is essential for the sustainability of a project. The sooner you start generating income, the sooner you can reinvest that income back into the business and grow your operations. Therefore, it's crucial to plan from the beginning various independent monetization strategies. This diversification will protect you from potential declines in any single revenue stream. Personally, I never start a project without having at least three different and independent ways to monetize it.

How do I monetize? That's a great question and a vast topic that I cannot address in detail here. However, at this point, understanding the concepts related to web monetization is much more important than the methods themselves.

Let's do some math...

First, in terms of monetization concepts, we need to discuss something that appears apparent to me but may not be to everyone: time and probability. At first, and this is the most common thing in the world, the websites you create and publish are unlikely to produce much traffic and thus no or very little money.

Let's define a few terms:

1. **Class A website:** A website that receives traffic and is monetized in a short time (6-12 months).

2. **Class B website:** A website that receives a lot of traffic but is poorly monetizable.

3. **Class C website:** A website that receives little traffic even after more than 12 months from publication.

The classic situation is that to find one Class A website, you need to try at least five different projects. If you're skilled and have already mastered the tools and SEO techniques from the book, you might find one Class A or B website every 2-3 attempts.

The odds are stacked against you, especially in the early stages, even if you put in your best effort by conducting extensive keyword research and flawlessly implementing all techniques.

Keeping this in mind, let's analyze a few different situations:

You create three different websites. Unfortunately, the three websites do not take off, generating only $100 in revenue per month after six months, which is approximately $33 per website.

You become discouraged because you believe that after six months, you have only earned $100 and could have made more money begging on the street. So you ditch the projects and return to sending out resumes in hopes of being hired as a shop assistant.

A "short-term ego" doesn't help in this work; you need to get rid of it because you didn't realize you were paying only $25 per year for hosting the three websites (a total of $75), and you're already making $525 in your first year, considering you only started in the sixth month. You also fail to consider that in the second year, assuming the same performance, you'd earn $1,125 each year for a 1500% ROI.

What would have happened if, instead of 10 websites, you had launched 30 different projects? Imagine if by the eighth month, the two websites you closed to save $5 a year had received a boost in the SERPs and transformed from Class B websites into Class A websites.

Another example:

You create just one website, which turns out to be a Class B website. After six months, it does not take off, and you ditch the entire project, believing that you cannot earn anything from the internet. This is a big mistake because you're fighting unarmed against the odds, which, as we mentioned, are 5 to 1.

Another example:

You create 10 websites and invest one year of work into them. Four of the websites are Class B; they fail to take off, and after a year, they make only $150 per month combined. Two of the websites become Class A, ranking high in a profitable niche, and each earns $800 per month through a variety of monetization techniques. The remaining four websites, Class C, struggle to take off but still manage to bring in $50 a month together.

Doing the math, you've worked "for free" for a year, but in reality, you haven't wasted time; you've invested it. From now on, you have a passive income of ($1,600 + $150 + $50 = $1,800) a month generated from your different websites. If you've done a good job, your rankings won't worsen after a year; in fact, they will improve even more, especially since you'll continue publishing content and implementing the strategies I've taught you correctly.

Visits and traffic will increase, as will all indirect earnings from various monetization. Those eight different Class B and C websites that weren't accomplishing anything may possibly start improving, while your entire system is supported by the two greatest Class A websites. *Do you understand the possibilities in a business like this?*
One last piece of advice on this topic: don't rush to monetize your website. First, focus on generating traffic and providing value to users. "Take your time to grow" and plan for at least two sources of income for each asset to diversify.

Monitoring

To optimize the performance and availability of your websites, it's wise to implement an automated monitoring system. These tools conduct regular check-ups on your websites, verifying server responses, content accuracy, and page accessibility. This way, you can promptly identify and resolve any anomalies.

There are various online services that monitor your websites for you. You simply need to sign up and provide the URLs of your websites, and these services will ensure that your websites are always online.

If the websites go offline, these services will detect it and notify you immediately via email or with a notification. You can also set the frequency of checks, which is usually automatic every "x" minute. The service I use for this type of monitoring is free for a limited number of domains.

It's not uncommon for a provider to perform maintenance on a server or restart the machine. In this case, the websites hosted on that server may go offline for a few minutes. The service alerts you when the website goes offline and when it comes back online, so you can quickly determine whether it was a scheduled maintenance event or something more serious.

Sometimes, the problem can be more severe, requiring your urgent intervention. If a website generating $200 a day in income goes offline and you don't notice it for two days, you could lose $400.

Additionally, the search engine will recognize that the website is down, and after a while, it will take action. You don't think Google will continue directing users to a website that doesn't work, *do you?*

Road Map

To simplify the process you are about to undertake, I have prepared a kind of map that should help you have a clear picture of all the steps you need to take if you're starting from scratch. The navigation route is already mapped out; you just need to begin following it.

When viewed as a whole, the work may seem overwhelming, but the trick is to tackle each step individually. Breaking a large task into smaller steps greatly helps prevent you from getting lost. Addressing any potential issues will also be easier with this approach. Perseverance, technique, and focus are all qualities you need to keep in mind and balance during the execution of your projects.

1) Try to understand the niche you want to focus on. Think of something you are passionate about and enjoy, but also consider something that is economically viable, even if it doesn't align with your interests. Conduct market and trend research.

2) Check if there are products within your chosen niche that people are selling profitably. To do this, look at affiliate networks in the vertical you are considering and see which products are selling the most. If there are many that belong to a niche you are also passionate about, that's even better—you're in luck. This gives you a general idea of the products or services you will need to promote when monetizing your website.

3) Start researching your competitors. Search Google for the products you found or the general terms related to the niche, and note down all the domains that have high traffic or are well-positioned. Take notes on how these websites manage their traffic, where they funnel it, and what they sell.

4) Deepen your keyword research. Check all the websites you listed and find out which pages generate the most traffic for each website. Record the pages and organize everything in a Google Doc file.

5) Research the traffic volumes. For each page you found, check all the keywords driving traffic to that page.

6) Select keywords with lower difficulty and competition levels, yet with high traffic volume and CPC. If a keyword is less competitive, you will rank faster; if the CPC is high, it means that the keyword converts well from visitor to buyer.

7) Check where the links to the pages you are analyzing come from and jot down the URLs. If you want to implement a backlink strategy, this data will be useful.

   For example, you might consider emailing those who have already linked to an article X, letting them know that you've addressed the same topic in more detail. This way, you have the chance to create links.

8) Create content for your website, always referencing the keywords and improving the articles already present in the search engine results. Include more text, more images, etc.

9) Implement all the SEO techniques described in phase 3 of this book, and at the same time, promote the content, for example via email or social media, and try to connect with other "content creators."

10) Monitor the incoming traffic, user behavior, and the functioning of the funnel. Identify system flaws, eliminate them, and restart the process in an endless refinement cycle with the aim of providing value to people.

Finally, here is another more schematic list of how you should chronologically approach a project, from the idea to the beginning of indexing.

1. You have an idea.
2. Market study.
3. Competitor study.
4. Keyword and volume study.
5. Funnel/marketing design.
6. Website structure design.
7. Page hierarchy design.
8. Internal link design.
9. Domain purchase.
10. Setting a closed robots.txt.
11. URL structure design.
12. Page template creation.
13. Page template optimization.
14. Integration of meta tags.
15. Integration of schema tags.
16. Content creation.
17. Internal link creation.
18. Content optimization.
19. Media optimization.
20. User experience optimization.
21. Setting an open robots.txt.
22. Sitemap creation.
23. Error checking with Screaming Frog.
24. Submission to Google Search Console.
25. Error checking with GSC.
26. Crawling initiation.
27. You can go on vacation for 3 months.

I hope this list helps you feel less confused and gives you a roadmap for every new website you want to create.

Check up routine

Whether you have one website or 40, you always need to keep an eye on them. Having two newly created websites is like having two newborns; you need to care for them, feed them, and change their diapers. On the other hand, having two established websites with active traffic is somewhat like having two older children; you still need to call daily to check on where they are and how they're doing.

What I do every day (more or less) is primarily check the earnings generated by the various websites. This helps; if the earnings are good, it sets a positive mood for the day and puts me in the right mindset. If the earnings are low, it motivates me to take immediate action and try to fix any issues.

If everything is average or better, that's fine; I take things easy. However, if the income from a particular asset has significantly decreased, I immediately check that website to understand the cause and resolve it.

I also take a look at Google Analytics or Google Search Console to monitor the traffic volumes of the larger websites.

That's it. I don't check my email, don't look at orders (in e-commerce), and absolutely don't check social media. All of this is done once or twice a week, or more frequently if there are orders to fulfill.

It's meaningless to check your email, Facebook page, and websites on a daily basis. *How would you manage if you had 100?* It's smarter to plan a weekly calendar and automate as much of the system as possible.

Once I complete this check-up, I review the tasks and goals I need to achieve for the day, all of which I noted down the day before in a diary. This way, the work is organized, and I can start working.

Section 6: Manage emotions

Small thoughts lead to big results

We are approaching the end of this journey, and you have already read and, I hope, learned what is necessary to achieve the goal of this book: bringing organic traffic to your website.

There are a few things I would still like to share with you. These are insights you will understand on your own as you navigate the path to creating websites and online assets.

There are other lessons you might find in another book in the future. Perhaps these are things you already know or concepts you may never have encountered.

In simple terms, I'll share some helpful advice below to help you develop your online business projects—concepts that apply regardless of the type of traffic you're attempting to generate. If I had known these when I was 25, my life would be very different today.

If I had to choose the most challenging aspect to learn and control throughout this journey, out of all the chapters I have written, I would undoubtedly choose this.

You are not dealing with HTML code, which, like any language, can be taught relatively easily, nor with a server that can be replaced if it fails. Here, you're dealing with yourself and your emotions, which is no laughing matter.

Invisible Results

In projects like these, where time and money are invested with an expectation of long-term revenue, there is a huge amount of imagination required, a laborious commitment, and a lot of stress from the wait.

Those who design online assets and work to drive traffic through search engine optimization techniques are not so naive as to think that results come immediately. Generating organic traffic is, as I have said, a "long-term" job.

A class C website can remain without traffic for up to 12 months. A class B website may have few conversions for as long as 24 months.

But what are 12 or 24 months if you can reap the rewards of your work and investments with no further effort over the next ten years?

What is the value of 12 months if your traffic skyrockets in the thirteenth month and your class B website transforms into a class A?

Remember one fundamental thing: at the beginning, results are never visible, but then they grow with an exponential curve. I repeat: at the start of a project, the results are never visible, and they may not be seen for months. However, if the project has been designed to succeed, something will change sooner or later, resulting in exponential growth.

And what is it that changes? It's possible that the website needed extra time to be properly indexed. Perhaps the week before, you made a substantial change, or even a small tweak, that made a difference. Or maybe you published the right article at the right time and experienced a visibility boom.

In short, always keep this in mind and maintain consistent efforts; don't give up. Look for examples of curves where results are not visible at first and then become exponential.

I like the quote, "The wise point to the moon, while the fool looks at the finger." Take a look at the graph representing Facebook's growth since its founding.

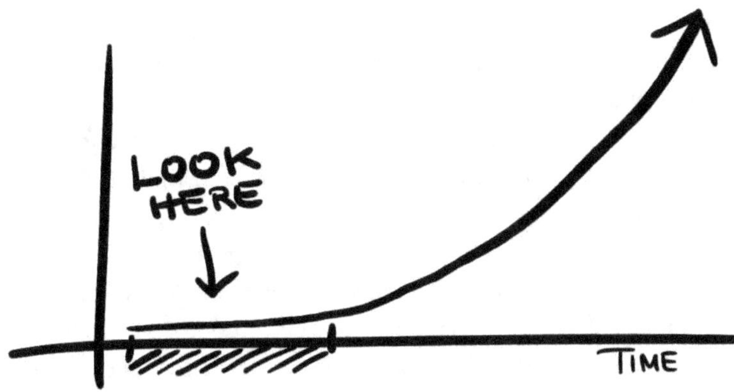

But don't just look at the climb, as everyone does. You see that the initial period was relatively flat, and then there was exponential growth. That first period is the key (the moon).

This curve and behavior can be found in a variety of fields and applications, not only technology. The curve of COVID-19 diffusion is a recent example.

The challenge here is to have patience, manage the fear of failure, and prevent it from making you give up too soon.

Law of Large Numbers

"The best way to have a good idea is to have lots of ideas." —— Linus Pauling

The guy who said that phrase was right; it's just a matter of probability. If 10 horses are running in a race and you bet everything on just one, you'll obviously have a 1 in 10 chance of winning. Clearly, if you bet on 8 different horses instead of just one, you'll have an 80% chance of winning. You need to find a way to stack the odds in your favor.

Similarly, if you work on only one project, your chances of success are slim. Are you familiar with the *"law of large numbers"*? It states that life on Earth is an inevitable consequence of the vastness of the universe. Or increasing the number of trials increases the likelihood that a specific event will occur.

To help you understand how probabilities work, remember that 90% of new companies close within the first 3 years. And of the remaining survivors, 9 out of 10 close within the following 10 years.

So, allow room for creativity and new ideas. In fact, whenever a new idea comes to mind, write it down and take notes. You might reconsider and implement that idea later. Leave extra room for new projects and keep your mind flexible, trying to make the most of the opportunities that sometimes appear before you.

Remember that it's best to start with just one project at first, but keep in mind that if you want the numbers and probabilities to work in your favor, you'll probably need to experiment more.

The objective is to plant a small seed on the web that will grow into a tree and provide you with fruits to harvest for years to come. So instead of a single seed, it's better to throw down a handful of seeds, *right?*

Mindset and goals

When working on complex projects, both online and offline, it's crucial not to lose sight of the goal. To stay focused on the goal, you must first have a clear understanding of it. To properly focus on my goals, I usually write them down in a diary or a file on Google Drive.

I don't write "things to do," but rather "goals." If I use Drive, I assign a score to each objective or goal and prioritize the list every day. This way, I can start working on the highest-priority item until it's done. If I write them in a diary, I cross them off once completed.

Writing and visualizing goals is very useful. It boosts productivity. Also, seeing goals achieved and surpassed helps visualize the path and see that you're "moving forward."

Yes, all of these goals are part of your strategy. The plan accounts for 20% of success, whereas mindset accounts for the other 80%. Napoleon Bonaparte said: "Everyone is capable of making a plan, but few are capable of following it through to the end." What a man.

By creating lists of objectives, or "goals," I always start the day already knowing what I need to do. If in the morning you start working, turn on the computer, and ask yourself, "So, what do I do today? Where do I start?" then something isn't right.

I am "goal-oriented" and work towards objectives. If a goal is too big, you can break it down into smaller, more manageable sub-goals.

Get into the mindset of "visualizing your goals," and then, write them down. Your work is long-term, and it takes a great deal of imagination to achieve it.

Your primary goal should be to create what is known as "brand assets. For example, creating your own brand and identifying your target audience—who will engage with you over time, instead of merely for a single visit or purchase.

By developing assets with a loyal audience that generates revenue, you can separate time from money. Separating time from money is revolutionary. It means that you are no longer trading your time for a paycheck but rather using it to create something that will benefit you.

The potential that this goal-oriented mindset offers is enormous. *Can you see it?* The ultimate goal, if you think about it, is to make yourself unnecessary.

I'll also share another thought. Something that always intrigued me in high school was how a nuclear fission bomb works. To keep it simple, to start nuclear fission, you need to gather a minimum critical mass of fissile material (uranium-235 or plutonium-239). But if the material doesn't reach "critical mass," the fission won't sustain itself, and there would not be a chain reaction.

Complete your goals, take those risks, and reach critical mass. At that point, your project will start a chain reaction, releasing a massive amount of energy.

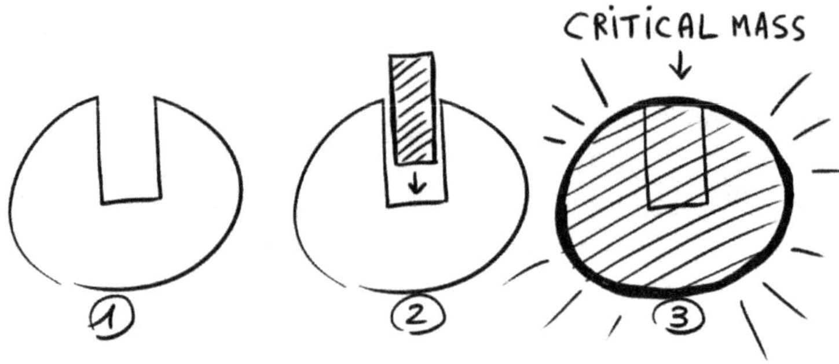

Paralysis by analysis

"Paralysis by analysis" is a status you'll have to face multiple times during the development of your projects, especially in the beginning when you have less experience. You'll have to confront it, accept the blocks you'll encounter, and know how to overcome them. It will be a battle against yourself.

It literally means "paralysis due to analysis," and it happens when we overthink something to the point that we can't make a decision. This is also known as "overthinking."

It's as if excessive analysis paralyzes us, preventing us from taking action. Often, this situation arises from indecision between various options, leading to an endless, unproductive analysis.

You can't move forward, either because what you're attempting to achieve is too complicated, or more likely because you've weighed yourself down. You keep analyzing different options until you end up in an infinite spiral of thoughts and reasoning that drains your time and energy.

Other times, the cause is an excessive focus on a specific problem. You want to dig deep into a problem and complicate your life when, in fact, the solution might simply be to solve it and move on.

In any case, if you're stuck in such a situation and are experiencing the effects of "paralysis by analysis," know that it's a normal deviation that happens in nearly every project. You find yourself wandering in a maze of thoughts and possibilities, unable to find a way out, and you start procrastinating.

How to resolve it? Clearly focus on the goal you've set. Set a maximum time limit to resolve it. Then, choose the solution that, all things being equal, seems the simplest.

Learn to delegate

During a complex project, it's inevitable to encounter a moment of standstill, a place I refer to as the "panic room." It's the point where you feel overwhelmed by the workload, surrounded by a chaos of ideas and worries. You'll fear not being able to get everything done, and this emotion might paralyze you.

It's like being in one of those white rooms you see in movies, where a maniac has scratched the padded walls with their nails, carving incomprehensible codes and messages—nonsensical things. If you find yourself sane and stay for more than a day, you'll eventually go mad.

An example that comes to mind is when you obsess over Core Web Vitals scores during the performance optimization phase of your pages. You constantly strive to get 100%, and perhaps you view it as a personal challenge. However, doing so increases the danger of burnout. Instead, delegate the work to your developer. Keep in mind, even Google's own homepage doesn't pass the Core Web Vitals test on mobile... So, draw your own conclusions.

The solution to this impasse is simple: build a team. By collaborating with others, you can divide the work, share responsibilities, and find more effective solutions.

Managing a project alone is tough and takes time, especially if it's your first one. Getting a new website off the ground requires effort. Consider how you would handle many websites, say 40, in different markets. You'll realize you need help because you can't do everything on your own.

I'm not simply talking about getting help with website content. You must adopt the appropriate mindset: you are creating assets that will work for you automatically.

Always consider the perspective of someone who will eventually need to step away from the project, either completely or essentially entirely.

Delegating is the solution to your overwork problems. At some point, you'll need to find collaborators—people who can help you push the projects forward. When that moment arrives, take advantage of it. Search for people who are better than you, who can stimulate your mind and assist you in developing new or complimentary skills to those you already possess.

Ideally, the members of your team should have completely opposite or unique abilities compared to yours, but share the same moral code. The people working with you should align with your company's "vision." This is the key foundation for building a successful team.

Laser focus mode

Building on what we've said about priorities and how to organize them, it's important to highlight a few tips regarding focus and distractions.

When you're working on something, do it seriously. Forget everything else and focus solely on your task. No distractions, no glancing at your phone, just you and your goal.

You need to channel all of your energy and attention toward one singular purpose: solving the problem or reaching the objective you've set for yourself. I call this the "laser focus" mode because you need to be like a laser—directing all your power to a single, specific point.

Only you can pick how and where you work, because each person and project is unique. Focus on your strengths, greatest abilities, and core skills, as they will produce the best results.

Some people prefer to tackle the toughest tasks first thing in the morning, while others leave them for later. I personally handle them at the start of my day, simply because when I wake up, my energy levels are at their peak, and I can give it my all. If I waited until the evening, I wouldn't have the same drive or energy left.

Workspaces and their organizations also play a role. Personally, I prefer a high level of isolation while switching into "laser" mode.

When I'm working on my computer and need to focus, I like to listen to natural sounds like the wind in the trees, the sea, or a thunderstorm. For example, I am currently listening to a tune titled "a blizzard storm sound." It helps me to relax and focus.

So, put on headphones with relaxing music, and work until you've finished what needs to be done.
Finally, let me give you a piece of advice that alone is worth a lot of money: eliminate all notifications from your phone. I'm not just saying to do this

when you're in "laser mode"—I mean, eliminate notifications permanently. Do it now.

Take your phone and delete all of the apps that you don't need and that send you notifications. Get rid of Facebook, Instagram, TikTok, and all those apps that are literally consuming your attention. Learn to use these tools from the perspective of someone who exploits them professionally, not as someone who uses and is enslaved by them. Become the creator, not the consumer of content. In terms of apps you use regularly, disable all of their notifications, especially the ones with sounds.

Chances are, you're using Facebook, Instagram, and TikTok out of habit. You should've already understood this when we discussed the section of the book about users seeking "solutions to needs."

These apps are the source of harmful habits. They were designed to consume your attention, and consequently, your energy—try to understand this. They create addiction; they reward you for using them.

Imagine that every time a notification pops up and grabs your attention, it triggers an automatic, involuntary behavior (you grab your phone, open it, unlock it, check the notification, dismiss it, close it again); and it drains a bit of your energy.

1 notification = -1 point of physical energy and -1 point of mental energy.

By the end of the day, your brain is fried, trust me. You might not even realize how many times you're distracted by notifications, sounds, lights, icons, or pop-ups on your phone. Maybe you don't notice how often you end up scrolling through social media feeds and reading useless things.

Use your time and energy in the best possible way.

Once you try eliminating all this clutter, I guarantee your productivity will improve drastically, you'll conserve energy, and both your life and business will get a significant boost.

Learn to lose

The entrepreneurial journey online, like any adventure, is filled with ups and downs. Despite your determination and best efforts, you will inevitably face failures. *Are these moments negative?* Yes, but they are also valuable opportunities for growth and learning.

The business world is constantly evolving. When we consider the online business landscape, this evolution is more than rapid. Conceptually and fortunately, we perceive that some standards will never change, although on a technological level, everything changes rapidly. An idea that works today may not capture users' interest in two years. A website you build today, generating traffic through SEO after 10 months, might see all its visitors taken by a competitor just one year later. These are the risks of the game.

However, failures push us to be flexible and adapt to changes. They help us focus on what is truly important and eliminate distractions. Facing and overcoming difficulties makes you stronger, more resilient, and teaches you to tackle challenges with a more positive and constructive attitude.

Every failure is like a scientific experiment, teaching you something new about yourself, your market, and the strategies that don't work.

So if a strategy or project doesn't work out, don't feel ashamed. Try to see it as an opportunity for growth. Certainly, analyze the reasons for your failure and consider what you could have done differently. Manage your emotions and gather useful information that you can apply next time. Implement the concept of a *"feedback loop"* that I explained earlier.

A successful entrepreneur is not someone who has never failed but someone who has the ability to rise again after every fall. It is important to cultivate a positive mindset and always believe in your abilities and the standard principles described in this book. Remember that failures are just a chapter in your story. Learn to lose and move forward; this is the right mindset.

Imagine a professional trader in technical analysis operating in the stock markets. Every day, they make decisions based on the analyses they conduct. They not only check prices and volumes of the stock on charts but also look for matches with hundreds of different strategies and indicators. They analyze price patterns, apply strategies based on moving averages, Fibonacci retracements, volume profiles, double bottoms and tops, Bollinger bands, and hundreds of other techniques.

Sometimes their predictions turn out to be wrong. Yet they do not get discouraged. Instead, they view each completed trade as an opportunity to refine their strategies. They keep a detailed journal of every trade, analyzing the factors that led to the success or failure of each individual operation.

Sometimes they will win, and other times they will lose. But it is through these continuous experiments that they will hone their skills and ultimately develop their own techniques and strategies, along with an increasingly sharp intuition that will tilt the odds in their favor.

In conclusion, true failure is not about failing or making mistakes but about giving up and not trying to improve. When you attempt to develop various web projects, do not fall in love with a single project too much, as it may be necessary to abandon it and focus on another.

Ignorance Bubble

Have you ever stopped to think about how much we really know about the world around us? Often, we move within a bubble, a kind of personalized informational ecosystem that shows us only what algorithms think might interest us. We don't know what we don't know. We are trapped in a bubble of ignorance.

This is the so-called "ignorance bubble," a concept that describes our tendency to underestimate the vastness of available knowledge and limit our exposure to new ideas.

Social media and search engines, with their increasingly sophisticated algorithms, create a tailored reality for us. This personalization offers numerous advantages, but it also exposes us to the risk of becoming trapped in a kind of digital funhouse mirror, where our opinions are constantly reinforced and dissenting voices are silenced.

Algorithms systematically personalize the user experience by showing you content related to your interests or behaviors. Imagine scrolling through videos on TikTok and accidentally pausing a few seconds longer than usual on a video of two cows grazing. The platform will start suggesting more cow-related videos, experimenting with different angles to keep you consuming more content. It might show you normal cows, cartoon cows, talking cows, or people dressed as cows at a carnival—any variation it can find to feed you.

If you've given consent, search engines may continuously listen to your conversations using your smartphone's microphone. Assume you discuss with a friend how you got sunburned at the beach. You'll suddenly notice sunscreen advertisements on social media or the next website you visit.

If one day you entertain the idea that the Earth is flat, rest assured you'll find like-minded individuals online who think the same. You can engage with them, discuss, reinforce your belief, and even create a community. But none of this changes the fact that the Earth is round. Objective reality exists independently of our opinions and the size of the communities that support them.

The web is an extraordinary tool, but it must be used with discernment. Not everything we read online is true, and not all opinions hold the same weight. It's crucial to develop critical thinking and verify information from multiple sources before accepting them as true.

The ignorance bubble makes us feel like we have control over our online experience. However, the reality is quite different. We are at the mercy of algorithms that, while trying to meet our needs, can limit our ability to explore new horizons or reinforce false beliefs. This illusion of control can lead to a distortion of reality, a danger that especially affects children.

But how can you break free from this ignorance bubble? You need to be proactive in your search for information. Stop relying solely on algorithms, diversify your sources, question your beliefs, and cultivate curiosity.

Working with search engine optimization, we know that search engine algorithms determine which websites are shown in response to a specific query. This means that companies looking to reach a broader audience via SEO must constantly adapt to algorithm changes and provide high-quality, relevant content.

To overcome the ignorance bubble and improve your online visibility, you need to step out of your comfort zone. Actively seek new information, challenge your beliefs, and open yourself to new perspectives to understand the complexity of the world around you and make more informed decisions.

Section 7: Managing problems

For every problem there are infinite solutions

In this brief section, I'd like to highlight the most common problems that will delay you or that you will inevitably face if you set out to develop one or more websites, regardless of the type of traffic you seek.

Knowing the difficulties is the first step to overcoming them. In this section, I offer you a comprehensive overview of the most common challenges in web development from an SEO perspective. *Why?* Because being aware of potential problems will allow you to address them proactively and avoid unnecessary losses of time and resources.

Throughout your journey, especially if you have little experience, you will encounter the following problems:

1. I cannot find the right niche.
2. I am afraid of competitors.
3. Where can I find the money?
4. Where can I find collaborators, and how do I delegate?
5. How do I overcome mental blocks?
6. How do I avoid procrastination?
7. How can I overcome confusion?

[1] Can't find the right niche

Before creating an asset in a niche you're unsure about, conduct thorough research. Often, I spend three months doing in-depth and meticulous keyword research.

Usually, if I have an idea, I jot it down, do a quick initial search, and note down the data roughly to see if the niche and market "inspire" me. I wait a bit, think it over, and let it simmer. Then maybe, two months later, I'll revisit the research and do a more in-depth analysis. If I'm not convinced, I leave it to stew. Some ideas can develop quickly in a few days, while others need more time.

I might abandon the idea, or after another month, I might pick it up again and decide to proceed with a website in that niche. The ideal ratio of the "thinking phase" compared to the "implementation phase" is at least 3 to 1.

Utilize tools like Google Trends, as discussed earlier, or other tools mentioned in the market research section.

Browse, read, explore, and take notes along the way. Ideas will start to flow, and among them, you'll find one that's original and will eventually be successful.

[2] I am afraid of competitors

Competitors existed before you and will undoubtedly exist after you. Therefore, this situation shouldn't scare you but rather motivate you.

If you see that there's a lot of competition in a niche, it means there's a lot of money involved. If you can spot a gap amid all this competition, you might consider entering it. Perhaps there are long-tail keywords with high volume and low competition that could present an opportunity.

In the beginning, you'll likely find niches with plenty of competitors. Look for those with fewer but still significant commercial value.

Leverage your competitors and use them to your advantage. They've already done what you'll need to do; therefore, you must outperform them. Study their weaknesses; learn how you can improve their content. Analyze their links and ask yourself:

- Where are they getting them from?
- Which pages get the most traffic?
- What are the keywords driving that traffic?

Use the crawler tool I showed you to manage your website and examine theirs on both structural and technical levels and find their flaws.

Many of the websites I've developed weren't anything new; they were simply much better versions of existing competitors. Don't see the glass as half empty; instead, try to see it as half full and use your competitors to fill the glass completely.

[3] Finding money

Finding funding at the beginning of web project development can be a challenge if you don't already have a stable income or a defined budget. However, it is not a major concern because the initial expenditures of developing websites are not prohibitively expensive.

As I mentioned before, you can create your first websites for free without purchasing a domain by using the free CMS WordPress. So, no excuses—you can start without spending a dime; all you need is a PC and an internet connection. *Don't have a PC?* Use your smartphone. *Don't have a PC or an internet connection?* Go to a public library.

If you already have a website or want to create a serious asset, a domain costs around $10, and economical hosting is about $40 a year.

Given that a well-researched niche website can be profitable with just 10 articles (if done correctly), let's do some quick math.

If you write the contents yourself, in your spare time, you only spend $40 a year. If you hire someone to write them, assuming you need ten 1,000-word articles at $15 each, the total cost would be $150.

In total, you can launch a niche website and start your digital journey for about $200. *Does that seem like a lot?* I don't know any other investment that offers such potential for growth and profit, starting with just $200.

[4] Finding collaborators

At the start of any operation, you need someone to show you how things are done and assist you along the way. It's difficult to succeed without precise and ongoing initial coaching.

But even after that, when you expand, you will always need help.

Whether you have a single large website or 20 small websites in different niches, you must consider and address this issue.

You will have other things to manage, new projects to launch, and niches to explore. You won't be able to do everything alone unless your goal is to spend all day at the computer working.

So, in addition to seeking guidance, you need to look for collaborators. They can help you with technological issues, social media, or writing new material.

Finding them can sometimes be straightforward and at other times a bit more complicated. I use Facebook groups to post ads. For example, if I'm looking for a copywriter to write articles, I'll post an ad in a copywriters' group. Sometimes I also use services like Upwork and Fiverr, especially for more specific tasks.

On these platforms, you'll find many people offering their services, and there's a decent system for managing projects, contracts, and payments for each freelancer. In any case, before hiring somebody, it is a good idea to have them sign an NDA (non-disclosure agreement).

[5] Mental Blocks

It may seem incredible, but "thought," and the resulting mindset, plays a fundamental role. Very often, you create mental blocks that don't actually exist. Or you get caught up in "paradigms" that limit you.

If you think you will never find the right niche, you probably won't, because you've created that belief and the resulting mental block.

If you believe your website will make no more than $30 per month, you will most likely fall short of that figure, which will create a roadblock for you.

Another common and truly silly block is the language barrier. The language of the web is English, but you can create websites for audiences in other languages using tools available today. So, blocks like these don't actually exist. If you don't know a language, learn it or use an AI tool to overcome the problem. Many of your competitors don't even speak English, so consider the competitive advantage you would have.

You can truly do everything; the possibilities for online growth and business are infinite. Set ambitious but achievable goals and decide on a specific timeline to reach them. Break down large goals into smaller sub-goals, with "sub-deadlines," and start.

Starting is the most important block to tear down first. After that, the rest will follow.

[6] Loss of perseverance

If you're feeling a bit confused while trying to absorb all this information, don't worry. It's normal, and it has happened to me too.

You can't imagine how many times I've reached the point of thinking I understood everything, only to fall into an abyss of doubts and uncertainties with no clear end in sight. This is part of the game.

Your performance as a professional, along with your assets, will not always be consistent. It's not a straight line that starts from zero and rockets upward. It's more like a sinusoidal line, with ups and downs. The lows are a normal part of the process; they've always happened and will always happen.

Do not fall into the trap of believing that everything is simple and that the journey will always be downhill. Instead, be aware of how business on the web operates and prepare yourself to face these "downturns."

Look at the following image. As you can see, the journey isn't straight, and there are cyclical periods of "negativity." What matters is the long-term trend.

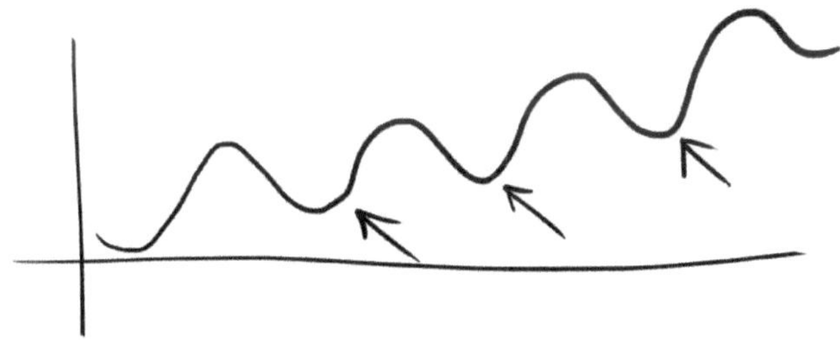

If you are unfamiliar with how things work, you may be able to endure the first and second downturns, but after the third, you will most likely become discouraged and give up.

The secret to overcoming these moments is "be consistent," meaning perseverance and continuous research and study.

Always remember that creating websites aimed at attracting the majority of organic traffic is a business model that requires time—a long-term investment. Consider how many times you'll need to face the downturns on the curve.

The great thing is that if you develop even just three assets, their curves, along with their declines, will balance out over time. On average (μ), you will maintain good performance.

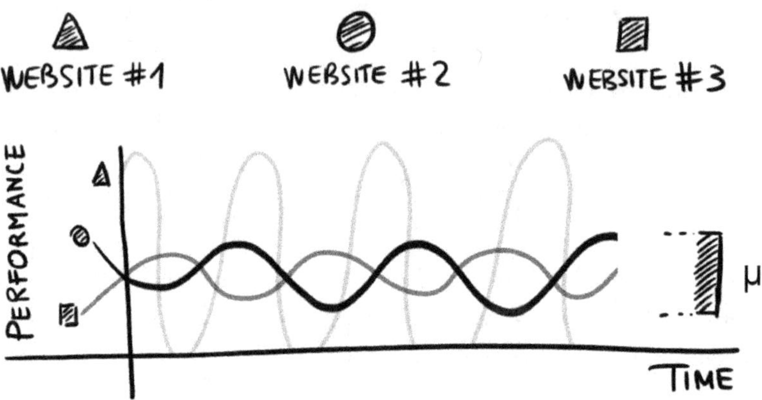

Remember that it's not a sprint; it's a marathon, and now you know how it works. Stay strong and keep moving towards your goal.

[7] Confusion

Congratulations! You've read almost 100,000 words in which I have shared my perspective on how a part of the web world operates. Given the vastness of the topic and the countless facets we've yet to explore, you might find yourself in a state of normal confusion. Perhaps you're unsure where to start, or if you've already begun, you're not sure where to focus your energies. I recommend you start by considering this question:

What is the truly important problem you want to solve?

To help you visualize your project more clearly, you can use "mind maps"—tools for generating, organizing, and memorizing ideas. A mind map is far more effective than a business plan because it helps you understand where the business can go and what direction it can take. Here's an example:

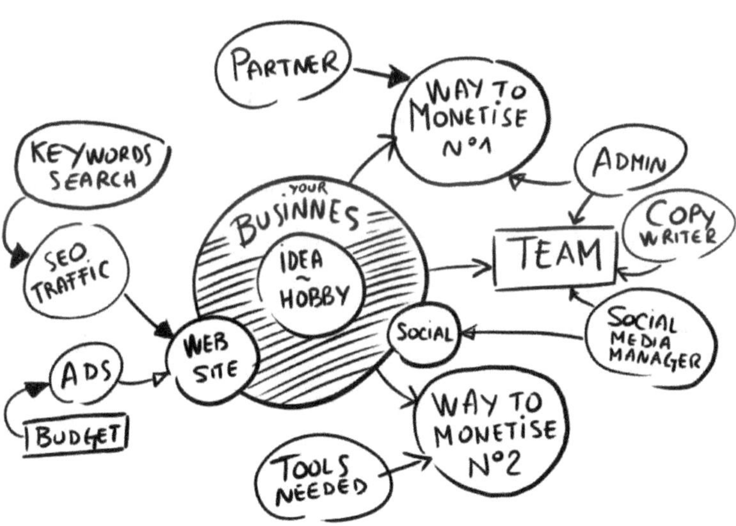

The map in this example consists of circles or bubbles. The innermost circle contains your idea, which preferably corresponds to one of your passions. The first outer circle represents your business, encompassing your business idea.

Then there are secondary circles connected to it, some of which represent "ways to make money," and gradually the map expands. You can also create connections between the outer bubbles; there are no limits. You can continue to add bubbles along the way as you develop the business and envision where it might lead.

Now, let's say your financial resources are the circle below. Here's how those resources could be allocated in an SEO project.

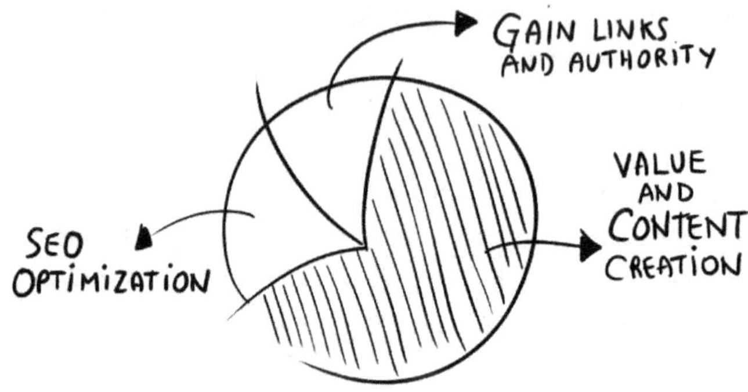

Here is the breakdown of time as it should ideally be once you are evaluating a project.

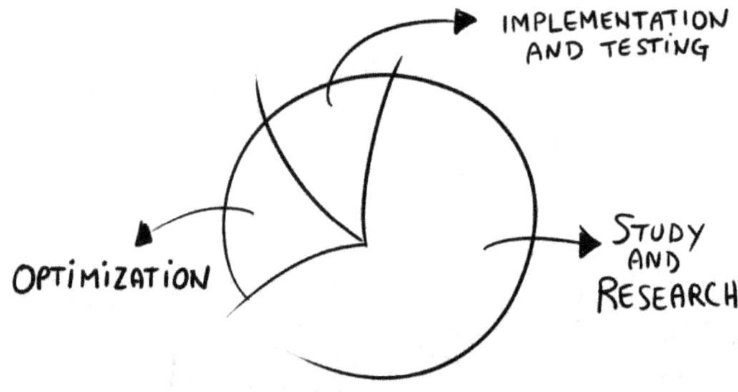

Conclusion

Our talking about SEO is complete. What a journey! Wasn't it? You now have the knowledge needed to fully comprehend the potential of your web projects by utilizing search engine optimization techniques and all of the other concepts learned.

I have particularly delved into the topic of organic traffic, given its complexity and centrality in SEO. Other topics have been covered more generally, and each of them deserves dedicated exploration.

I chose to thoroughly explain the traffic that I always seek and the techniques that I use every day. If you can position your website well organically, you can truly dominate a particular niche. You won't spend anything to get traffic, and once the website is monetized, you can achieve huge profit margins. *Can you imagine a more exciting business than this one?*

Now you have the tools, the knowledge, and the standards to start your journey on the web. Don't think of SEO merely as a set of rules and techniques to follow to ensure that your website appears in the top search results. SEO is much more: it's a journey, not a destination. It's a way of thinking, a philosophy that guides you in creating valuable content for users, but also an art that allows you to do it in a creative and personalized way.

The rules of the game may change, but the value of great content remains timeless. Focus on the game's standards you have learned and make exceptional content; success will follow.

Enjoy your adventure!

SEO STANDARD AUDIT

If you need help with your website, check out my private mentorship services.

They are reserved for small businesses and marketing agencies.

If you run a small business, I can help you to:

1. Understand why your website is not growing.
2. See what is blocking visitors from search engines.
3. Save time identifying top problems right away.

If you run an agency, I can help you to:

1. Quickly spot problems on your clients websites.
2. Increase the quality and expand your service offering.
3. Save time and resources with professional external service.

Get in touch!

Glossary

The word *"asset"* refers to *"a property that holds value"* and is any resource you own that can be monetized. A website is an online asset. The ideal online asset is something that you no longer have to edit, for example, a pillar post or video on YouTube.

Traffic refers to the visitors to your website. Traffic is defined as those who browse the internet and seek information. Traffic includes users of websites, social networks, and online services. Traffic is made up of people; in fact, *traffic is people.*

Flow is a term that describes something moving continuously from point A to point B along a path. It's exactly how users behave on the web, and that's why we refer to the flow as the pathway we want to guide traffic (users) through, directing them from where they start (A) to where we want them to end up (B).

A *link* is a connection between one page and another. It usually appears as blue-colored or underlined text, but it can also be an image. When you click on it, you are taken to another web page. In the world of the web, links and their structure are important; we will discuss this further later.

The *search engine* is nothing more than a website or service like Google, Bing, or similar that is used to search the web. In this book, when I talk about search engines, I am mainly referring to Google, which is the most dominant today. However, the best practice when performing SEO optimizations is to consider and check which search engine is most used in the country or market of interest.

The *"snippet"* is the search result you see on search engine pages. It usually consists of a title and a description that help you determine if the proposed website contains what you're looking for. However, it can be much more complex, containing videos or images, structured data, or even becoming an informational card.

SEO, short for "Search Engine Optimization," literally means "optimizing pages for search engines." It refers to all the techniques used to optimize websites, pages, or web resources to make them easy for search engines to find and index.

It's commonly said that a user "lands" on a web page when they open it. Landing pages are specific pages designed for users to arrive at.

The *advertiser* is the person or company that purchases ad space to publish their ad.

The "SERP" (Search Engine Result Page) is the list of websites that a search engine displays for a specific search query. Most web traffic comes from the top 8-10 results on the SERP (around 91%). You will encounter the term SERP hundreds of times in this book.

The term *"brand awareness"* is used to measure how well the public knows us, how familiar they are with our brand, and therefore our company or business. If a user, when thinking of a product, immediately thinks of your brand (which produces that product), you will have excellent *brand awareness* as well as perfect *positioning* in your market.

The word "feed", which you'll read multiple times in the following pages, refers to the social network pages where information is listed in a column. The Facebook feed is the page where, as you scroll, you see posts from the people and groups you follow.

"Spider" is another term for the crawler, the robot, or the automated software used by search engines to analyze pages.

The term *"revenue"* comes from the Latin "re-venire" (to return), and it is always used to indicate a return, specifically in the sense of an economic return.

The term *"niche"* refers to a topic, category, or field in which you will try to carve out a space for your online business.

The *"trend"* is the general progression of a particular sector over a specific period of time.

422

The term *"seasonality"* describes the general pattern of recurring interest in a specific sector over a given period.

In this field the term *"keyword"* or *"key"* refers to the set of words that a user has searched. One or more keywords make the "query" that a user asks the search engine. These are fundamental concepts.

The *"volume"* refers to the number of searches for a single keyword during a specific period of time.

When a user types a word into the search engine's search field, they are "querying" its database for an answer. That is a *"query."*

The term *"long tail"* refers to keywords that are in the "long tail" of the graph below, which means searches that consist of four, five, or even more words.

"Conversion Rate," or "CR," is one of those truly important indicators among all that you'll come across. For example, if you have 100 visitors on your site and 1 visitor purchases a product, you have a CR (conversion rate) of 1%.

CTR (*Click Through Rate*) is the ratio between the number of clicks and page views. If a page is viewed 10 times and receives 1 click, it has a CTR of 10%.

"Copywriting" is the art of writing optimized texts that are both valuable for people searching for information, attractive to search engine algorithms, and, at the same time, through persuasive action, useful for converting people in your target audience. This means that first, you need to know who your target audience is; otherwise, you won't know whom to persuade or what to write.

By *"click baiting,"* we mean something that tries to convince the user to click with too much insistence, aggression, or deception.

"CMS" stands for "Content Management System" and is an application created to manage web content, in our case pages, categories, and articles. Joomla, Drupal, in addition to WordPress, which is the most popular, are also CMSs.

The term KPI (Key Performance Indicator) refers to those "key indicators" we consider to determine the success or failure of a performance. CTR, for example, is a KPI, but there can be many others.

When I talk about "ranking," I'm referring to the classification of results in the search engine results pages (SERPs).

When talking about the web, *embed* means inserting a multimedia element (such as a video, an interactive image, a social media post, a form, or an application) within a webpage. Instead of creating a link that redirects the user to an external page, the embedded element is displayed directly within the page itself.

"Pareto" was an Italian economist who formulated the well-known principle stating that "the majority of effects are caused by a small number of factors," later summarized as "20% of the causes result in 80% of the effects."

Marketing is the strategy and process you use to satisfy and retain customers over time (branding). The marketing system consists of three phases: attraction (or profiling), education (nurturing), and sales. Without a market, there is no marketing.

The term *reciprocity* refers to the principle that makes someone feel "indebted" to you. The classic example is when you invite a friend over for dinner, and they say, "Next time it's on me." You treated them to dinner, so they feel a sense of obligation and want to return the favor in some way. Maybe they even brought a bottle of wine to the dinner as a result of this reciprocity.

Headings are relevant both for the reader, as they make the text more readable, and for SEO, as they determine the topic or subtopic of the content, making crawling more efficient.

Batch refers to a list or series of identical commands executed sequentially. For example, you decide on a command or action once and have it automatically repeated X number of times on Y different elements.

User experience can often be found abbreviated as UX and indicates the overall quality of experience when using a website.

Reach is a word for the number of people potentially reached by an action, e.g., an advertising campaign or a simple post on a social page.

"Pagerank" is nothing more than the value that determines the "rank" position of "pages" in SERP results. PageRank, often called 'link juice', is transmitted from one page to another through links and measures the importance of a page in the eyes of Google.

'*Link juice*' is a term used to describe how much influence one link has over another. For example, a link from a PR7 website is said to have more 'juice' (value) than one from a PR2 site.

"Link building" is the set of processes and techniques aimed at creating external links that point to the pages of another website to increase its authority.

The terms "*White Hat*" and "*Black Hat*" are used to describe, respectively, ethical and legitimate techniques or intentions (white) and their opposite (black). It's similar to referring to white magic and black magic.

'URL' is short for "Universal Resource Locator" and is the address of a page on the web.

The term "*prompt*" in the context of artificial intelligence applications refers to a question, command, or text input that you provide to the language model in order to receive a response or trigger an action.

The term 'evergreen' conveys the idea of content with constant value.

Both '*authority*' and '*authoritativeness*' are important. The former indicates the degree of power you actually have; the latter indicates the degree of power others recognize in you.

The word "geo" refers to a geographic area. For example, Italy would be "geo IT," and the United States would be "geo US." The term is used to refer to groupings of different geos, such as "tier 1 geo," "tier 2 geo," and so on.

"*Tier*" indicates the level of difficulty of different geos. The wealthiest and most competitive countries are classified as "tier 1." Developing countries, where purchasing power is negligible or very low, are classified as "tier 3."

The word "*pixel*" refers to a tracking tool that is implemented on a website by installing a code, which records visitors' activity and converts it into useful data for optimizing ad campaigns.

A/B testing, or split testing, is a common technique in digital marketing that involves comparing two (or more) versions of an element to determine which one delivers better results.

"*Influence marketing*" is a marketing strategy that relies on individuals (influencers) who have an influence on a potential customer base.

The "engagement rate" is the ratio between the number of followers and the number of people interacting with the content.

Referral traffic is called this because the traffic source, meaning the originating website, is called the "referrer," as it sends part of its visitors to your website.

A "*guest post*" is the practice of publishing a post as a guest on another website. Essentially, you write content and publish it on another website. You get a link on a website that targets your audience, and the website receives original content and compensation.

An *infographic* is a visual representation of information. It is a technique for gathering various types of data into tables, concept maps, diagrams, graphs, and histograms, making the information easily readable.

The *feed* is the "board" of the social platform, the section where notifications or new content appear when they are published.

Remarketing means carrying out a marketing operation on someone who has already performed a tracked action, such as watching one of your videos or visiting your website.

Forums (the word comes from the Latin "forum," meaning public place) are online platforms that host discussions divided into groups or sections, where users can post messages to share common interests, and these messages remain permanently accessible.

A *"squeeze page"* is a short landing page with minimal content, perhaps just a title, a brief text, and a form, designed solely to capture contact information.

Follow-up sequences are called this because the succession of emails "follows" the user, aiming to inform, educate, and persuade them to take the action you want them to take.

"Social proof" is the element that shows the user that what they are viewing has been valuable to many other people before them.

The term *"giveaway"* often refers to a type of contest where something is "given away" to users to capture their attention and stimulate their interaction.

"Customer journey" is the path a customer takes during their relationship with a company. It's the story of the relationship between the customer and the brand, representing the interactions and experiences a customer goes through during all phases of the marketing process.

The *"footer"* is an HTML element of any web-page that delimits the lower part of a page.